18468

LENIN
LIFE AND WORKS

Facts On File Chronology Series

LENIN
LIFE AND WORKS

Gerda and Hermann Weber

Edited and translated by Martin McCauley

Facts On File, Inc.
119 West 57 Street, New York, N.Y. 10019

First published in 1980 by

Facts On File, Inc.
119 West 57 Street
New York, N.Y. 10019

ISBN 0-87196-515-1

Typeset by Leaper and Gard Ltd, Bristol

Printed in Great Britain

Contents

General Introduction to the Chronology Series

The aim of this series is to provide an accurate, succinct, in-depth account of the central figure's life and ideas and the impact he had on the events of his day. Personal details are included when they shed light on character and personality. The subject's own writings and speeches are the main source of information, but letters and the opinions of his contemporaries are used when they add a useful extra dimension to the study. An attempt has been made only to record verifiable facts and to provide a reliable, up-to-date account of the subject's activities and influence. The main events of the time are included so as to set the person in historical perspective and to provide a rational context for his ideas and actions. Bibliographical references are given so as to permit readers, should they so desire, to follow up the quotations; a detailed bibliography of works by and about the subject is also included.

Martin McCauley, Series Editor

Preface

Vladimir Ilich Lenin, who has probably altered the course of the history of our time more than anyone else, died almost 60 years ago. Lenin's life is today more than ever surrounded by myths, and the picture of his personality determined by where a party stands politically. A detailed chronology of his life and works would appear to be of use and to be justified, given these circumstances. The most important confirmed dates of his life and work are used to portray the leading revolutionary of our century, the Bolshevik Party Leader and Soviet statesman, Lenin.

The richness of the material on the political career of Lenin has, of necessity, led to a selection being made which must remain subjective even when objectivity was the aim. Lenin's personal life, however, has been much less researched; here all ascertainable information has been included.

The most important scource for Lenin's writings is the 45-volume English translation of the Russian fourth edition. All direct quotations are followed by the source (CW). Another valuable source is *Vladimir Ilich Lenin Biograficheskaya Khronika* (Khr. I-III). Where it has not been possible to clear up contradictory information, this has been stated. All dates are given according to the Gregorian calendar which was adopted in Soviet Russia on 1 February 1918. In the 19th century the Julian calendar, then in use in Russia, was twelve days behind the Gregorian and in the 20th century thirteen days behind.

Mannheim   Gerda and Hermann Weber

Abbreviations

AS	Lenin *Ausgewählte Schriften* (Munich 1963)
Biographie	W I Lenin *Biographie* (Berlin DDR 1971)
Briefe I-VIII	W I Lenin *Briefe* Band I-VIII (Berlin DDR 1967-73)
CW	V I Lenin *Collected Works* (Moscow 1963-70) 45 volumes. Translated from the Russian fourth edition
Gautschi	Willi Gautschi *Lenin als Emigrant in der Schweiz* (Zürich 1973)
Haas	Lenin *Unbekannte Briefe 1912-1914* Hrsg. von Leonhard Haas (Zürich 1967)
Khr I-III	*Vladimir Ilich Lenin Biograficheskaya Khronika* (Moscow 1970-2) 3 volumes
Krupskaya	Nadezhda Krupskaya *Memories of Lenin* (London, 1970)
Krupskaya I and II	N K Krupskaja *Erinnerungen an Lenin* I and II Band (Moscow-Leningrad 1933)
Krupskaya 1959	Nadeshda Krupskaja *Erinnerungen an Lenin* (Berlin DDR 1959)
PSU	Presse der Sowjetunion (Berlin DDR 1969) Supplement Zu Ehren Lenins
SW	W I Lenin *Sämtliche Werke* (Vienna-Berlin-Zürich 1927-34 and 1940-41)
Tagebuch	*Tagebuch der Sekretäre W I Lenins 21. November 1922-6. März 1923* (Berlin DDR 1965)
W	W I Lenin *Werke* (Berlin DDR 1955-65)

1870

22 April: Vladimir Ilich Ulyanov, who later adopted the pseudonym Lenin, is born in Streletskaya Ulitsa, Simbirsk (now Ulyanovsk), the son of Ilya Nikolaevich Ulyanov (26 July 1831–24 January 1886), an inspector of schools, and Maria Aleksandrovna Ulyanov (née Blank) (18 March 1835–25 July 1916). Lenin's father was the son of the tailor and former serf Nikolai Vasilevich Ulyanov (1765–1838) from Astrakhan and of Anna Aleksevna Ulyanov (née Smirnov), 25 years younger than her husband and of Kalmyk origin. Ilya, in spite of his poor circumstances, was able to study and taught mathematics and physics in Penza where he married Anna Blank in August 1863. She came from a Russified Volhynian German family; her father Aleksandr Dmitrievich Blank (1802–1873) was a doctor and her mother, Anna Ivanovna Groschopf, came from a family which traced its origins back to a well-to-do middle class family in Lübeck. The Ulyanovs moved to Nizhny Novgorod (now Gorky) in 1863 where Ilya again taught and then moved, in the autumn of 1869, to Simbirsk where Ilya Ulyanov became an inspector of primary schools.

Vladimir Ilich was the fourth child. Those born before him were: Anna (1864–1935), Aleksandr (1866–1887) and Olga (born and died 1868). After Vladimir came Olga (1871–1891), Nikolai (born and died 1873), Dmitri (1874–1943) and Maria (1878–1937).

1874

Ilya Ulyanov, a loyal and religious man, becomes director of schools in Simbirsk. He also becomes an active state counsellor in the hereditary service nobility.

1878

14 August: After moving several times in Simbirsk the Ulyanovs acquire a house in the Moskovskaya Ulitsa.

1879

28 August: Vladimir Ulyanov (Lenin) becomes a pupil in the first class of the grammar school in Simbirsk.

1882

13 January: His father, Ilya, receives the Order of Vladimir, Third Class. He only then becomes a nobleman according to a recent Soviet source (Khr. I p. 11) but this is contrary to all previous accounts.

1886

24 January: Lenin's father dies of a brain haemorrhage.
Spring–Summer: According to his own account, given later, he breaks with religion and becomes an atheist.

1887

13 March: Lenin's brother Aleksandr is arrested for planning an attempt on the life of Tsar Alexander III.
17 May–18 June: Vladimir Ulyanov sits his final grammar school examinations.
20 May: Aleksandr Ulyanov is hanged in the Schlüsselburg prison in St Petersburg.
22 June: The academic council of Simbirsk grammar school awards Lenin certificate no 468 and a gold medal. In his report the headmaster, Fyodor Kerensky (father of the later Prime Minister), writes: 'Quite talented, invariably dilligent, prompt and reliable, Ulyanov was first in all his classes, and upon graduation was awarded a gold medal as the most meritorious pupil in achievement, growth and conduct. There is not a single instance on record, either in school or outside of it, of Ulyanov evoking by word or deed any adverse opinion from the authorities and teachers of the school . . . The guiding principles of his upbringing were religion and rational discipline.' (Trotsky, *The Young Lenin* p. 94)
End of June: The Ulyanovs move to the estate of the Blank family at Kokushkino, near Kazan.
Before 10 August: Lenin moves to Kazan.
25 August: Lenin becomes a law student at the University of Kazan. He has a reference from Fyodor Kerensky, headmaster of Simbirsk grammar school.

16–17 December: Lenin takes part in student demonstrations; he is arrested and sent down from university. 'I was arrested for the first time in December 1887 and sent down from the University of Kazan because of student unrest; later I was expelled from Kazan.' (PSU 58, 1969 p. 15)

19 December: Lenin receives confirmation of his expulsion from the university and is directed to Kokushkino where he is placed under surveillance by the secret police.

1888

18 September: Lenin writes to the Ministry of the Interior and asks for permission to travel abroad to continue his studies. The request is refused on 28 September (Khr. I p. 39; according to CW 1 p. 540 the rejection occurred on 5 October)

Before 26 September: Lenin moves with his mother and Dmitri to Kazan. He 'surrounded himself with books and spent most of the day poring over them' and then 'Volodya gave up smoking straight away and never smoked again.' (Wolodja, *Unser Bruder und Genosse* pp. 38, 40)

Autumn–May 1889: Lenin apparently belongs to a Marxist circle, organised by N E Fedoseev.

Winter: Lenin studies Marxist literature for the first time, including Marx's *Das Kapital*. He is most struck, however, by the views of N Chernyshevsky whose *What is to be Done?* he reads and rereads.

1889

3 May: Lenin and his family move from Kazan to Alakaevka, a village near Samara, where his mother has inherited a small estate and a mill. 'My mother would have liked me to have taken up farming. I started but soon realised that things were not going right. Relations with the peasants were abnormal.' (Krupskaya I p. 40)

End of May–June: Lenin puts an advertisement in the *Samarskaya Gazeta* (Samara Newspaper). 'Former student will give private lessons, will also teach outside the confines of the city.' (Biographie p. 37)

Summer: Lenin writes in 1922: 'In the spring of 1889 I went to live in Samara Gubernia, where at the end of the summer, I heard of the arrest of Fedoseev and other members of study circles in Kazan, including the one to which I belonged. I think that I too might easily have been arrested had I remained in Kazàn that summer.' (CW 33 p. 452)

17 September: Lenin and his family move from Alakaevka to Samara (Khr. I p. 43; according to CW 1 p. 540 on 23 October). Besides law he

occupies himself further with Marxist literature and apparently translates *The Communist Manifesto*. Lenin grows a (reddish) beard and
gradually loses his hair.

1890

29 May: As a result of an application (24 May) by his mother Lenin
receives permission to sit his final examinations at a Russian university
as an external student.
24 June: Lenin applies to the Ministry of Education for permission to
take his final examinations in law at the University of St Petersburg.
Summer: Lenin, together with his family, spends the summer once
again in Alakaevka. He reads *The Condition of the Working Class in
England* by Engels and practises the *Internationale* in French with his
sister Olga.
After 1 September: Lenin travels for the first time to St Petersburg and
has discussions about his examinations. He breaks his journey (7-14
September) in Kazan.
5 November: Lenin returns to Samara from St Petersburg.

1891

Mid March: Lenin takes part in an illegal meeting at the house of a
dentist called Kaznelson in Samara. He opposed the Populists (Narod-
niki) on the subject of the economic development of Russia.
Between 2-7 April: Lenin travels from Samara to St Petersburg. On 7
April he hands the chairman of the examination board in law an application to sit the examination as an external student; he includes an
essay on criminal law.
16 April-6 May: Lenin sits five examinations in seven subjects during
the spring semester (Marks: very good).
20 April: Lenin's sister Olga writes to their mother: 'I think, darling
Mamochka, that you have no reason to worry that he is over-exerting
himself. Firstly, Volodya is reason personified and secondly, the
examinations were very easy. He has already completed two subjects
and received a 5 [top marks] in both. He rested on Saturday (the
examination was on Friday). He went early in the morning to the river
Neva and in the afternoon he visited me and then both of us went
walking along the Neva and watched the movement of the ice.' (*Vom
Alltag des Uljanows* p. 60)
20 May: Olga Ulyanova, Lenin's younger sister, dies of typhoid in St
Petersburg. His mother comes to St Petersburg.
29 May: Lenin travels with his mother back to Samara and spends the

4

summer in Alakaevka.
13 September: Lenin travels from Alakaevka to Samara and from there
to St Petersburg.
28 September–21 November: Autumn semester examinations in St
Petersburg. Lenin sits eight examinations in eleven subjects and obtains
first place and very good marks. Apparently he also makes contact with
Marxists, having obtained their addresses from his Samara acquaintance,
A Shukht.
23 November: Lenin returns to Samara from St Petersburg.

1892

26 January: Lenin is awarded a first class degree by the St Petersburg
Board of Education.
30 January: Lenin is admitted as a lawyer's assistant by the Samara area
court. He works as assistant to the lawyer A N Khardin from February–
August 1893.
4 August: Lenin acquires the right to handle his own cases in court.
Summer–end of year: Lenin prepares lectures attacking the Populists,
preparatory work for future writings.

1893

Spring: Lenin is a leader of a Marxist circle in Samara. He writes his
first extant work (first published in 1923) 'New Economic Developments in Peasant Life (On V Y Postnikov's *Peasant Farming in South
Russia*)' (CW 1 pp. 11-73). Lenin attacks the view of the Populists that
there is no development towards capitalism in Russia.
1 September: Lenin leaves Samara and moves to St Petersburg. He
breaks his journey in Nizhny Novgorod, where he meets Marxists, and
in Moscow where the Ulyanov family now lives (Dmitri is studying
there). Lenin, the revolutionary, is now a Marxist. Trotsky wrote later:
'It is thus, between his brother's execution and the move to St Petersburg, in these simultaneously short and long six years of stubborn work
that the future Lenin was formed . . . all the fundamental features of
his person, his outlook on life and his mode of action were already
formed during the interval between the seventeenth and twenty-third
years of his life.' (Trotsky *The Young Lenin* p. 207)
15 September: Lenin becomes assistant to the lawyer M F Volkenstein.
Autumn: Lenin writes the pamphlet: 'On the so-called Market Question', first published in 1937. He had already expounded the main
points in St Petersburg Marxist circles. He criticises G B Krasin but
mainly opposes the Populists and the Legal Marxists. (CW 1 pp. 75-125)

17 October: In a letter Lenin informs his mother that he has found a 'good room' and is 'quite satisfied'; however he asks his mother for money since he has 'not been living carefully.' (CW 37 pp. 65-6)

Autumn-Winter: Lenin is active in a Marxist circle and he also has contact with workers.

Second half of December: In a letter to the economist P P Maslov Lenin writes: 'The disintegration of our small producers (the peasants and handicraftsmen) appears to me to be the basic and principal fact explaining our urban and larger scale capitalism, dispelling the myth that the peasant economy represents some special structure.' (CW 43 p. 37)

1894

January: Lenin spends the Christmas holidays with his family in Moscow.

21 January: Lenin opposes V P Vorontsov, a Populist, at an illegal meeting in Moscow. A police agent reports to the authorities: Vorontsov silenced the Marxist Davydov 'so that the defence of his views were taken over by a certain Ulyanov (allegedly the brother of the hanged Ulyanov) who then carried out the defence with a complete command of the subject.' (Wolper *Pseudonyme Lenins* p. 38)

End of February: At an illegal discussion, disguised as a celebration during Shrovetide, Lenin meets for the first time his future wife Nadezhda Konstantinovna Krupskaya (26 February 1869-27 February 1939)

March-June: Lenin writes his first extended work: 'What the "Friends of the People" are; How they Fight the Social Democrats.' He began the preparatory work in Samara in 1892 and 1893. The first part is ready in April and is hectographed during the spring and illegally distributed and also printed in August. Parts Two and Three appear during the autumn. The work is a defence of Marxist views and an attack on the Populists, the Russian agrarian socialists. (CW 1 pp. 129-332)

26 June: Lenin leaves for Moscow and so ends the summer with his relations in a house outside Moscow.

8 September: Lenin returns to St Petersburg.

Autumn: Lenin has a discussion with P B Struve, the leading theorist among the Legal Marxists, in Lesnoe, near St Petersburg; he takes issue with him over his book *Critical Remarks on the Subject of Russia's Economic Development*. Lenin takes part in several Marxist meetings. He gives lectures, as in the house of S P Nevsorova, where Krzhizhanovsky first met him: 'He [Lenin] drowned us in a torrent of statistics which he used to illustrate his points . . . His tall forehead and his great

erudition earned him the nickname "the old man".' (PSU 75, 1969 p. 18)
End of year: Potresov meets Lenin for the first time. In 1927 he describes the meeting: 'He had doubtless passed his twenty fifth birthday
when I met him for the first time during the 1894-95 Christmas and
New Year holidays, at a meeting in a St Petersburg suburb, in the Okhta
quarter. Lenin was only young according to his birth certificate. One
could have taken him for at least a 35-40 year old. The face withered,
the head almost bald, a thin reddish beard, eyes which observed one
from the side, craftily and slightly closed, an unyouthful, coarse voice.
A typical merchant from any north Russian province — there was
nothing of the "radical" intellectual about him, so many of whom were
making contact with the workers in those years just when the workers
were beginning to stir. No trace either of the service or noble family
from which Lenin came.' (*Die Gesellschaft* Berlin 1927 II p. 406)

1895

After 5 January: Together with Babushkin, a worker, Lenin writes a
handbill, addressed to the workers of the Semyannikov Works on the
disturbance in their factory.
2 or 3 March: Lenin takes part in a meeting of members of social
democratic groups from St Petersburg, Moscow, Kiev and Vilno. Passing
from propaganda work in Marxist circles to mass agitation work is
debated.
April: Lenin's work 'The Economic Content of Narodism (Populism)
and the Criticism of it in Mr Struve's Book' (CW 1 pp. 333-507)
appears in the volume *Material on the Nature of our Economic Development* under the pseudonym K Tulin, Vladimir Ulyanov's first
pseudonym. The volume was jointly prepared by the Marxists Lenin,
Starkov, Radchenko, Potresov and the Legal Marxists Struve and
Klasson. Lenin regarded it as permissable to enter into an alliance with
the Legal Marxists against the Populists. The volume was seized and
burnt due to its 'pernicious intention'; only 100 of the 2,000 copies
were saved.
Spring: Lenin falls ill with severe pneumonia.
7 May: After his recovery Lenin makes his first trip abroad to establish
contact with the 'Emancipation of Labour' group.
14 May: Lenin writes a letter to his mother during a two-hour stop
in Salzburg. He complains that his command of German is 'not up
to much', the pronunciation is unfamiliar and the people speak so
quickly. But 'despite this disgraceful fiasco I am not discouraged and
continue distorting the German language with some zeal'. (CW 37 p.
72)
15 May-8 June: Lenin travels to Switzerland; he meets Potresov in

Geneva and travels with him to see Plekhanov who is on holiday in the mountain village of Les Ormonts, near Les Diablerets. Protresov wrote later that Lenin showed himself 'overawed in the presence of the great theoretician, of the doyen of Marxism' and Plekhanov looked, 'not without warm sympathy, at the able practitioner of revolution', Lenin. (*Die Gesellschaft* 1927 II p. 409) Lenin visits Axelrod in Zürich and spends a week with him in Affoltern, a village near Zürich.

20 May: Lenin raves about the Swiss Alps in a letter to his mother: 'The fare is not much and the scenery is splendid.' He reports that he has seen his god-daughter (Anna Shukht) and her family in Geneva. Servants are 'very expensive here' and they have to be 'well fed'. (CW 37 p. 73)

Before 8 June: Lenin travels to Paris and gets to know Paul Lafargue, Karl Marx's son-in-law, there.

8 June: Lenin writes, in a letter to his mother: 'I am only just beginning to look around me a bit in Paris.' (CW 37 p. 74)

June-beginning of July: During his stay in Paris Lenin does some research on the Paris Commune and copies extracts from *Étude sur le mouvement communaliste à Paris en 1871* by G Lefrancais.

July: Rests at a spa in Switzerland.

18 July: In a letter to his mother from the Swiss spa Lenin writes: 'I have decided to take advantage of the fact and get down seriously to the treatment of the illness (stomach) . . . I have been living at this spa for several days and feel not at all bad.' He has 'already exceeded' his budget and asks for 'another 100 roubles or so' to be sent to Zürich. (CW 37 p. 75)

End of July-Mid September: Stays in Berlin. Lenin works in the reading room of the Prussian Staatsbibliothek. In Paris and Berlin Lenin writes a conspectus of *The Holy Family* by Marx and Engels. (CW 38 pp. 19-51)

3 August: Lenin hears a talk by Arthur Stadthagen on the agrarian programme of the SPD at an SPD meeting in Niederbarnim, near Berlin.

10 August: Lenin writes to his mother from Berlin-Moabit, Flensburger Strasse 12, II (c/o Frau Kurreick). He lives 'a few steps away from the Tiergarten . . . the Spree, where I bathe every day . . . I understand far less conversational German than French . . . the day before yesterday I was at the theatre, they played Hauptmann's *The Weavers*.' (CW 37 p. 77)

29 August: He writes in a letter to his mother from Berlin: 'I am still working in the Königliche Bibliothek and in the evenings I wander about studying the Berlin mores and listening to German speech . . . In general I much prefer wandering around and seeing the evening amusements and pastimes of the people to visiting museums, theatres, shopping centres, etc.' Lenin is again in 'financial difficulties'. He asks his mother 'if you can send me 50 to 100 roubles?' CW 57 pp. 78-9)

7 September: Lenin, in a letter to his mother, thanks her for the money she has sent.

14 September: In a letter to Wilhelm Liebknecht, Plekhanov recommends Lenin as 'one of our best Russian friends' and requests that Lenin be received because of an 'important matter' as he is returning to Russia. Lenin visits Wilhelm Liebknecht in Charlottenburg between 14-19 September. (Khr. I p. 105)

19 September: Lenin returns to Russia. He brings Marxist literature with him in a suitcase with a false bottom. He breaks his journey in Vilno, Moscow and Orekhovo-Zuevo and has discussions about the publication of the periodical *Rabotnik*. He informs Axelrod about this journey in a letter in November. (CW 34 pp. 20-22)

After 19 September (20 December at the latest): Lenin writes a memorial article on the occasion of the death of Friedrich Engels and it is published in the periodical *Rabotnik* (The Worker) in spring 1896. Nos 1 and 2 appear. (CW 2 pp. 15-27)

11 October: Arrival in St Petersburg.

Autumn: Lenin is a co-founder of the League of Struggle for the Emancipation of the Working Class.

Autumn: Lenin writes the brochure: 'Explanations of the Law on Fines Imposed on Factory Workers'. The printing of the brochure beings in St Petersburg on 15 December (CW 2 pp. 29-72)

20 December: The leadership of the League of Struggle discusses the first number of the organ *Rabochee Delo* (The Working Matter) which has been prepared for printing. Lenin has two articles in it ('To the Working Men and Women of the Thornton Factory' and 'What are our Ministers Thinking about?' CW 2 pp. 81-92). The leadership is arrested during the night by the police.

21 December: Lenin is remanded in custody.

End of 1895-Summer of 1896: Lenin writes the draft programme and explanatory notes of the programme of the social democratic party (first published in 1924) in prison in St Petersburg. He calls 'communal socialist production' and 'political power' for the working class the 'goal of the struggle of the working class' and the 'prerequisite for its liberation'. (CW 2 pp. 93-121)

1896

2 January: Lenin is interrogated in prison for the first time.

Beginning of January: Lenin begins preparatory work on his book *The Development of Capitalism in Russia*.

14 January: Lenin writes to A K Chebotareva from prison in St Petersburg about his plans for a book on economic questions and asks for reading matter.

24 January: Lenin, in a letter to his sister Anna, writes that he has enough to eat in prison (his family provided him with generous amounts of food), his health is 'quite satisfactory . . . I sleep about nine hours a day and see various chapters of my future book in my sleep'. (CW 37 p. 85)

After January: During his imprisonment Lenin has permission to see members of his family and acquaintances twice a week (Mondays and Thursdays).

27 March: Lenin's sister Anna reports: 'We chatted for a whole hour today with V[olodya]; he is as usual in good spirits.' (*Vom Alltage der Uljanows* p. 62)

11 April: Second interrogation in prison.

19 May: Third interrogation in prison.

8 June: Fourth interrogation in prison.

Before 24 August: Lenin asks Nadezhda Krupskaya, in a note in code, to walk along a street with Appolinaria Yakubova (Lenin may originally have intended to marry her) so that he can see them from a window in the corridor. Nothing came of it. Krupskaya wrote: 'Even Vladimir Ilich was affected by prison melancholy.' (Krupskaya p. 29)

November (before 7 December): Lenin writes a handbill: 'To the Tsarist Government' which was distributed by the League of Struggle for the Emancipation of the Working Class. (CW 2 pp. 122-7)

14 December: Lenin files a request to the Attorney General, asking for permission to give his sister Anna a letter and two manuscripts, one of them being his (lost) work: 'Outline of Political Economy at the Beginning of the 19th Century.'

1897

10 February: Lenin is exiled, by government order, to east Siberia for three years and placed under police surveillance.

22 February: Lenin's mother requests that he be allowed to travel to Siberia at his own cost and not under police escort. Permission is granted on 24 February.

26 February: Lenin is released from prison. He received his order of exile the day before. He may remain in St Petersburg until 1 March.

Between 26 February–1 March: Lenin writes a letter, in chemical ink, to Nadezhda Krupskaya (who is temporarily in prison) and confesses his love for her.

1 March: Lenin leaves St Petersburg. On his way to exile he may break his journey in Moscow (the result of a request by his mother).

2–6 March: Lenin stays with his family in Moscow. He overstays his permitted time by two days.

6 March: Lenin asks the Moscow Okhrana for permission to stay longer in Moscow. However he receives his travelling papers and undertakes to leave Moscow by 11 pm.

7 March: Lenin leaves Kursk station at 2.30 pm (whence his brother Dmitri had accompanied him) on the Moscow–Kursk railway for Siberian exile. In Tula, Lenin takes leave of his mother, his sisters Maria and Anna and her husband Mark Elizarov, they having accompanied him to Tula.

9 March: Lenin arrives in Samara.

14 March: Lenin writes to his mother from Ob station (two previous letters never arrived) that he had crossed the Ob in a horse sleigh and had bought a ticket to Krasnoyarsk. The journey had been less tiring than expected. 'The country covered by the West Siberian railway . . . is astonishingly monotonous – bare, bleak steppe . . . Snow and sky – and nothing else for the whole three days.' (CW 37 p. 92)

16 March: Arrival in Krasnoyarsk where Lenin lives in K G Popova's house until 12 May.

18 March: Request to the Governor General of Irkutsk for permission to stay in Krasnoyarsk until his place of exile has been decided and 'because of my weak state of health to place me in Eniseisk province, if possible in Krasnoyarsk or Minusinsk county'. (Briefe I pp. 458-9)

22 March: Lenin writes, in a letter to his sister Maria, that he has been in the 'famous local library belonging to Yudin'. (CW 37 p. 94)

27 March: Lenin writes to his mother that he spends his time in two ways: 'First, in visiting Yudin's library, and second, in getting to know the town of Krasnoyarsk and its inhabitants (many of them exiles).' (CW 37 p. 95) Among Lenin's acquaintances in Krasnoyarsk are P A Krasikov, N A Merkholev and A A Filippov.

16 April: Lenin's closest comrades in the League of Struggle in St Petersburg, G M Krzhizhanovsky, L Martov, A A Vaneev and V V Starkov, not travelling at their own expense, arrive in Krasnoyarsk.

29 April: Lenin reports, in a letter to his mother and his sister Anna, that he has been exiled to Shushenskoe village, in Minusinsk county (on 17 April he had praised the local climate and the low cost of living there). He asks for many books and journals which are due to him in payment for his article: 'A Characterisation of Economic Romanticism.'

April: The first part of Lenin's article (written during the spring): 'A Characterisation of Economic Romanticism (Sismondi and our native Sismondiists)' appears in the April issue (no. 7) of the Legal Marxist journal *Novoe Slovo* (New Word), under the pseudonym K T-n. The other parts appear in the following numbers. (CW 2 pp. 129-265)

11 May: Lenin asks for the governor for the 'legally stated level of support' since he has no means of his own. (Briefe I p. 459)

12 May: Together with Krzhizhanovsky and Starkov (who have been exiled to Tesinskoe) Lenin leaves Krasnoyarsk by steamer to get to his place of exile Shushenskoe, travelling via Minusinsk.

20 May: Arrives at his place of exile, Shushenskoe. Lenin lodges in the house of the peasant Zyryanov. During his exile Lenin works chiefly on his book *The Development of Capitalism in Russia*.

30 May: In a letter to his mother and sister Maria, Lenin refers to Shushenskoe as 'not a bad village . . . not far away there is a forest . . . and there is a fairly big tributary of the Enisei not far away . . . where you can bathe . . . Yesterday I travelled about 12 versts to shoot duck and great snipe.' (CW 37 pp. 107–8)

6 June: Lenin writes to his mother and sister Anna: 'Life here is not bad.' Besides hunting and bathing he 'spends a lot of time walking.' (CW 37 p. 112)

20 June: To his mother and sister Anna Lenin writes: 'I am very satisfied with my board and lodging.' He expects visits from comrades: 'I shall not be bored.' (CW 37 p. 116)

21 June: Lenin is informed that he will receive the requested maintenance of 8 roubles per month, beginning in May 1897.

Summer: Lenin writes 'The New Factory Law' (the manuscript reaches the outside world during the autumn and is published as a pamphlet in Geneva in 1899). (CW 2 pp. 267–315)

27 June: In a letter to his brother-in-law, Mark Elizarov, Lenin is concerned about the sale of the 'unprofitable' Kokushkino estate (part of which belongs to his mother). (CW 37 p. 118)

31 July: Lenin writes to his mother and his sister Maria that work on *The Development of Capitalism in Russia* is 'progressing very, very slowly.' (CW 37 p. 122)

11 August: Lenin travels to the village of Tesinskoe to attend the wedding of fellow revolutionary V V Starkov and A M Rosenberg.

28 August: Lenin sends a letter, hidden in the spine of a book, to Axelrod in Zürich. 'There is nothing I have wanted so much, or dreamed of so much, as an opportunity of writing for workers.' (CW 34 p. 24)

29 August: In a letter to his mother Lenin writes that life in Shushenskoe, his place of exile, is 'very monotonous'. He has been 'distracted from his main work [*The Development of Capitalism in Russia*] by writing an article.' (CW 37 p. 124) He writes 'The Handicraft Census in Perm Gubernia and General Problems of "Handicraft" Industry' and it is published in the volume *Economic Studies and Essays* in October 1898. (CW 2 pp. 355–458)

9 and 10 October: Lenin meets other political exiles in Minusinsk.

11–16 October: Lenin travels to Tesinskoe village and meets exiled social democrats. On 12 October he writes to his mother from Tesinskoe: 'Everybody here also says that I have put on a lot of weight, am sunburnt and look like a real Siberian. That is what shooting and village

life do for you! All the St Petersburg ailments have been shaken off!'
(CW 37 p. 129)

24 October: In a letter to his mother: ' . . . I have acquired a dog myself
— I got a pup from an acquaintance here and hope that I shall be able
to train it by next summer.' (CW 37 p. 130)

End of the year: Lenin writes the pamphlet 'The Tasks of the Russian
Social-Democrats', published in Geneva in 1898, one of his most
important early writings. In it Lenin takes an orthodox Marxist stand
against the Economists and Revisionists but he already underlines the
leading role of the Party in the revolution. (CW 2 pp. 323-51) He also
writes 'The Heritage we Renounce' which appears in *Economic Studies
and Essays* in 1898. (CW 2 pp. 491-534)

22 December: In a 'Christmas' letter to his mother and sisters Maria and
Anna, Lenin reports: 'I am reading Labriola's *Essais sur la conception
matérialiste de l'histoire*. It is a very sensible and interesting book.' (CW
37 p. 135)

1898

2 January: Writing to his mother and sisters Lenin asks for a volume of
Saint Simon and various works by Marx in French.

5–14 January: Krzhizhanovsky is Lenin's guest in Shushenskoe.

8 January: Lenin receives two sums of money forwarded by his mother.

20 January: A request, by telegram, to the St Petersburg Director of
Police: 'I have the honour to request that my fiancée, Nadezhda Krupskaya, be permitted to move to Shushenskoe. Ulyanov, in administrative
exile.' (Briefe I p. 460) Krupskaya had been sentenced to three years'
exile in Ufa.

19 February: In a letter to his mother Lenin answers his sister Anna's
question about the date of the wedding. 'Isn't she in a hurry! First of
all Nadezhda Konstantinovna has to get here and then we have to get
permission from the authorities to marry — we are people without any
rights at all.' (CW 37 p. 151)

13–15 March: The 1st Congress of the All-Russian Social Democratic
Labour Party (RSDLP) meets in Minsk. When Lenin hears of it he
declares, 'from now on I am a member of the RSDLP.' (Biographie
p. 86)

Beginning of March–August: Lenin translates volume one of the *History
of Trade Unionism* by Sidney and Beatrice Webb (it comes out in
Russian in September 1899).

20 March: In a letter to his mother and sister Anna, Lenin asks Krupskaya to bring a chess set with her. 'There are some players among our
comrades in Minusinsk and I have once already recalled old times most
enjoyably.' Also he asks for 'as much money as possible.' (CW 37 p.

165)

9 April: Lenin writes to his brother-in-law, Mark Elizarov, that because of the strict censorship in Moscow he would like to publish *Economic Studies and Essays* in St Petersburg. 'My work [*The Development of Capitalism in Russia*] has come to a complete standstill.' (CW 37 p. 170)

19 May: Nadezhda Krupskaya, accompanied by her mother Elizaveta, arrives in Shushenskoe.

22 May: Lenin informs his mother that the guests have 'at last' arrived. Krupskaya, on the same day, writes to Lenin's mother: 'Volodya . . . is a picture of health and looks very much better than he did in St Petersburg. One of the local inhabitants, a Polish woman, says "Pan Ulyanov is always in a good mood". He is terribly taken up with shooting.' (CW 37 pp. 171, 558)

12 July: Lenin submits a request to the head of Eniseisk province for permission to marry.

22 July: Lenin and Nadezhda Konstantinovna Krupskaya marry. It is a church wedding, the only possible form of marriage in Russia. Peasants from Shushenskoe act as witnesses. Lenin and Krupskaya move into their new home.

27 July: Lenin writes to his sister Anna: 'Nadya and I are making a fair copy of the Webbs' book. I have to post it, by the terms of the contract, in the middle of August. I am utterly fed up with this copying (about 1,000 pages for the two of us). The translation is interesting, for it is a very, very useful book.' (CW 37 p. 179)

21 August: Lenin completes the first draft of his major work *The Development of Capitalism in Russia*, which he had begun in 1896. Krupskaya writes to Lenin's sister Anna: 'Today Volodya finished his "markets"; now he has only to cut it down and the job is done. In a few days too the Webbs' book will come safely to an end.' (CW 37 p. 561)

28 August: Lenin informs his mother: 'Today I am sending my translation of the Webbs' book to St Petersburg.' On Fedoseev's suicide he writes: 'For people in exile, these "exile scandals" are the worst thing of all.' (CW 37 p. 185)

7 September: Lenin posts the article which he has written in the last few days: 'On the Question of our Factory Statistics (Professor Karyshev's New Statistical Exploits)'. It is included in *Economic Studies and Essays*. (CW 4 pp. 13–45) In a letter to his mother he expresses delight at the release from prison of his brother Dmitri.

23 September–7 October: Lenin is in Krasnoyarsk. He had received permission to see the dentist there. He meets other exiles, plays chess and goes shopping.

Autumn: The pamphlet 'The Tasks of Russian Social Democrats', written in 1897 (see end of 1897), appears in Geneva.

9 October: Krupskaya informs Lenin's mother: 'At last we have engaged a servant, a fifteen year old girl, for two and a half roubles a month + boots; she is coming on Tuesday and that will be the end of our independent housekeeping.' (CW 37 p. 568)

Between 21–27 October: Lenin's first book to appear in Russia is published under the title *Economic Studies and Essays* (first print 1200 copies). It contains five articles and appears under the pseudonym Vladimir Ilyin.

13–16 November: Krzhizhanovsky is Lenin's guest; they go hunting and read the first chapter of *The Development of Capitalism in Russia*.

Between 19–23 November: In a letter to his sister in Podolsk, Lenin writes: 'Today I am sending to mother's address two notebooks of the "markets". These are the first two chapters.' Lenin also gives instructions about the printing. (CW 37 p. 193)

23 November: Lenin writes to his sister Maria in Brussels: 'During the first part of my exile I decided not to look at a map of European Russia, there was always such a bitter taste in my mouth . . . During the first half of my exile I looked mostly backwards, I suppose, but now I am looking ahead.' (CW 37 p. 196)

4 December: Krupskaya writes to Lenin's sister Anna: 'Volodya is carving chessmen from bark, usually in the evenings when he has "written himself to a standstill" . . . the chessmen are turning out splendid.' (CW 37 p. 573)

10 December: Lenin writes to his mother and his brother Dmitri: 'I have finished one half of my book.' The new pastime is skating, it 'takes me away from shooting quite a lot.' (CW 37 pp. 203–4)

18 December: Lenin informs his sister Anna that four chapters are finished, the first draft 'I have scratched about and abridged most ruthlessly.' (CW 37 pp. 206, 208)

1899

1 January: Krupskaya writes to Lenin's mother that after *The Development of Capitalism in Russia* is finished they plan to devote themselves 'to the study of languages in general and German in particular.' (CW 37 p. 212)

5–14 January: Lenin and Krupskaya are in Minusinsk and meet other exiles. Chess and skating occupy their free time.

15 January: Lenin informs his mother about the holiday 'but tomorrow we shall set to work again.' (CW 37 p. 217)

7 February: Lenin orders a new gun through his brother Dmitri; he informs him that he skates with 'the greatest zeal' and 'I have been practising with such industry that once I hurt my hand and could not write for two days.' (CW 37 p. 227)

11 February: Lenin completes *The Development of Capitalism in Russia*. He writes to his mother: 'I finished them (the "markets") at long last today.' (CW 37 p. 228)

19 February: Lenin asks his mother for dictionaries. 'I want to make a real study of German.' (CW 37 p. 233)

25 February: Lenin writes to his sister Anna. The title *The Development of Capitalism in Russia* is too bold, 'too broad and promises too much.' He adds: 'Our finances are again at rock bottom. Please send 200 roubles.' (CW 37 pp. 235, 237)

Mid March: Lenin writes the article 'Once More on the Theory of Realisation', an attack on Struve. It appears in the journal *Nauchnoe Obozrenie* (Scientific Review) No 8, August 1899, under the pseudonym V Ilyin. (CW 4 pp. 74-93)

8-12 March: So as to celebrate 'Shrovetide in style', six exiled comrades arrive at the Lenins'. 'Our quiet Shusha suddenly became crowded and noisy.' (Krupskaya to Maria Ulyanova in Brussels on 19 March) (CW 37 p. 245)

5-12 April: Lenin's book *The Development of Capitalism in Russia: The Process of the Formation of a Home Market for Large Scale Industry* is published in St Petersburg under the pseudonym Vladimir Ilyin. (CW 3 pp. 21-607) Lenin has been working on it since 1896. The newspaper *Russkie Vedomosti* (Russian News), on 27 and 28 April, carries the announcement: 'From the publishing house of M I Vodovosova: Vladimir Ilyin *The Development of Capitalism in Russia The Process of the Formation of a Home Market for Large Scale Industry*. Price: 2 roubles 50 kopeks 480 pages' (SW III p. 612).

16 April-21 May: Lenin writes two articles entitled 'Capitalism in Agriculture (Kautsky's book and Bulgakov's Article)' which appear in January and February 1900 in the monthly *Zhizn* (Life, the organ of the Legal Marxists). (CW 4 pp. 105-59)

16 April: In a letter to his mother and sister Anna, Lenin writes: 'Shooting is the only form of amusement here and some sort of "loosening-up exercise" is necessary because of my sedentary life.' (CW 37 p. 252)

9 May: Lenin writes to Potresov: 'In general all this "new critical trend" in Marxism, espoused by Struve and Bulgakov . . . looks highly suspicious to me: resounding phrases about "criticism" against "dogma" and so forth — and absolutely no positive results of the criticism.' (CW 34 pp. 32-7)

14 May: A sudden search of the Lenins' house in Shushenskoe but the police do not uncover the secret exchange of letters.

2 July: Lenin writes to his mother: 'Life here goes on as usual. I am not working much at present and soon when the shooting season opens, I shall probably work even less.' He remarks, in a letter to his brother Dmitri, that Tugan-Baranovsky's 'refutation' of Marx is 'monstrously foolish and nonsensical'; he himself is becoming a 'more and more determined opponent of the latest "critical stream" in Marxism and of neo-Kantianism.' (CW 37 pp. 266-8) Krupskaya reports to Lenin's mother: 'Volodya is busy reading all kinds of philosophy (that is now his official occupation), Holbach, Helvétius, etc.' (CW 37 p. 579).

9 July: Lenin writes to Potresov that he is finding it harder to restrain himself vis-à-vis neo-Kantianism. However he is 'only too well aware' of his 'lack of philosophical training.' He has begun to study Holbach and Helvétius and then wants to start on Kant. (CW 34 pp. 39-43)

Before 3 September: Lenin writes the article 'A Protest by Russian Social Democrats', attacking the Economists' 'Credo', and defends the orthodox Marxist position. Lenin's article appears in December as an offprint from No 4-5 of the journal *Rabochee Delo*. (CW pp. 167-82)

1-3 September: In Ermakovskoe Lenin's protest is approved, after a lively debate, by 17 exiled social democrats from Minusinsk county. Besides Lenin and Krupskaya, Lepeshinsky, Starkov, Krzhizhanovsky, Shapovalov, Lengnik and others were present. Lenin and Krupskaya return to Shushenskoe on 3 September.

Beginning of September: Lenin and Krupskaya begin the translation of volume two of the *History of Trade Unionism* by Sidney and Beatrice Webb.

13 September: Lenin and Krupskaya read *Die Voraussetzungen des Sozialismus* by Eduard Bernstein. Lenin writes to his mother: 'Its contents astonish me more and more as we go on. It is unbelievably weak theoretically . . . There are phrases about criticism but no attempt at serious independent criticism. In effect it is opportunism . . . Bernstein's statement that many Russians agree with him . . . made us very indignant.' (CW 37 pp. 281-2)

22 September: Lenin delivers the funeral oration at the burial of A A Vaneev, an exiled member of the St Petersburg League of Struggle, in the village of Ermakovskoe.

October: Lenin accepts an invitation to work on *Rabochaya Gazeta* (Worker's Newspaper, recognised by the 1st Congress as the official organ of the RSDLP). He writes 'Letter to the Editorial Group' and the articles 'Our Programme', 'Our Immediate Tasks' and 'An Urgent Question'. (CW 4 pp. 207-26) In 'Our Programme' he writes: 'We take our stand on the Marxist theoretical position. Marxism was the first to transform socialism from a utopia into a science.' (CW 4 p. 210) The newspaper did not appear then, however; the articles were first published in 1925.

End of the year: Lenin writes 'A draft Programme of Our Party' — first published in 1924. (CW 4 pp. 227-54) He wants to 'imitate the Erfurt Programme of the SPD.' (CW 4 p. 235)

1900

31 January: Krupskaya and Lenin inform his mother that 'no further term of exile is envisaged'; they are making preparations to leave. (CW 37 p. 286) They send the translation of the Webbs' book to St Petersburg.

10 February: Lenin's exile ends. The three years of exile were useful preparation for Lenin, the revolutionary, who besides completing his fundamental work *The Development of Capitalism in Russia* intervened, through his articles, directly in the policy of the socialist movement. He recovered his health in exile. He also worked as a lawyer in Siberia. 'I was an illegal lawyer since I had been sent into administrative exile and so it was forbidden to work. Since there was nothing else to do people came to see me and told me things.' (W 33 p. 282) The creation of a revolutionary party was to be Lenin's major concern when he returned. He 'corresponded about it with Martov and Potresov' from his place of exile (Krupskaya p. 43); 'full of enthusiasm' he told Krzhizhanovsky about his 'thoughts and plans.' (*Lenin, wie wir ihn kannten* p. 29)

11 February: Lenin, Krupskaya, her mother and other exiles leave Minusinsk. 'We travelled hundreds of kilometres on the Enisei and then by road in a horse drawn cart.' (Biographie p. 109) They catch the train at Achinsk.

18 February: Lenin and Krupskaya arrive in Ufa where Krupskaya (and her mother) must remain since her exile is not yet over. Lenin travels to Pskov since he is not permitted to stay in any large city. 'It was a great pity to have to part, just at a time when "real" work was commencing. But it did not even enter Vladimir Ilich's head to remain in Ufa when there was a possibility of getting nearer to St Petersburg.' (Krupskaya p. 45)

After 21 February: Lenin travels illegally to Moscow and stays with his relatives.

Before 9 March: Lenin travels illegally to St Petersburg where he meets Vera Zasulich, who likewise is staying there illegally, and discusses the publication of an all-Russian newspaper.

10 March: Arrives in Pskov. Lenin moves into the Arkhangelskaya Ulitsa where he is placed under surveillance by the Okhrana. Lenin works in the provincial statistical administration.

28 March: Lenin writes, from Pskov, to his mother in Moscow that he intends to consult a doctor about his catarrh. 'I go frequently to the library, and do some walking.' (CW 37 p. 288)

End of March: Krupskaya, from Ufa, tells Lenin that she is constantly ill. He sends her money.

1–17 April: Lenin writes 'Draft of a Declaration of the Editorial Board of *Iskra* (Spark) and *Zarya*' (Dawn). (CW 4 pp. 320–30)

Beginning of April: Pskov meeting of Legal Marxists (Struve, Tugan-Baranovsky) and revolutionaries (Lenin, Martov, Potresov, Radchenko) about participation on *Iskra* and *Zarya*.

15 April: Lenin travels to Riga and discusses *Iskra* with Latvian social democrats.

19 April: Lenin informs his mother that a German is giving him lessons in German 'at 50 kopeks an hour'. Krupskaya is confined to bed (gynaecological illness); he is sending her more money as he has received 100 roubles in royalties for *The Development of Capitalism in Russia* (CW 37 p. 290).

3 May: Request by 'Vladimir Ilich Ulyanov, a member of the hereditary nobility, resident in Pskov, to the Director of Police for permission to spend a month and a half with his sick wife in Ufa.' (Briefe I p. 463) The request is rejected. His mother obtains permission later.

18 May: Lenin receives a passport for a trip to Germany from the Governor of Pskov.

31 May: Lenin informs his mother that he is coming to Podolsk to visit her.

1 June: In the evening Lenin together with Martov travels illegally to St Petersburg to discuss problems of revolutionary activity.

3 June: In the morning Lenin is arrested in St Petersburg, interrogated and imprisoned until 13 June. After his arrest letters from Krupskaya, books and 1300 roubles are taken from him. (Khr. I p. 254: Krupskaya p. 47 gives the sum as 2000 roubles).

13 June: After his release Lenin travels to his family at Podolsk, near Moscow, where he stays until 20 June.

20 June: Lenin travels to Ufa to visit Krupskaya. He breaks his journey in Nizhny Novgorod where he has discussions with local social democrats about support for the planned *Iskra*. He continues his journey from Nizhny Novgorod to Ufa by steamer.

28 June: Arrives in Ufa and sees Krupskaya. Lenin stays until 15 July and also meets local social democrats.

15 July: Lenin leaves Ufa and stays in Samara until 23 July and has talks with local social democrats.

23 July: Lenin arrives in Podolsk to see his family.

26 July: Lenin leaves Podolsk to go into emigration. He meets Babushkin and Rozanov in Smolensk and discusses the publication of *Iskra* until 28 July.

29 July: Lenin leaves Russia, his first foreign exile begins and will last five years.

1 August: Lenin sends Krupskaya in Ufa a post card from Austria.

Beginning of August: Lenin has talks with Axelrod about the publication of *Iskra* during a two-day stay in Zürich. Then he travels to Geneva where he confers with Plekhanov. He describes his differences in September in 'How *Iskra* Was Nearly Extinguished'. (CW 4 pp. 333–49)

Before 24 August: Discussions with N E Bauman, Plekhanov, Potresov, Steklov, Zasulich and others about collaboration on *Iskra* and *Zarya* take place at Bellerive, near Geneva.

Second half of August: Lenin and Potresov share lodgings in the village of Vésenaz, near Geneva.

Before 24 August: Lenin writes to Krupskaya in Ufa that he lives 'almost, one might say, in solitude – and yet there is this bustle.' He gives a detailed account of the differences among Russian social democrats and demands 'a resolute struggle against Economism, an open protest again the threatening vulgarisation and narrowing of Marxism, an irrevocable break with bourgeois "criticism".' (CW 34 pp. 44–7)

24–26 August: Talks take place in Corsier, near Geneva, with members of the Emancipation of Labour group on joint editing of *Iskra*. Lenin's 'Declaration of the Editorial Board of *Iskra*' almost leads to a break. Agreement is reached after the meeting. It is agreed, opposed originally by Plekhanov and Axelrod, to set up the editorial office of *Iskra* in Munich. The editorial board consists of Plekhanov (two votes), Axelrod and Vera Zasulich, the older leading members of the Emancipation of Labour group, and Lenin, Martov and Potresov, the younger leading members. Smidovich is secretary but Lenin's wife Krupskaya takes over in April 1901.

27 August: Lenin meets Potresov and Axelrod in Vésenaz, near Geneva.

28 August: Lenin attends a meeting of the Emancipation of Labour group in Geneva. In the evening he leaves Geneva for Nuremberg where he discusses the printing of *Iskra*.

30 August: Lenin meets his sister Anna Ulyanova-Elizarova in Nuremberg.

31 August: Lenin writes to his mother in Podolsk, from Nuremberg. For conspiratorial reasons he describes a 'trip down the Rhine' which never took place. (CW 37 p. 298)

After 2 September: Lenin writes a report on his discussions with Plekhanov 'How *Iskra* was Nearly Extinguished'. (CW 4 pp. 333–49)

4 or 5 September: Lenin meets Adolf Braun, a leading German social democrat and at that time editor of *Fränkische Tagespost*, in Nuremberg, to get advice on technical matters in connection with the publication of *Iskra*. He keeps up a correspondence with Braun.

5 September: Lenin writes from Nuremberg to an unknown addressee about the difference between 'our group' (Lenin, Martov, Potresov) and other social democratic organisations and his attitude to the split in the Union of Russian Social Democrats Abroad. His group does not wish to 'forego even a particle' of its independence. (CW 34 pp. 48–50)

6 September: Lenin travels from Nuremberg to Munich. He stops in Prague to visit Modrăček, a printing worker whose address Lenin uses for mail from Russia.

7 September: Lenin arrives in Munich and writes to his mother (he gives

Paris as the place of posting for reasons of secrecy). Lenin concentrates in Munich wholly on the publication of *Iskra* and *Zarya*. He lives in Munich first, under the name of Meyer, at an inn owned by a social democrat called Rittmeyer in Kaiserstrasse 53 (now 46).

End of September–Beginning of October: Lenin joins an English language class and advises Krupskaya, in a letter, to learn English.

September: Lenin writes 'The Declaration of the Editorial Board of *Iskra*' which appears as an offprint in October (CW 5 pp. 351-6).

3 October: Lenin writes, in a letter to his mother in Moscow: 'I am now quite well. I got over my influenza long ago and am working more regularly.' (CW 37 p. 302)

18 October: Lenin writes to Axelrod in Zürich about the difficulties of publishing *Iskra* and about contacts with Russia. 'We [Lenin and Potresov] are both quite well, but very edgy: the main thing is this astonishing uncertainty; these German rascals keep putting us off daily with "tomorrows". What I could do to them!' (CW 36 p. 37). Of the editorial board, only Lenin, Zasulich and Potresov are in Munich (Martov is in Russia, Plekhanov in Geneva and Axelrod in Zürich). However the main work of editing falls on Lenin's shoulders.

Autumn: Lenin spends most of his time on organisational preparation of the newspaper *Iskra* and the journal *Zarya*. Julian Marchlewski, a Polish revolutionary, helps Lenin in Munich and they meet frequently.

26 October: Lenin writes, in a letter to A A Yakubova: 'And those who are beginning the struggle at the present time are by no means *destroying* unity. There is no longer any unity, it has already been destroyed all along the line. Russian Marxism and Russian Social Democracy are already a house divided against itself and an open, frank struggle is one of the essential conditions for restoring unity.' (CW 34 pp. 51-4) Lenin writes to his former girl friend who, in the meanwhile, has become one of the leading Economists: 'Perhaps it is very inappropriate that in a letter to *you* of all people I have to speak so often of a struggle (literary struggle). But I think that our old friendship most of all makes *complete frankness* obligatory.' (p. 54)

2 November: Lenin lists the main tasks, in a letter to V P Nogin: ' . . . 1) transport of literature across the frontier . . . 2) delivery throughout Russia . . . 3) organisation of workers' groups to circulate the paper and collect information.' (CW 36 p. 42).

16 November: Lenin writes the article 'The Urgent Tasks of Our Movement' and it appears as the leading article in the first number of *Iskra*. (CW 4 pp. 366-71) Lenin explains that just as before 'the immediate political task' is the 'overthrow of the autocracy, the achievement of political liberty'. Social Democracy is 'the combination of the working class movement and socialism'; the most pressing task is the linking of the economic struggle to the political struggle which a 'strongly organised party' must lead.

First half of December: Lenin is in Stuttgart to prepare the publication of the journal *Zarya* (it is printed by the SPD publishing house J H W Dietz as of March 1901).

6 December: Lenin writes to his mother from Munich: 'Life goes on here as usual.' (CW 37 pp. 306-7)

7 December: Lenin writes to Axelrod in Zürich and exhorts him to 'send therefore *immediately* all that is available, everything possible [for *Iskra*].' (Briefe I p. 71) Address: Georg Rittmeyer, Kaiserstrasse 53 O Munich (inside: for Meyer).

14 December: Lenin travels from Munich to Leipzig and remains there until 23 December. He is there because of the first number of *Iskra*, which is set up on 24 December, in the printing works of Hermann Rauh, a social democrat, who prints the *Arbeiter-Turn-Zeitung*, in Leipzig-Probstheida, Russenstrasse 48. Lenin also organises the distribution. The newspaper is sent from various post offices. A co-worker reports: 'Each packet went to a different address in Switzerland and in Belgium.' (Donath *Auf Lenins Spuren* pp. 16, 17)

24 December: The first issue of *Iskra* appears carrying Lenin's articles 'The Urgent Tasks of Our Movement', 'The War in China' and 'The Split in the Union of Russian Social Democrats Abroad'. (CW 4 pp. 366-79)

26 December: Lenin writes to his mother that he is 'rather lonely'. (CW 37 p. 311)

30 December: Lenin writes: 'Sunday 2 am. I should like to set down my impressions of yesterday's meeting with the twin [Struve]. It was a remarkable meeting, "historic" in a way, (Arsenev, Velika [Zasulich], the twin + wife + myself) — at least it was historic as far as my life is concerned; it summed up, if not a whole epoch, at least a page in a life history and it determined my conduct and my life's path for a long time to come.

'As the case was first stated by Arsenev, I understand that the twin was coming over to us and wished to take the first steps, but the very opposite turned out to be the case . . .

'The twin revealed himself in a totally new light, as a "politician" of the purest water, a politician in the worst sense of the word, an old fox and a brazen huckster. He arrived *completely convinced of our impotence*.' (CW 4 pp. 380-2)

1901

30 January: An *Iskra* editorial meeting with Struve accepts the latter's condition for co-operation between the liberal 'democratic opposition', led by Struve, and *Iskra*. Discussions take place throughout January between Lenin, Potresov, Zasulich and Struve. Plekhanov and Axelrod also came to Munich during the first half of January. Lenin opposes the agreement, he writes Plekhanov: 'If the majority expresses itself in favour − I shall, course, submit, but only after having washed my hands of it beforehand.' (CW 34 p. 57)

January: Valdimir Ulyanov, in a letter to Plekhanov, uses the pseudonym Lenin for the first time and he is known by this name from 1901–2 onwards. Previously Lenin had written under the name Tulin and then under Ilyin; in all he uses about 150 pseudonyms.

Mid February (not before 21): The second number of *Iskra* appears; it contains Lenin's article 'The Drafting of 183 Students into the Army'. (CW 4 pp. 414–19) The paper appears in Munich where Lenin has been conducting negotiations since January with the printing firm of Max Ernst (Senefelder Strasse). The paper is finally printed there.

7 February: Lenin goes to the theatre in Munich, he sees the opera *Die Tochter des Kardinals* by Halewy.

9 February: In a letter to his mother, Lenin writes of several visits to the theatre. The opera *La Juive* brought him 'the greatest pleasure'. (CW 37 p. 317)

20 February: Lenin writes his mother about the Munich carnival: 'People here do know how to make merry publicly in the streets.' (CW 37 p. 319)

28 February: Lenin goes to Prague for a few days to make preparations for Krupskaya's arrival from Russia.

2 March: Lenin travels from Prague to Vienna to have his application for a passport for Krupskaya witnessed by the Russian consul there.

4 March: Lenin writes his mother from Vienna, this is 'a huge, lively and beautiful city'. (CW 37 p. 323) He returns to Munich.

20 March: Lenin informs Axelrod that difficulties have arisen over the publication of *Zarya* by the SPD publishing house Dietz in Stuttgart. 'When shall we get rid of the "tutelage" of these gutter comrades?' (CW 34 p. 58) He is pleased that no 2 of *Iskra* has arrived safely.

22 March: In a letter to F I Dan in Berlin he writes: 'Collect money. We are now just about as poor as beggars.' (Briefe I p. 91)

23 March: The first number of *Zarya* appears in Stuttgart containing three articles by Lenin under the general heading 'Casual Notes'. (CW 4 pp. 383–413)

14 April: Krupskaya arrives in Munich. She finally joins Lenin after going by mistake to Prague (to Modràček's address).

May: Lenin begins work on his pamphlet *What is to be Done?*

2 May: *Iskra* no 3 appears in Munich containing Lenin's article 'The Workers' Party and the Peasantry'. (CW 4 pp. 420–8)

Between 7–14 May: Lenin's plan to set up a League of Revolutionary Russian Social Democrats Abroad is debated by the editorial board.

18 May: Lenin, Krupskaya and her mother move into a new flat in Schwabing, Siegfriedstrasse 14. They are now living officially under the name 'Dr jur Jordan Jourdanoff and Frau Maritza' and have a Bulgarian passport. Krupskaya reports that she is buying furniture and 'again living in our own way. Martov (in Munich since March) and others arrived after lunch and the so-called meeting of the "editorial" took place.' (Krupskaya p. 59)

24 May: A letter, signed Lenin, is sent to G Leiteisen.

26-28 May: *Iskra* no 4, containing Lenin's important article 'Where to Begin?', appears in Munich. It contains, in embryonic form, Lenin's theses on party organisation which he is to develop in *What is to be Done?* (CW 5 pp. 13-24)

May: First meeting of Lenin and Rosa Luxemburg in Munich. They discuss the possibility of her contributing to *Zarya*. According to Krupskaya the meeting took place at Parvus's home. Parvus and Lenin meet often.

7 June: Lenin reports, in a letter to his mother that he has 'received 250 roubles' from his publisher 'and the financial side of things is now not bad.' (CW 37 pp. 329-30)

11 June: Krupskaya writes to Lenin's mother that their suburb, Schwabing, combines the advantages of a large city, 'shops, trams, etc.' with the proximity of the countryside. 'Yesterday, for instance, we went for a good walk along the road.' (CW 37 p. 601) Lenin receives 600 marks from his publisher, Vodovosova.

Before 7 July: Lenin meets Karl Kautsky, who breaks his journey in Munich, and they discuss the possibility of Kautsky contributing to *Zarya*.

9 July: Lenin, in a letter to Axelrod, describes his meeting with Kautsky ('on his way for a holiday in the Tyrol'). (CW 36 p. 88)

21 July: Lenin informs Axelrod: 'The Rittmeyer address is *no longer good*.' The new address of the editorial board is: 'Herrn Dr med Carl Lehmann, Gabelsbergerstrasse 20 a/II, Munich.'

25 July: In a letter to Plekhanov Lenin takes up the matter of their dispute about the relationship with the liberals, a dispute which has been going on since the beginning of July. Lenin sticks to his stern criticism of the liberals. 'But since there is "irritation" . . . I am no longer able to conceal it, and cannot exercise cunning here. I shall try to tone it down still more and make still further reservations; perhaps something will come of it.' (CW 34 pp. 80-2)

2 August: Krupskaya writes to Lenin's mother: 'Volodya is now working quite hard and I am glad for his sake; when he throws himself completely into some task he feels well and strong — that is one of his natural qualities; there does not seem to be a trace of the catarrh and no insomnia. Every day he takes a cold rub down and we go bathing almost every day, too.' (CW 37 pp. 603-4)

30 August: Lenin's article 'The Lessons of the Crisis' appears in *Iskra* no 7. (CW 5 pp. 89-94) It concerns the industrial crisis which is 'ever so much greater' in Russia than in any other country.

1 September: Lenin writes to his mother: 'It was very sad to learn that our people's affairs are in such a sorry state [his sister Maria and brother-in-law Mark Elizarov had been arrested]. I embrace you again and again, my dear, and wish you good health and vigour.' (CW 37 pp. 334-5)

29 September: Lenin travels with Krupskaya and Martov from Munich to Zürich to attend the 'unification' conference of Russian Social Democratic Organisations Abroad and remains there until 5 (or 6) October.

4 and 5 October: Lenin, under the name of Frey, addresses the conference at which representatives of *Iskra*, *Zayra*, *Sotsial Demokrat* and the Bureau Abroad take part. This is Lenin's first public speech before Russian social democrats abroad (the speech on 4 October is in CW 5 pp. 225-9). Representatives of *Iskra*, *Zarya* and *Sotsial Demokrat* declare that unification is impossible because of the opportunism of the Bureau Abroad and leave the conference.

21-22 October: Lenin writes to Plekhanov that he has contracted flu after his trip. 'I am indisposed.' (CW 34 p. 87) The letter is signed Lenin; normally he signs himself Petrov or Frey at this time.

October: *Iskra* no 9 appears. It contains Lenin's article 'Fighting the Famine Stricken', 'A Reply to the St Petersburg Committee' and 'Party Affairs Abroad'. (CW 5 pp. 231-42)

3 November: Lenin informs Plekhanov: 'Our finances are now in good shape', there are 'very good prospects of greater income from periodicals.' If Plekhanov ever needs money he should write 'without embarrassment.' (Briefe I pp. 150-1)

27 November: Lenin writes to Lyubov Axelrod that he has 'lately been very busy with a pamphlet' (*What is to be Done?*) but that once again he is 'going down with some "undetermined" illness.' (CW 36 p. 100)

1 December: In a letter to Plekhanov Lenin states: 'I am still unwell, and "struggling" with the pamphlet . . . [*What is to be Done?*] which is advancing almost in crab-like fashion.' (CW 36 p. 103)

17 December: Lenin writes to Axelrod: 'The whole burden of our newspaper [*Iskra*] now rests on my shoulders; also administrative matters due to delays in transport and the confusion in Russia have become more complex. My pamphlet is suffering. I am terribly behind.' (Briefe I p. 158)

21 or 22 December: Issue no 2-3 of *Zarya* appears in Stuttgart, printed by Dietz. It contains Lenin's article 'The Persecutors of the Zemstvo and the Hannibals of Liberalism' which had started the conflict with Plekhanov. (CW 5 pp. 31-80) It also carries under the title 'The "Critics" in the Agrarian Question' the first four chapters of his future pamphlet 'The Agrarian Question and the "Critics of Marx"'. (CW 5 pp. 103-22) This article is signed Lenin and one can from now on speak of Lenin. Finally Lenin's 'Review of Home Affairs' (signed T Kh) also appears in *Zarya* (CW 5 pp. 251–301)

23 December: Lenin asks Axelrod: 'Could you possibly have a look at my pamphlet (my book?) against the Economists? . . . I should like to discuss it with you.' (Briefe I p. 164)

December: The pamphlet 'Documents of the "Unity" Conference', containing a preface by Lenin, appears in Geneva.

End of the Year: Lenin writes his theses on 'Anarchism and Socialism'. (CW 5 pp. 327–30) Anarchism is a 'product of despair'.

1902

2 January: *Iskra* no 13 appears in Munich containing Lenin's articles 'Demonstrations Have Begun' (CW 5 pp. 322–5) and 'On a Letter from "Southern Workers"'. (CW 5 p. 326)

3 January: Lenin receives a copy of *Iskra* no 10 which had been printed on a secret printing press in Kishinev.

13 January: Lenin reacts critically to Plekhanov's draft party programme. (CW 6 pp. 19–26)

21 January: Lenin lays before the editorial board of *Iskra* in Munich his proposals for changes in Plekhanov's draft programme. Plekhanov and Axelrod are also present and considerable discord ensues.

End of January–Beginning of February: Lenin works on a new draft of the party programme. (CW 6 pp. 27–33)

14 February: *Iskra* no 16 appears and contains Lenin's article 'Political Agitation and the "Class Point of View"'. (CW 5 pp. 337–43) Lenin states: 'We must untiringly combat any and every bourgeois ideology.'

28 February: *Iskra* no 17 appears with Lenin's articles 'Signs of Bankruptcy' and 'From the Economic Life of Russia'. (CW 6 pp. 79–96)

First half of March: Lenin writes 'The Agrarian Programme of Russian Social Democracy'. It appears in August 1902 in *Zarya*. (CW 6 pp. 107–50)

Mid March: Lenin's pamphlet 'What is to be Done? Burning Questions of Our Movement' is published by Verlag J H W Dietz in Stuttgart. (CW 5 pp. 347–520) In this work, one of his most important and influential, Lenin intervenes directly in the discussion on the development of Russian social democracy. He presents his conception of Party organisation. In 'What is to be Done?' the striking sentence 'Give us an organisation of revolutionaries and we shall turn Russia upside-down' appears. The demand for an organisation of professional revolutionaries, the thesis of the Party as the conscious and organised avant garde of the working class and the concept of the necessity of bringing socialist consciousness to the workers from outside are developed. Lenin clearly has the special circumstances of Russia in mind.

23 March: *Iskra* no 18 appears with Lenin's article 'A Letter to the Zemstvoists'. (CW 6 pp. 151-9) *Iskra* also publishes an annoucement about the publication of Lenin's pamphlet 'What is to be Done?' by Dietz Verlag, Stuttgart.

Before 27 March: Discussions take place about transferring the printing of *Iskra* away from Munich as the printer is no longer willing to accept the risk and the editorial board fears discovery by the Russian secret police and persecution by the German police. Plekhanov and Axelrod are for moving to Switzerland; London is also mentioned.

10 April: Lenin, in a letter to his sister Anna in Berlin, tells her of his intended move to London on 12 April. His new address: Mr Alexejeff, 14 Frederick Street, Gray's Inn Road, London WC1 (inside: for Lenin). (CW 37 p. 343)

12 April: Lenin and Krupskaya leave Munich for London.

13 April: They break their journey to London in Cologne and visit the cathedral there, and then travel on to Liège and Brussels.

14 August: Lenin and Krupskaya arrive in London. They live initially under the name of Richter in a furnished room. British socialists support the printing of *Iskra*. Lenin writes later: 'British social democrats, led by Quelch, readily made their printing plant available. As a consequence Quelch himself had to "squeeze up". A corner was boarded off at the printing works by a thin partition to serve him as editorial room.' (CW 19 pp. 369-71) Lenin often visits the printers in 37a Clerkenwell Green.

18 April: Lenin writes from London to Axelrod in Zürich. 'We are taken up with settling in. Lots of trouble . . . The first impression of London: hideous. And everything is so expensive!' (Briefe I p. 177)

April-May: Lenin and Krupskaya get to know London, visit Speaker's Corner in Hyde Park and eat in restaurants. Krupskaya reports: 'Soon my mother was due to arrive and we decided to live in family style . . . What is more, we were at that time on the payroll of our organisation, which meant that we had to look after every penny . . . We assumed the name of Richter . . . and our landlady took us for Germans the whole time. After a while Martov and Vera Zasulich arrived.' (Krupskaya pp. 68-69)

20 or 21 April: Lenin receives a recommendation to the director of the British Museum from Isaac Mitchell, secretary of the General Federation of Trade Unions. On 25 April he receives permission to use the reading room (reader's card no A 72453).

April: In 'A Letter to the Northern League' Lenin comments critically on the programme of the Russian Northern League. (CW 6 pp. 161-71)

8 May: Lenin expresses hope, in a letter to his mother, that he will 'see her soon' and wishes her bon voyage. He advises her to 'take express trains in Germany and Austria.' (CW 37 pp. 344-5)

10 May: Lenin inserts the following notice in *The Athenaeum*, a weekly journal: 'Russian doctor of laws and his wife seek English lessons from an Englishman (or English woman) in return for lessons in Russian. Replies to: J Richter, 30 Holford Square, Pentonville.' (Khr. I p. 387) They find someone and improve their command of English.

14 May: Lenin writes a very critical letter to Plekhanov about the latter's editorial changes of his article 'The Agrarian Programme of Russian Social Democracy'. 'If you have set yourself the aim of making our common work impossible, you can very quickly attain this aim by the path you have chosen. As far as personal and not business relations are concerned, you have already definitely spoilt them or, rather, you have succeeded in putting an end to them completely. N Lenin.' (CW 34 p. 103)

7 June: Lenin writes to his mother in Samara: 'We are all expecting you, my dear.' (CW 37 pp. 346-7)

14 June: The draft programme of the RSDLP, written by the editors of *Iskra* and *Zarya*, including Lenin, appears in *Iskra* no 21.

23 June: Lenin writes to Axelrod that his health is bad. 'I am almost completely incapable of working, my nerves are at breaking point.' (Briefe I pp. 186-7) On the same day he writes to Plekhanov and they are reconciled. 'A great weight fell from my shoulders when I received your letter, which put an end to thoughts of "internecine war" . . . That I had no intention of offending you, you are of course aware . . . My nerves are worn to shreds and I am feeling quite ill.' (CW 34 pp. 104-5)

26 or 27 June: Lenin arrives in Paris from London.

27 June: Lenin addresses Russian émigrés on the programme and tactics of the Russian socialist revolutionaries and on the programme of the social democrats.

End of June: Lenin travels to Loguivy, in Brittany and holidays there until 25 July. His mother, Maria Ulyanova, arrives from Russia and his sister Anna Ulyanova-Elizarova from Germany.

Before 16 July: Lenin writes two letters to I I Radchenko (CW 6 pp. 176-85) 'I personally am particularly interested, in this connection, in what the workers will think of 'What is to be Done?', because I have not yet had any views from workers.' (CW 36 p. 119)

24 July: Lenin writes, in a letter to G D Leiteisen from Loguivy: 'I was a bit premature in imagining myself well again.' (CW 34 p. 106)

25 July: Lenin travels to London from Loguivy.

2 August: In a letter to P G Smidovich, Lenin develops ideas about the form of the illegal organisation, about professional revolutionaries, mass organisations and so on.

14 August: *Iskra* no 23 appears in London and contains the first part of Lenin's article 'Revolutionary Adventurism' (CW 6 pp. 186-96) directed against the social democrats and their concept of 'terror'.

15 August: Lenin has discussions, in London, with representatives of the St Petersburg committee of RSDLP, the Russian *Iskra* organisation and the Northern League of the RSDLP. The organisation committee for convening the 2nd Congress is formed.

24 August: Lenin writes a letter to the Moscow committee of the RSDLP (which agrees with 'What is to be Done?'). He gives advice about immediate tasks. 'For an illegal writer it [solidarity] is all the more valuable since he is isolated from his readers.' (Briefe I p. 220)

August: *Zarya* no 4 appears containing Lenin's article 'The Agrarian Programme of Russian Social Democracy'. (CW 6 pp. 107–50) Lenin writes the preface to the second edition of 'Tasks of the Russian Social Democrats', which is published in December 1902. (CW 6 pp. 211–16)

14 September: *Iskra* no 24 appears containing Lenin's article 'The Draft of a New Law on Strikes' and the second part of 'Revolutionary Adventurism'. (CW 6 pp. 217–26 and 196–207)

16 September: In a letter to the editors of *Yuzhny Rabochii* (Southern Worker), Lenin stresses the need to merge the local party committees in an all-Russian organisation.

27 September: Lenin writes to his mother in Samara that he has been trying to spend more time in the library; they have also 'travelled and walked around a great deal of the surrounding country.' (CW 37 p. 349)

27 September: Lenin writes to A M Kalmykova in Dresden. 'At present, we are very hard up for money, and there are some *urgent* expenses.' He asks for 2000 marks to be sent. (CW 36 p. 123)

Between 14–24 September: Lenin writes the pamphlet 'A Letter to a Comrade in Our Organisational Tasks'. Lenin replies to the social democrat A A Shneierson, a future Menshevik, who had drafted a plan for the organisation of the work in St Petersburg. Lenin demands a 'disciplined party of struggle'. His letter is hectographed and widely distributed. The Siberian committee of the RSDLP publishes it in January 1903. Lenin himself publishes it as a special pamphlet in Geneva in January 1904. (CW 6 pp. 231–52)

9 November: Lenin leaves London for Switzerland. En route he stops in Liège and addresses a meeting.

10 November: Lenin gives a talk on the programme and tactics of the Socialist Revolutionaries in Lausanne.

11 November: Lenin writes from Geneva to Axelrod in Berne that he had spoken the day before in Lausanne but had to speak in Geneva the same day. A discussion is scheduled for the 12th in Geneva so his talk in Berne will be given not later than the 15th.

14 November: *Iskra* no 27 appears containing Lenin's article 'Vulgar Socialism and Narodism as Resurrected by the Socialist Revolutionaries'. (CW 6 pp. 263–70)

15 November: Lenin speaks on the Socialist Revolutionaries in Berne.

20 November: Lenin speaks in Zürich.

28 November: After his return to London Lenin thanks Axelrod 'for your letter and the money.' (Briefe I p. 232)

29 November: Lenin speaks in London on the Socialist Revolutionaries. He writes to Plekhanov on 14 December that the talk 'did not interest our people here.' (CW 34 p. 124)

3 December: Lenin's mother writes to her daughter Anna that a letter from Krupskaya had arrived. 'She describes her small flat which has considerable drawbacks. In all they have two small rooms and one of them, that of El. Vasilevna [Krupskaya's mother], serves both as kitchen and dining room. Water and coal, the fuel they use, are both downstairs and have to be brought up; the washing-up water has to be taken outside and so on . . . they had first of all thought of looking for a larger place but Nadenka added that she and V[olodya] have become like cats which get used to a particular spot.' (*Vom Alltag der Uljanows* pp. 140, 143)

17 December: Lenin writes to his mother: 'Our life goes on just the same as before . . . we all caught colds. But we are all right now.' (CW 37 pp. 352-3)

18 December: Lenin informs Axelrod that he is going to send him 'from here a young, very energetic and capable comrade to help him (cover name The Pen).' He has Trotsky in mind. (Briefe I p. 239)

27 December: Lenin demands, in a letter to Lengnik in Kiev, that the struggle against the Economists, who have taken over the Kiev committee of the RSDLP, be stepped up.

1903

10 January: Lenin writes to Plekhanov that he has received an invitation from the Paris College (the Russian College for Social Sciences in Paris) and would like to discuss the planned lectures with Plekhanov. 'Our' people should have nothing at all to do with the college but it is important 'to speak there too' as a counterbalance. 'What do you think?' (CW 43 pp. 103-5)

28 January: *Iskra* no 32 appears and contains Lenin's article 'Announcement of the Formation of an Organising Committee'. (CW 6 pp. 307-11)

4 February: In a letter to his mother, Lenin writes: 'We recently went to our first concert this winter and were very pleased with it — especially with Chaikovsky's latest symphony (Symphonie Pathétique). Are there any good concerts in Samara? We went once to a German theatre but what we should like would be to visit the Russian Art Theatre and see *The Lower Depths*.' (CW 37 p. 355)

5 February: Lenin writes to Martov in Paris and informs him about the discussions with the Union of Russian Social Democrats Abroad. The letter ends: 'All the best, Lenin.' Martov was one of the few people whom Lenin addressed in the second person singular (ty).

14 February: *Iskra* no 33 appears and contains Lenin's articles 'Concerning the Statement of the Bund' and 'On the Manifesto of the Armenian Social Democrats'. (CW 6 pp. 319–29)

22 February: Lenin writes to his mother that he 'expects to take a trip to Germany in a few days.' (CW 37 pp. 356–7) Actually he travelled to Paris.

23 February: Lenin travels from London to Paris. He delivers four lectures on the topic 'Marxist views on the agrarian question in Europe and Russia' at the Russian College of Social Sciences, until 26 February. Lenin remains in Paris until 9 March.

25 February: Lenin addresses members of the *Iskra* group in Paris on the agrarian programme.

28 February: *Iskra* no 34 appears containing Lenin's article 'Does the Jewish Proletariat Need an "Independent Political Party?"'. It is directed against the Bund, the Jewish social democratic organisation in Russia. (CW 6 pp. 330–6)

2 March: Lenin writes from Paris to Plekhanov in Geneva: 'I am submitting to all members of the editorial board a proposal to co-opt the "pen" as a full member of the board . . . We are *very much in need* of a seventh member both because it would simplify voting (six being an even number) and reinforce the board. The "pen" has been writing in every issue for several months now . . . A man of more than average ability, convinced, energetic and promising.' (CW 43 pp. 110–2) The 'pen' was Trotsky's cover name. However nothing came of the proposal.

3 March: Lenin speaks at a meeting of Russian political émigrés in Paris on the agrarian programme of the Socialist Revolutionaries. The discussions last three days.

4 March: Krupskaya writes to Lenin's mother from London and informs her that he is away. 'You will probably think that we have no amusements here at all but we go somewhere almost every evening; we have been to the German theatre a number of times and to concerts, and we study the people and the local way of life. It is easier to observe here than anywhere else. Volodya is very keen on these observations and gets as enthusiastic about them as about everything he does.' (CW 37 pp. 605–6)

9 March: Lenin returns to London from Paris.

14 March–10 April: Lenin works on 'To the Rural Poor. An Explanation for the Peasants of What the Social Democrats Want'. It appears in Geneva in May. Lenin has been concerned about the peasant question for some time. He tries to write as simply as possible. On the goals of the socialists he writes: 'We want to achieve a new and better order of society; in this new and better society there must be neither rich nor poor; all will have to work . . . The teachings about this society are called *socialism*.' (CW 6 p. 366) Lenin writes of class struggle in the countryside and of the alliance of workers and peasants. As Krupskaya reports this was one of the few pieces of work 'which did not get on Vladimir Ilich's nerves, but gave him a certain amount of satisfaction.' (Krupskaya p. 79)

18 March: Lenin addresses a meeting at Whitechapel on the occasion of the anniversary of the Paris Commune.

29 March: Lenin tells his mother that Krupskaya and he are taking lots of walks. 'We are the only people among the comrades here who are exploring *every bit* of the surrounding countryside.' (CW 37 p. 358)

14 April: Lenin's article 'Mr Struve Exposed by his Colleagues' appears in *Iskra* no 37. (CW 6 pp. 354-60) Lenin opposes Struve's liberalism and writes that it is important to 'subordinate *everything without exception* to the interests and demands of the *revolutionary struggle.*'

28 April: Lenin's article 'Les Beaux Esprits se Rencontrent. (Which May be Interpreted Roughly as: Birds of a Feather Flock Together)' appears in *Iskra* no 38. Lenin again criticises the Socialist Revolutionaries. (CW 6 pp. 433-7)

Beginning of May: The editorial office of *Iskra* is moved from London to Geneva, a decision opposed by Lenin. Lenin and Krupskaya move to Geneva in May. He is ill for about two weeks in Geneva and they live in the Morar pension until he recovers. Krupskaya writes later that Lenin 'was so overwrought that he developed a nervous illness called "holy fire", which consists of inflammation of the nerve terminals of back and chest ... [probably shingles] On the way to Geneva Vladimir Ilich was very restless; on arriving there he broke down completely, and had to lie in bed for two weeks.' (Krupskaya p. 79)

May: The pamphlet 'To the Rural Poor' is published in Geneva (see 14 March–10 April). (CW 6 pp. 361-432)

End of May–June: Lenin writes the first draft of a Party statute. The second draft is written in July, the final version at the end of July.

12 June: Lenin and Krupskaya move into a new flat in Geneva, Sécheron, Chemin du Foyer 10. The live here until 1 July 1904.

June: Lenin speaks on the agrarian programme in Geneva and Berne.

June–July: Lenin is involved in preparations for the 2nd Congress of the RSDLP. He drafts the rules of procedure and the agenda, also a draft Party statute and a report on the activities of *Iskra*. He attends meetings of delegates and makes himself known to delegates who are arriving for the congress.

29 June: Lenin writes to Karl Kautsky and sends him a copy of his pamphlet *Die soziale Revolution* translated into Russian by N Karpov, edited by Lenin and published in Geneva.

June–July: Lenin writes the 'Reply of Criticism of Our Draft Programme'. He defends his views on the agrarian question against the criticisms of P P Maslov. The article appears in July in pamphlet form in Geneva.

28 July: Lenin's article 'The National Question in Our Programme' appears in *Iskra* no 44. (CW 6 pp. 454–63)

30 July: The 2nd Congress of the All-Russian Social Democratic Labour Party opens in Brussels. The RSDLP splits at this congress, which lasts until 23 August, into Bolsheviks and Mensheviks. The Congress takes place in Brussels in a large store, a 'big flour warehouse'. (Krupskaya p. 83) Lenin is elected deputy chairman, to the presidium and to the credentials commission, at the first session. There are 43 delegates with collectively 51 mandates and 14 delegates with a consultative voice. The *Iskra* organisation with 27 delegates (and 33 votes) is in the majority, the Jewish Bund has 5 representatives, the Economists 7 and there are 4 undecided delegates (with 6 votes).

31 July: Lenin speaks on the agenda at the second session of the Congress (morning) and on the organisation committee at the third session (afternoon).

1–5 August: Lenin participates in the 4–12th sessions of the 2nd Congress in Brussels; he speaks on the Party programme and on the Jewish Bund. Lenin is elected to the programme commission, which meets between 3–11 August, at the eighth session (3 August)

6 August: The Congress adjourns after the 13th session in Brussels and moves to London since the police had discovered it and had expelled some of the delegates.

7 August: Lenin travels with Krupskaya, Bauman and Lyadov, via Ostend–Dover, to London.

11 August: The 14th Session of the 2nd Congress of the RSDLP convenes in the morning in London. Lenin speaks on the Party statute. Lenin is elected to the editorial commission of the statute at the 15th session in the evening.

12–14 August: Lenin takes part in the 16–21st sessions of the Congress and intervenes often on the agrarian programme.

15 August: The 22nd and 23rd sessions of the Congress debate paragraph 1 of the statute during which it almost comes to a split. Although the majority of the *Iskra* organisation had previously accepted the programme, agrarian programme and so on, the *Iskra* group now splits. Lenin and Martov have submitted opposing draft statutes. Martov wants a relatively broad Party; a member should be someone 'who regularly supports one of its organisations'. Lenin, on the other hand, demands a narrow, restricted Party membership with 'personal work in one of the Party organisations' a precondition for membership. (AS p. 234) Lenin has to accept defeat, Martov's proposal for paragraph 1 is adopted by 28 votes to 23; 19 *Iskra* votes go to Lenin and 14 to Martov, the votes of the Bund and the Economists are cast for Martov.

16 and 17 August: The statute is further debated at the 24th–26th sessions. Lenin intervenes often.

18 August: 27th and 28th sessions of the Congress. The Bund delegates and two representatives of the Economist *Rabochee Delo* quit the

Congress during the 27th session. This changes the voting balance; the 'hard line' Iskrists, Lenin's supporters, now dominate. From now on Lenin's supporters call themselves, after their fortuitous majority, Bolsheviks (majoritarians) and the supporters of Martov, Mensheviks (minoritarians). During the evening, after the 28th session, the fourth, and last, meeting of *Iskra* supporters takes place. (Khr. I p. 479 — previously the date of this session was always incorrectly given as 'the 15–16 August'.) The final break between Lenin's supporters, the Bolsheviks, and Martov's, the Mensheviks, takes place at this meeting. Differences occur between the nine 'hard line' Iskrists, Lenin's supporters, and the seven 'soft line' on the question of election to the Central Committee; the *Iskra* group splits on who should be elected to the leading organ.

19–23 August: The Bolsheviks with 24 delegates are numerically stronger than the Mensheviks with 20 delegates during the last days of the Congress (29–37th sessions). With the Boksheviks in the majority, elections take place to the central organ, the Central Committee and to the Council of the Party. Lenin's supporters, Krzhizhanovsky, Lengnik and Noskov are elected to the CC and Lenin, Plekhanov and Martov are elected to the editorial board of *Iskra*. Lenin's resolutions and speeches at the Congress are in CW 6 pp. 467–509.

The splitting of the RSDLP makes Lenin, leader of the Bolsheviks, the leader of the Party. He writes later: 'Bolshevism exists as a political movement and as a political Party since 1903.' (AS p. 984)

24 August: Lenin and congress delegates visit Karl Marx's grave in Highgate cemetery. Lenin leaves London for Geneva after 24 August.

28 August: Lenin's articles 'An Era of Reform' and 'The Latest Word in Bundist Nationalism' appear in *Iskra* no 46. (CW 6 pp. 510–21)

13 September: Lenin writes, in a letter to Potresov: 'The refusal of Martov to serve on the editorial board . . . the refusal of a number of persons to work for the CC . . . are bound to lead to a split in the Party'. Lenin confirms that he had 'often behaved and acted in a state of frightful irritation, frenziedly' at the Congress and he was willing to 'admit this *fault of mine*' but in the results of the Congress there was nothing injurious to the Party. (CW 34 p. 164)

14 September: Lenin's article 'The Law on Compensation Payable to Workers Injured in Accidents' appears in *Iskra* no 47. (CW 41 pp. 96–103)

Mid September: Lenin writes the 'Account of the Second Congress of the RSDLP', a description of the split 'intended for personal acquaintances only.' (CW 7 pp. 19–34)

25–28 September: Lenin and Plekhanov try to reach agreement with the minority but without success.

30 September: Lenin writes to Kalmykova about the Congress: 'I would not think of denying the personal aspect but that is no reason for demanding a *political* correction.' (CW 34 p. 169)

September: Lenin's article 'The Tasks of Revolutionary Youth' appears in the paper *Student* no 2-3. (CW 7 pp. 43-56)

4 October: Lenin, Plekhanov and Lengnik have discussions with Martov, Axelrod, Potresov and Zasulich from the minority but they end without agreement.

5 October: In a letter to Krzhizhanovsky and Noskov, Lenin reports on the session of 4 October. 'There is no longer any hope, absolutely no hope of peace. You can't imagine even a tenth of the outrages to which the Martovites have sunk here.' They are 'encroaching on our contacts, *money*, literary material, etc. War has been declared.' (CW 36 p. 128)

6 October: Lenin and Plekhanov, in a letter, inform Martov that they are ready to co-opt him as a member of the editorial board of *Iskra*. (CW 34 pp. 173-4)

14 October: Lenin's article 'Maximum Brazenness and Minimum Logic', directed against the Bund, appears in *Iskra* no 49. (CW 7 pp. 59-65)

October: Lenin has an accident before the conference of the League. 'Vladimir Ilich, who had become engrossed in thought, ran into the back of a tram, and very nearly had his eye knocked out. He appeared at the conference pale and bandaged.' (Krupskaya pp. 93-4)

26-30 October: Lenin attends the 2nd Conference of the League of Russian Social Democrats Abroad in Geneva.

27 October: Lenin delivers a report to the Conference on the 2nd Congress of the RSDLP.

28 October: Lenin explains, at the fourth session of the Conference, why he is not making any concluding remarks to his speech.

30 October: Lenin protests at the Conference of the League against the 'crying violation of the Party Rules.' (CW 41 p. 107)

1 November: Lenin hands a declaration to Plekhanov: 'In as much as I do not share the opinion of G V Plekhanov . . . that it will be in the interest of Party unity at the present time to make a concession to the Martovites . . . I hereby resign from the Party Council and from the editorial board of the Central organ.' (CW 7 p. 91) On the same day Lenin writes to Plekhanov: 'Do not withdraw and do not give everything away to the Martovites.' (CW 34 p. 185)

4 November: Lenin's article 'The Position of the Bund in the Party' appears in *Iskra* no 51. (CW 7 pp. 92-103) In a letter to Krzhizhanovsky in Kiev Lenin asks him to come immediately to Geneva because Plekhanov has 'cruelly and shamefully let me down' and has gone to 'haggle with the Martovites.' Lenin states that 'the situation is desperate.' (CW 34 p. 186)

6 November: In a letter to Plekhanov, Lenin repeats his 'resignation from the editorial board' of *Iskra*. (CW 34 p. 189) He sends Plekhanov all the editorial documents.

10 November: Lenin informs M N Lyadov, in a letter, of Plekhanov's

move to the Mensheviks. On *Iskra* he writes that of the 45 issues which
the editorial board of six published '*not a single* issue was made up (in
the sense of technical editorial work) by anyone other than Martov or
myself'. Martov had written 39 articles, Lenin 32, Plekhanov 24 but
Potresov only 8, Zasulich 6 and Axelrod 4. (CW 34 p. 195)
18 November: Lenin requests the editorial board of *Iskra* to insert the
following announcement: 'As from November 1 (New Style) 1903
N Lenin is no longer a member of the *Iskra* editorial board.' (CW 7 p.
113)
Between 19-21 November: Lenin is co-opted, as representative abroad,
to the CC of the Party; Galperin as well. Already in October Zemlyachka, Krasin, Essen and Gusarov had been co-opted to the CC to
which Krzhizhanovsky, Lengnik and Noskov had been elected at the
2nd Congress.
27 November: The CC, at a session in Geneva, adopts Lenin's declaration which contains a protest against Plekhanov's behaviour in the
editorial question.
29 November: Lenin, as a CC member, joins the Council of the Party.
In a letter to Martov, Lenin is prepared, through a statement, to resolve
the 'personal aspect' of the conflict. 'I did not and do not question the
integrity and sincerity of Martov.' (CW 43 p. 115)
8 December: Lenin's article 'Letter to *Iskra*' appears in *Iskra* no 53. In
it he asks that the masses be given the opportunity of getting to know
their leaders and of placing each of them in the right position. 'Let the
columns of the Party organ and of all Party publications indeed be
thrown open hospitably to all opinions'; only in this way can 'a really
harmonious ensemble of leaders' appear. (CW 7 pp. 115-8)
Between 8-12 December: Lenin sends the editorial board of *Iskra*, now
Menshevik, an open letter 'Why I Resigned from the *Iskra* Editorial
Board'. As the editorial board did not print it, it is published as a pamphlet. (CW 7 pp. 119-25)
10 December: In a letter to members of the CC in Russia, Lenin asks
for the convocation of the 3rd Party Congress; it must '*be held not later
than January*.' (CW 34 p. 201)
14 December: Lenin's article 'The Narodnik-Like Bourgeoisie and
Distraught Narodism' appears in *Iskra* no 54. (CW 7 pp. 104-12)
22 December: In 'To the Central Committee of the RSDLP' Lenin
protests again the CC announcement to the committees that peace has
been restored with the Mensheviks. The struggle is 'just beginning'.
(CW 7 pp. 211-2)
30 December: In a letter to the CC of the RSDLP, Lenin complains
about its tactics and again asks for the convocation of the 3rd Congress.
This must not necessarily 'legitimise a split', but would be 'better
than the present situation.' Lenin concludes: 'Don't bother me about
leaflets. I am not a machine and in the present scandalous situation I

can't work.' (CW 34 pp. 216-7)

1904

2 January: Lenin reacts to Axelrod's article in *Iskra* no 53 in a post-script to his letter of 30 December 1903. He calls the newspaper, now published by the Mensheviks, until issue no 112 in October 1905, the 'new *Iskra*'. In it he is reproached for 'bureaucratic centralism in the Party organisation'. 'If all efforts are at once directed towards Nikolaev, Siberia and the Caucasus' then we can restrict the Martovites to one third of the votes. The Martovites control Kiev, Kharkov, Gornoza-vodsky, Rostov and the Crimea. (CW 34 pp. 218-9)

4 January: Lenin writes, in a letter to Krzhizhanovsky, that Martov 'is a pawn in the hands of cunning persons.' (CW 34 p. 221)

8 January: Lenin informs his mother that he, Krupskaya and F V Lengnik, 'a few days ago . . . had a wonderful outing to Salève.' (CW 37 p. 359)

15 January: Krupskaya writes to Lenin's mother that she is shocked that Lenin's sisters and brother (Anna, Maria and Dmitri) have been arrested in Kiev. 'We feel unsettled somehow and the work goes badly.' (CW 37 p. 607)

28-30 January: Lenin attends a session of the Council of the RSDLP, proposes resolutions and speaks on peace in the Party and the convoca-tion of the 3rd Party Congress. (CW 7 pp. 145-87)

31 January: Lenin reports to the CC of the RSDLP on a meeting of the Party Council. 'Plekhanov sided with the Martovites, outvoting us on every question of any importance.' (CW 34 p. 227)

First half of February: Lenin drafts the appeal 'To the Party Member-ship' (CW 7 pp. 140-4)

February: Lenin writes, in a letter to the CC in Russia, that 'the Party is virtually torn apart . . . I believe that we really do have in the CC bureaucrats and formalists, instead of revolutionaries. The Martovites spit in their faces and they wipe it off and lecture me: "it is useless to fight!" . . . Forget all idiotic formalities, take possession of the commit-tees, teach *them* to fight for the Party.' (CW 34 p. 233)

20 February: Lenin writes 'Circumstances of Resignation from the *Iskra* Editorial Board'. (CW 7 pp. 193-8)

February-March: Lenin writes the pamphlet 'One Step Forward, Two Steps Back'.

13 March: Lenin resigns temporarily (until 26 May) from the Council of the Party.

19 March: Lenin's pamphlet 'One Step Forward, Two Steps Back: The Crisis in our Party' (CW 7 pp. 203-425) appears in Geneva. In this important publication Lenin comments on the minutes of the Party

Congress and again gives his version of the split. Furthermore he develops his concept of the role and especially the organisation of the Party in very blunt language. His concept of the narrow, cadre Party with its core of professional revolutionaries, a Party which is true to its principles and united in action, becomes the basis of Bolshevism.

13 and 18 June: Lenin attends sessions of the Council of the Party and delivers three speeches. (CW 7 pp. 435-44)

After 21 June: Lenin, Krupskaya and M M Essen travel by steamer to Montreux and go walking in the mountains.

25 or 26 June: Lenin and Krupskaya travel to Lausanne, then take an extended holiday around Switzerland. Krupskaya reports later: 'At the end of June (3 July) 1904 Vladimir Ilich and I put on our rucksacks and headed, without any plan, into the mountains for a month. We stayed about a week in Lausanne . . . and went up into the mountains near Montreux . . . The new impressions, the natural tiredness and the healthy sleep had a healthy effect on Vladimir Ilich. His thoughts, his joie de vivre, his good humour returned. We spent August near Lac de Brêt where Vladimir Ilich and Bogdanov drafted the plan for the continuation of the struggle against the Mensheviks.' (W 37 pp. 615-6)

2 July: Krupskaya and Lenin write to his mother from Lausanne.

7-8 July: Lenin sends a card to his mother from Frutigen, Switzerland. 'Greetings from the tramps.' (CW 37 p. 363)

Between 4-12 August: Lenin edits the Bolshevik report of the Amsterdam Congress of the Second International.

15 August: In a letter to M K Vladimirov in Gomel, Lenin writes that 'some of the CC members have adopted a "conciliatory" attitude.' (CW 34 pp. 245-7) The conciliators, Noskov, Krasin, Gusarov, Galperin and Krzhizhanovsky had already outvoted the 'hard' Bolsheviks, Lenin, Lengnik, Essen and Zemlyachka in February. The conciliators had adopted, in July, a motion for Party unity with the Mensheviks. They now completely dominate the CC, Zemlyachka has resigned and Lengnik and Essen are in prison.

18 August: In a letter to five CC members, Lenin opposes the July motion of the CC and 'cannot acknowledge these decisions [as] lawfully adopted.' (CW 7 pp. 462-3)

28 August: Lenin tells his mother that he has begun to translate Hobson's book on imperialism.

August (July?): Lenin and Krupskaya take part in the Conference of the Twenty Two. The conference, attended by 19 Bolsheviks (Bogdanov, Lunacharsky, Olminsky, Lyadov, Lepeshinsky among others) and joined later by three others, adopts Lenin's appeal 'To the Party' concerning the convocation of the 3rd Congress. (CW 7 pp. 454-61) The precise date of the conference remains unclear. It may have taken place in the first half of August in a suburb of Geneva. Gautschi, on the other hand, (p. 58) thinks, on the basis of police archives, that it took place at Hermance between 23–28 July. However the police list, with the exception of Lenin, does not contain the name of any Bolshevik who attended the Conference of the Twenty Two. It is possible that the conference mentioned by Gautschi is a different one and Lenin's name incorrectly given. According to Khr. I p. 534 Lenin was in Brunnen, Switzerland, on 28 July. A letter dated 26 July to V D Bonch-Bruevich (CW 36 pp. 133–4) was sent to Geneva but it is not known where it was sent from.

11 September: In a critical letter to Noskov, Lenin opposes the 'conciliatory' majority of the CC. He declines to rejoin the *Iskra* editorial board; the Mensheviks are agreeable to this, as requested by the CC.

15 September: Lenin returns to Geneva from his summer holidays. He and Krupskaya move into a new two-room flat nearer the centre of the city, 'Rue Carouge 91'. (Gautschi p. 58) The annual rent is 600 francs.

20 September: Lenin, in a letter to M Leibovich, accuses the 'conciliatory' CC majority of going over to the Mensheviks.

Second half of September: Lenin writes the article 'One Step Forward, Two Steps Back: Reply by N Lenin to Rosa Luxemburg'. (CW 7 pp. 474–85) In her article 'The Organisational Question of Russian Social Democracy', which first appeared in *Iskra* and then in German in *Neue Zeit*, Rosa Luxemburg attacks the pamphlet 'One Step Forward, Two Steps Back' and accuses Lenin of 'ultra-centralism . . . it is full of the sterile spirit of the overseer' and is aimed at 'binding' the movement rather than developing it. (Luxemburg p. 94)

10 October: Lenin sends his anti-Rosa Luxemburg article to Karl Kautsky and writes that he 'is aware that the sympathies of the editors of *Neue Zeit* are with my opponents' but he thinks that 'it would be only fair to grant me the right to correct some of the inaccuracies in Rosa Luxemburg's articles.' (CW 43 p. 127)

26 October: Lenin writes again to Kautsky and asks him if his article has appeared. Kautsky tells Lenin that the editorial board has declined to accept the article. The article is published for the first time in 1930.

2 November: Lenin writes to A A Bogdanov that the financial position of the Bolsheviks is bad. 'This is now the only hitch; everything else we have. Without a big sum we are doomed to the introlerable, depressing vegetable existence we are leading here. We must get that money if it kills us.' (CW 43 pp. 132–3)

Between 12–21 November: Lenin's pamphlet 'The Zemstvo Campaign and *Iskra*'s Plan' is published in Geneva. (CW 7 pp. 497–518)

2 December: Lenin goes on a speaking tour; he reports on the situation in the Party. On 2 December he speaks in Paris.

3 December: Lenin, from Paris, writes to Krupskaya that he had met S D Leiteisen who has shown him a letter from Plekhanov. 'Plekhanov, of course, swears at Lenin for all he is worth.' (CW 34 p. 269) In a letter to A A Bogdanov, R Zemlyachka and M M Litvinov Lenin writes that the main task is to bring out a Bolshevik organ. 'First and foremost comes an organ, and again an organ, and money for an organ.' (CW 34 p. 272)

5 December: Lenin travels from Paris to Zürich.

6 and 7 December: He speaks on the situation in the Party in Zürich.

8 December: He speaks on the situation in the Party in Berne.

10 December: Lenin, in Zürich, writes to R S Zemlyachka in Russia that an announcement about the setting up of a Bolshevik Bureau in Russia should be made. 'May I speak here in the name of the Bureau? May I call the *Bureau* the publisher of the new organ?' (CW 34 p. 278)

12 December: The small circle of the Bolshevik leadership around Lenin decides to publish their own organ *Vperyod* (Forward). Lenin then writes the pamphlet 'A Letter to the Comrades (With Reference to the Forthcoming Publication of the Organ of the Majority)'. (CW 7 pp. 523-8) Lenin becomes a member of the Société de Lecture in Geneva and remains a member until December 1908. In this readers' association he can read books and journals and work with the minimum of formalities.

13 December: Lenin writes to R Zemlyachka: 'Money is desperately needed. Please do everything you can at once to send at least 1,000–2,000 roubles, otherwise we shall be in the air and everything will be left to chance.' (CW 43 p. 146)

14 December: Lenin writes to Lev Kamenev: 'I was especially happy to receive your letter since we hear so rarely from Russia . . . Please write more often and collaborate more closely with our new organ.' (CW 43 p. 146)

24 December: Lenin writes to M M Essen that the mood has changed. 'Yesterday the announcement concerning publication of our newspaper *Vperyod* came out. The entire majority rejoices and is heartened as never before.' (CW 34 p. 282)

End of 1904: Lenin, Krupskaya and Lyadov visit the theatre and see *La Dame aux Camelias* by Dumas with Sarah Bernhardt.

1905

4 January: Krupskaya informs the Moscow Party organisation of the appearance of the newspaper *Vperyod*.

5 January: A representative of the Party (either Zemlyachka or Bogdanov) writes to Lenin from St Petersburg. 'The "letter" (Gorky) will give 3,000 immediately to the organ and promises more in the future when he is convinced that the organ is not given to petty polemics. He is giving 5,000 for the Party Congress and promises to use all his connections to ensure that the material side of the affair is taken care of.' (*Lenin und Gorki* p. 388) Lenin's pamphlet 'Statement and Documents on the Break of the Central Institutions with the Party' appears in Geneva. In it he attacks the 'conciliatory' Bolsheviks in the CC, Noskov, Krasin and Galperin. 'I accuse the three members of the CC . . . of having systematically deceived the Party.' (CW 7 pp. 529-35)

6 January: The first number of the Bolshevik newspaper *Vperyod*, edited by Lenin, appears in Geneva. Lenin published 40 articles and smaller contributions in the 18 issues of the newspaper which appears until 18 May. In the first number he writes the leading article 'The Autocracy and the Proletariat' and the article 'Good Demonstrations of the Proletarians and Poor Arguments of Certain Intellectuals' and 'Time to Call a Halt'. (CW 8 pp. 17-39) *Vperyod* should have appeared on 4 January but it was held up two days because of delays in the setting-up process.

8 January: The publishers of *Vperyod* receive a cheque for over 700 roubles from Gorky (via Bogdanov).

14 January: Lenin's articles 'The Fall of Port Arthur' and 'Fine Words Butter no Parsnips' appear in *Vperyod* no 2. (CW 8 pp. 47-62)

19 January: In a letter to E Stasova in a Moscow prison, Lenin expresses his thoughts on how prisoners should behave in court.

22 January: Bloody Sunday in St Petersburg. The beginning of the first Russian revolution.

23 January: Lenin learns of the events in St Petersburg and writes the article 'Revolution in Russia'. (CW 8 p. 71) Krupskaya reports: 'Vladimir Ilich and I were on our way to the library and met the Lunacharskys, who were on their way to us . . . Lunacharsky's wife . . . was so excited that she could not speak . . . we went to the Lepeshinskys' émigré restaurant. We wanted to be together. The people gathered there hardly spoke a word to one another, they were so excited.' (Krupskaya p. 103)

24 January: *Vperyod* no 3 appears and contains several articles by Lenin including 'Revolution in Russia'. (CW 8 p. 71)

31 January: *Vperyod* no 4 appears and under the heading Revolutionary Days includes several articles by Lenin. He describes the revolution under way as a 'turning point in the history of Russia' and asks 'as long as we have to linger at such an accursed distance that the situation be accurately presented.' (CW 8 pp. 101-23)

3 February: Lenin presents a short analysis of the split in the RSDLP in a letter in reply to the Swiss socialist leader Hermann Greulich. (CW 8 pp. 125-31) The letter is signed by the editorial board of *Vperyod* (Lenin, Lunacharsky, Vorovsky and Bogdanov).

8 February: Lenin replies to August Bebel. Bebel had informed Lenin on 3 February that the executive committee of the SPD had instructed him to convene a court of arbitration, consisting of Bolsheviks and Menshviks, with the aim of ending the split in the RSDLP. Lenin writes that only the 3rd Party Congress can adopt the binding decrees and undertake the necessary steps. 'Thus your proposal can be submitted only to this Party Congress.' (CW 34 p. 295)

11 February: Lenin writes to Bogdanov and Gusev that he has the impression 'that 9/10 of the Bolsheviks are actually formalists.' The split has been made known; a Party Congress of *Vperyod* supporters called. 'We want to organise an Vperyod-ist Party — and break off all relations with the Mensheviks — and yet we are having "loyalty" dinned into our ears — we are being asked to act as though a joint congress of *Iskra* and *Vperyod* were possible. What a farce!' (CW 8 pp. 143-7)

14 February: Lenin's article 'Two Tactics', directed against the 'rearguard policies' of the Mensheviks, appears in *Vperyod* no 6. (CW 8 pp. 148-57)

17 February: Lenin has discussions in Geneva with the priest Gapon.

21 February: Lenin's articles 'A Militant Agreement for the Uprising' and 'Should We Organise the Revolution?' appear in *Vperyod* no 7. (CW 8 pp. 158-76)

28 February: Lenin's article on 'The Convening of the 3rd Party Congress' appears as the leading article in *Vperyod* no 8. In it he proposes the agenda for the Congress, in the name of the editorial board. (CW 8 pp. 177-80)

8 March: Lenin's article 'New Tasks and New Forces' appears in *Vperyod* no 9. In it Lenin, for the first time, develops his thesis on the 'democratic dictatorship of the proletariat and the peasantry' as the goal of the 1905 revolution. (CW 8 pp. 211-20)

11 March: In a letter to S I Gusev, Lenin writes: 'Many thanks especially for the scolding . . . I love to hear people scold — it means they know what they are doing and have a line to follow.' (CW 34 p. 302)

18 March: Lenin addresses the Russian colony in Geneva on the Paris Commune.

25 March: Lenin writes to the Odessa committee of the RSDLP: 'Not a single worker writes to *Vperyod*. *This is a scandal*.' (CW 34 p. 307)

2 April: The Odessa organisation elects Lenin as their delegate to the 3rd Party Congress, the Kursk committee does the same.

5 April: Lenin's article 'The Second Step' appears in *Vperyod* no 13 and in it he welcomes the fact that 'as well as the Bureau of the Committee of the Majority' the conciliatory CC supports the convocation of the 3rd Party Congress. (CW 8 pp. 262-6)

12 April: Lenin's article 'The Revolutionary–Democratic Dictatorship of the Proletariat and the Peasantry' appears in *Vperyod* no 14. It appears later as a pamphlet in Russian, Georgian and Armenian. The second part (the first part appeared in no 13), of 'Social Democracy and the Provisional Revolutionary Government' is also published. (CW 8 pp. 275-303)

23 April: Lenin writes, in the name of the CC of the RSDLP, an 'Open Letter' to comrade Plekhanov 'chairman of the Council of the RSDLP.' It is printed in *Vperyod* no 16 of 30 April. Lenin requests that the

Council, according to the statute, should immediately convene the Party Congress since the majority of the committees and the CC have called for this. The subordination of thè CC to the Council would mean the indefinite postponement of the necessary Party Congress. 'Placing its loyalty to the Party above loyalty to three foreign resident members of the Council, the CC submits the entire conflict to the judgment of the Party itself.' (CW 8 pp. 335-43)

24 April: Lenin travels to London from Geneva to take part in the 3rd Party Congress.

25 April: The 3rd Party Congress opens in London with only Bolsheviks present. Lenin is elected chairman of the Congress; it lasts until 10 May.

26-28 April: Lenin speaks several times during the first seven sessions of the Congress. (CW 8 pp. 359-70)

29 April: Lenin speaks on armed uprising. (CW 8 pp. 371-4)

1-3 May: Lenin speaks several times, on the peasant movement and on revolutionary government, for instance, during the 10-15th sessions of the Congress. The speeches are in CW 8 pp. 375-407. Lenin is in favour of participation in a revolutionary government and defends his theory of 'revolutionary dictatorship' against the Mensheviks. A delegate reports that towards the end of the speech 'standing, the whole congress listened to him in deep silence as the iron logic of the theoretician, speaker and organiser of the revolution overwhelmed them.' (Biographie p. 175)

4 May: The 16-17th sessions of the Congress debate the Party statute. Lenin's formulation of paragraph 1 is now adopted.

5-6 May: 19-21st sessions of the Congress; Lenin intervenes several times in the debates. (CW 8 pp. 411-2, 416-21)

8 May: The Congress elects A A Bogdanov, L Krasin, V Lenin, D Postalovsky and A Rykov to the CC. The publication of a new Party organ, *Proletarii* (The Proletarian), is agreed.

10 May: Lenin closes the 3rd Party Congress; he is elected editor of the new organ and is the unquestioned leader of the Bolsheviks.

Before 15 May: Lenin breaks his return journey from London to Geneva in Paris; he visits the 'wall of the Communards', the Eiffel tower and the Louvre.

27 May: The first number of *Proletarii*, the Bolshevik newspaper, appears in Geneva, edited by Lenin. The paper appears until 25 November 1905; 26 numbers, containing about 90 articles and notes by Lenin. *Proletarii* no 1 contains 'Report of the 3rd Congress of the RSDLP', 'How the Congress Was Constituted' and 'The 3rd Congress'. (CW 8 pp. 433-49)

Between 27 May-November: Lenin edits *Proletarii* on Mondays, Wednesdays and Fridays.

1 or 2 June: Lenin writes from Geneva to L A Fotieva that he has to travel to Paris 'on business' and wants to deliver a lecture there on the 3rd Congress. 'If you can, hire the biggest hall . . . and inform the maximum number of people.' (CW 36 p. 148)

2 June: Lenin informs the International Socialist Bureau in Brussels, by letter, that the 3rd Party Congress has taken place, that *Iskra* is no longer the central organ of the Party, that *Proletarii* has replaced it and that shortly a representative will be named to sit on the Bureau. (CW 8 p. 456)

3–6 June: Lenin is in Paris; he speaks on the 3rd Party Congress on 6 June, goes to the Grand Opera and the Folies Bergères (Freville *Lenine à Paris* p. 240. According to Khr. II p. 91, this trip took place before 30 March and lasted until after 1 June, the speech being delivered on 30 May; but this is improbable).

3 June: The first part of Lenin's article 'On the Provisional Revolutionary Government' appears in *Proletarii* no 2. The second part is printed in no 3 of 9 June. (CW 8 pp. 461–81)

17 June: Lenin's articles 'A New Revolutionary Workers' Association' and 'The Democratic Tasks of the Revolutionary Proletariat' appear in *Proletarii* no 4. (CW 8 pp. 499–518)

June–July: Lenin works on his pamphlet 'Two Tactics of Social Democracy in the Democratic Revolution'.

After 25 June: Lenin protests in an 'Open Letter' to the *Leipziger Volkszeitung* about Kautsky's presentation of the split in the RSDLP. 'Comrades . . . do not believe a word of what the so-called impartial Germans tell you about our split. Insist on seeing the documents, the authentic documents.' (CW 8 pp. 521–3) The letter is first published in 1931.

3 July: Lenin complains, in a letter to the secretary of the International Socialist Bureau, about money being sent to Plekhanov. '*Iskra* has ceased to be the organ of the Party and Mr Plekhanov is no longer the representative of the Party in the International Bureau . . . in all cases you should get in touch with Mr Ulyanov.' (CW 43 p. 159)

Beginning of July: Lenin discusses with Gapon the purchase and transfer of weapons to Russia. (SW VII p. 676)

8 July: Lenin confirms, in a letter to Camille Huysmans, secretary of the International Socialist Bureau, that half of the money has arrived. In future all questions should be addressed 'to the CC of our Party, that is, with Mr Oulianoff, 3 rue de la Colline, Geneva.' (CW 43 p. 160)

12 July: Lenin writes, in a letter to the CC, that 'Kautsky has written a mean article.' (CW 34 p. 318)

13 July: Lenin moves his family, Krupskaya and her mother, to a house in the country near Geneva; he travels 3–4 days per week to Geneva.

26 July: Lenin's articles 'Revolution Teaches' and 'Wrathful Impotence' appear in *Proletarii* no 9. (CW 9 pp. 146–60)

28 July: Lenin reports, in a letter to the CC, that foreign social democrats

(Bebel and others) want the International Socialist Bureau to 'bring pressure to bear on us' to effect a reconciliation with the Mensheviks. He proposes that 'mediation should be agreed with thanks. A binding decision by arbitration should be refused.' Only the 4th Party Congress can agree on amalgamation. (CW 34 pp. 320-2)

2 August: Lenin complains, in a letter to Lunacharsky, about his own Party. 'In political struggle a halt is fatal ... We are *impossibly* short of people.' (CW 34 p. 324)

7 August: Lenin's pamphlet 'Two Tactics of Social Democracy in the Democratic Revolution' appears in Geneva. (CW 9 pp. 15-140) In it Lenin develops the basic points of Bolshevik policy in the Russian Revolution of 1905-1907. The Mensheviks speak of a bourgeois revolution in which the liberal bourgeoisie will take power and introduce democratic capitalist development, which will afford the working class movement the opportunity of leading the struggle for socialism. Lenin however declares that the backward Russian bourgeoisie will not be able to complete the revolution; hence the proletariat and the peasantry must establish a 'democratic dictatorship of the proletariat and the peasantry' which will permit Russian capitalism to develop at American tempi and provide opportunities for the struggle for socialism. The pamphlet was reprinted twice in Russia in 1905 and also included in the volume *Twelve Years* (1907).

16 August: Lenin's article 'The Boycott of the Bulygin Duma and Insurrection' appears in *Proletarii* no 12. (CW 9 pp. 179-87)

29 August: Four articles by Lenin appear in *Proletarii* no 14. In 'The Black Hundreds and the Organisation of the Uprising' he goes into the question of the significance of combat groups and writes: 'Be prepared for the coming armed uprising!' (CW 9 pp. 200-4)

16 September: Lenin writes to Camille Huysmans, secretary of the International Socialist Bureau, and agrees to a conference to discuss 'conciliation' with the Mensheviks, provided that it takes the form of a preparatory conference. (Briefe II p. 72)

4 October: Lenin speaks in Geneva on the SPD Party Congress in Jena in September 1905.

10 October: Several articles by Lenin, including 'Socialism and the Peasantry' appear in *Proletarii* no 20 (CW 9 pp. 307-15)

11 October: Lenin writes, in a letter to Lunacharsky, that if there were a parliament in Russia it would be proper to support the liberals, for example, when balloting. However during the revolution it is quite a different story. 'A detailed analysis of the relation of "parliamentarism to revolution" would be appropriate.' (CW 34 pp. 352-4)

16 October: Lenin demands, in a letter to the combat committee of the St Petersburg committee, more activity. 'It horrifies me — I give you my word — it horrifies me to find that there has been talk about bombs for over six months yet not one has been made ...

Form fighting squads at once everywhere!' (CW 9 pp. 344-6)

25 October: Lenin says, in a letter to the CC, that he has received his nomination, by the CC, to the International Socialist Bureau.

27 October: Lenin informs the International Socialist Bureau that Lengnik, Rumyantsev and he are the CC representatives to the planned 'conciliation' conference with the Mensheviks.

30 October: The tsar declares the end of his personal autocracy and the advent of civil rights in Russia. Lenin prepares to return to Russia.

End of October: Lenin writes to Plekhanov that he is convinced 'that the need for social democratic unity is a question that can no longer be put off . . . We are in agreement with you on approximately nine tenths of the questions of theory and tactics, and to quarrel over one tenth is not worth while.' He has never attempted to impose his views on any social democrat and 'none, positively none of the new editors has entered into an engagement to be "Leninist".' (CW 34 pp. 363-6) Lenin writes the article 'Tasks of the Revolutionary Army Contingents', published for the first time in 1926. (CW 9 pp. 420-4) Lenin proposes the creation of contingents which will arm themselves as best they can, 'rifles, revolvers, bombs, knives, knuckle-dusters, sticks, rags soaked in kerosene for starting fires, or rope ladders, shovels for building barricades'. He also demands unarmed sections and the 'study of military science'. Lenin distinguishes between 'preparatory work and military operations' of the 'sections of the revolutionary army'. Lenin wants as well as the acquisition of weapons 'funds for the uprising (confiscation of government funds)'.

7 November: Lenin's attitude to the Imperial Manifesto 'The First Victory of the Revolution' appears in *Proletarii* no 24. Also included is 'Petty Bourgeois and Proletarian Socialism', (CW 9 pp. 427-46)

Mid November: Lenin travels from Geneva to Russia; he travels first to Stockholm where he waits for the necessary papers.

18 November: Leaves Stockholm for Helsinki.

21 November: Arrives in St Petersburg.

22 November: Lenin chairs an illegal meeting of Bolshevik functionaries in St Petersburg. They discuss the programme of the newspaper *Novaya Zhizn* (New Life). The paper appears for about a month and carries 13 articles by Lenin. A meeting of the CC adopts unanimously the appeal 'To all Party Organisations and to all Social Democratic Workers' to convene the 4th Party Congress.

23 November: The first part (the second and third parts appear on 28 and 29 November) of Lenin's article 'The Reorganisation of the Party' appears in *Novaya Zhizn* no 9. It is Lenin's first piece of writing after returning from emigration. He favours a democratisation of the Party after freedom of association and of the press have been granted. (CW 10 pp. 29-39)

26 November: Lenin's article 'Party Organisation and Party Literature' appears in *Novaya Zhizn* no 12. In it Lenin defends placing Party literature under 'Party control'. (CW 10 pp. 44–9)

End of November: Lenin attends, as a guest, the 2nd All-Russian Menshevik Conference in St Petersburg.

Between 1–6 December: Lenin meets Krupskaya several times illegally. She arrived in St Petersburg ten days after Lenin and is working as secretary of the CC. They live apart for reasons of secrecy.

8 December: Lenin's article 'Socialism and Anarchism' appears in *Novaya Zhizn* no 21. It attacks the anarchists. (CW 10 pp. 71–4)

9 December: Lenin takes part in a session of the St Petersburg Soviet.

10 December: Lenin attends an editorial board meeting of *Novaya Zhizn* in Gorky's home. Lenin and Gorky meet for the first time.

14 December: Lenin and Krupskaya move, for a few days, into a flat at the home of an acquaintance of Lenin's mother. Lenin reports to the police.

16 December: Lenin's article 'Socialism and Religion' appears in *Novaya Zhizn* no 28. This is the last number and because of a police ban is appearing illegally. In it Lenin describes religion as the 'opium of the people.' (CW 10 pp. 83–7)

17 December: Lenin and Krupskaya go into hiding because of police surveillance.

23 December: Lenin and Krupskaya travel to Tampere (Tammerfors) to attend the Ist All-Russian Bolshevik Conference.

25–30 December: The Ist All-Russian Bolshevik Conference takes place at Tampere, Finland. Lenin speaks on the political situation and on the agrarian question; his resolutions are adopted. Lenin comes out in favour of a reunification with the Mensheviks on the basis of equality. The conference decides to boycott the first Duma (parliament). Its business is speedily ended because of the armed uprising in Moscow.

30 December: Lenin returns to St Petersburg on a false passport.

1906

Mid–End of January: Lenin travels to Moscow and discusses the tactics of the boycott of the first Duma with Moscow Bolsheviks.

17 January: Lenin's article 'The Workers' Party and its Tasks in the Present Situation' appears in *Molodaya Rossiya* (Young Russia), a social democratic student newspaper. (CW 10 pp. 93–6) In it Lenin opposes 'constitutional illusions', regards the political strike as 'played out' and points to the uprising.

January: Lenin writes the article 'Should We Boycott the State Duma?' and it appears as a leaflet. (CW 10 pp. 97–100) In this article, described as the 'platform of the Party', Lenin develops the tactics of actively boycotting the first Duma.

5 February: Lenin meets Maxim Gorky in Helsinki.

20 February: Lenin's article 'The Present Situation in Russia and the Tactics of the Workers' Party' appears in *Partiinie Izvestiya* (Party News) no 1, a jointly published Menshevik-Bolshevik organ to prepare the reunification. (CW 10 pp. 112-9) In it he opposes Plekhanov's view that recourse should not have been made to weapons and writes that the 'question of the uprising' is 'placed on the agenda.'

24 February: Lenin speaks at the St Petersburg city Conference of the RSDLP, at which the Bolsheviks are in the majority. His draft resolution on boycotting the Duma is adopted by a majority.

Mid March: Lenin stays in Kuokkala, Finland; he works on draft resolutions for the reunification Party Congress.

End of March: Lenin discusses in Moscow and then in St Petersburg the draft resolution for the reunification Party Congress with leading Bolsheviks.

Beginning of April: Lenin writes the pamphlet 'Revision of the Agrarian Programme of the Workers' Party'. (CW 10 pp. 165-95) It is published in April.

2 April: Lenin's article 'The Russian Revolution and the Tasks of the Proletariat' appears in *Partiinie Izvestiya* no 2. (CW 10 pp. 135-46) Lenin writes: 'Either we must admit that the democratic revolution is at an end, shelve the question of insurrection and take the constitutional path. Or we recognise that the democratic revolution is still in progress . . . develop and apply in practice the slogan of insurrection, proclaim civil war and ruthlessly denounce all constitutional illusions. It is scarcely necessary to tell the reader that we are emphatically in favour of the *latter* solution of the problem that now confronts the Party.' Besides this Lenin's drafts of the tactical platform for the reunification Party Congress (CW 10 pp. 147-63) also appear in the newspaper. He states in them: 'The principle of democratic centralism in the Party is now universally recognised.'

6-10 April: Lenin writes the pamphlet 'The Victory of the Cadets and the Tasks of the Workers' Party'. It appears in April. (CW 10 pp. 199-276)

8 April: The St Petersburg organisation elects Lenin as its delegate to the 4th (Reunification) Party Congress.

Before 23 April: Lenin arrives in Stockholm for the Party Congress. He calls himself Magister Weber (Gautschi p. 34). In a private meeting of Bolshevik delegates he opposes the proposal to wreck the Congress just because the Mensheviks are in the majority.

23 April-8 May: Lenin attends the Reunification Congress of the RSDLP in the House of the People in Stockholm. The Mensheviks have 62 mandates and the Bolsheviks only 46. He is elected to the presidium and to the commission to draft the statutes. Lenin is in the chair for the 3rd and 4th sessions; in the 5th he speaks on the agrarian question. He is again in the chair for the 7th and 8th sessions and, at times, chairs the 9-12th sessions. In the 13th he speaks on the current situation, chairs the 15th session and delivers the final speech in the 16th. Lenin chairs the 18th and 21st sessions and speaks in the 22nd on the armed uprising. He is in the chair again for the 24th session and welcomes the Polish social democrats when they join the RSDLP. The 27th session, the last, adopts Lenin's version of paragraph 1 of the Party statute. Several Mensheviks but only four Bolsheviks are elected to the CC. Lenin no longer sits in the CC; most adopted resolutions reflect Menshevik views. The unity is only formal, the split remains and Lenin is as before leader of the Bolsheviks.

8 and 9 May: Lenin writes 'An Appeal to the Party by Delegates to the Unity Congress who Belonged to the Former "Bolshevik" Group' (CW 10 pp. 310-6). The appeal maintains that 'there is a split no longer'; Bolshevik delegates from 26 Party organisations sign it and it is then published as a leaflet.

Between 9-17 May: Lenin leaves Stockholm and returns, via Turku, Finland, to St Petersburg where he lives with Krupskaya in hiding.

18 May: Lenin's article 'The Fight for Freedom and the Fight for Power' (CW 10 pp. 383-5) appears in *Volna* (The Wave) no 9, a legal Bolshevik daily newspaper which appears in St Petersburg during the spring of 1906. It carries several articles by Lenin.

22 May: Lenin speaks publicly, under the name of Karpov, for the first time in Russia before 3,000 people at a meeting of the social-political club at the residence of Countess Panina in St Petersburg. Krupskaya writes later: 'Ilich was very excited. For a minute he stood silent, terribly pale. All the blood had flowed to his heart. One immediately felt how the excitement of the speaker was being communicated to the audience. Suddenly tremendous hand clapping commenced – the Party members had recognised Ilich . . . At the end of Ilich's speech, all those present were swept with extraordinary enthusiasm – at that moment everyone was thinking of the coming fight to the finish.' (Krupskaya pp. 135-6)

May: Lenin writes the pamphlet 'Report on the Unity Congress of the RSDLP'. (CW 10 pp. 317-82) It is published in June.

3 June: Lenin's article 'Bad Advice' appears in *Volna* no 23. (CW 10 pp. 444-9) In it he maintains that Plekhanov has made 'a great mistake by going much too far to the right and by calling upon the proletariat to support the Cadets and the Cadet Duma fully, completely and without reservation.'

8 June: The first number of *Vperyod*, like *Volna* and *Ekho* (Echo), a legal Bolshevik daily newspaper, appears in St Petersburg. Lenin plays an active role on the editorial board; he writes 14 articles for a newspaper which only appears in June. His article 'How Comrade Plekhanov Argues About Social Democratic Tactics' appears in the first number. (CW 10 pp. 460-80)

19 June: Lenin, calling himself Karpov, speaks to the delegates of the All-Russian Congress of School Teachers on the agrarian question. He also delivers the closing speech on the same subject.

23 June: Lenin's article 'Unity' appears as the leader in *Vperyod* no 14. In it he writes that the social democratic group in the Duma 'renders . . . the revolution a great service'; unity must not be made more difficult by introducing 'unnecessary and controversial slogans.' (CW 11 pp. 20-3)

24-25 June: Lenin attends the Conference of the St Petersburg Organisation of the RSDLP in Terijoki, Finland. He speaks on tactics and on unity in the Party. F I Dan, a Menshevik, is co-speaker but the St Petersburg committee comes down on the side of Lenin and the Bolsheviks.

5 July: The first number of the legal Bolshevik daily newspaper *Ekho* appears in St Petersburg. In all 14 issues appear for which Lenin writes 20 articles.

20 July: Lenin speaks, under the pseudonym of Karpov, at a meeting of functionaries of the St Petersburg RSDLP.

21-23 July: Lenin, Krupskaya and her mother holiday at Sablino, a suburb of St Petersburg. Krupskaya's mother writes to Anna: 'Our people came on the 8th [21st], Volodya went swimming and then we all sat together in the arbour. They spent the next day with us as well, V[olodya] . . . had intended to spend a week with us but he found the newspapers so interesting on Monday morning that he and N[adya] packed and left.' (*Vom Alltag der Uljanows* pp. 150-1)

23 July: Lenin attends a meeting of Party leaders in Kuokkala, Finland.

Between 26-30 July: Lenin writes the pamphlet 'The Dissolution of the Duma and the Tasks of the Proletariat' and it is published in August. (CW 11 pp. 109-31) The Duma was dissolved on 21 July which led to an uprising in Kronstadt and, on 30 July, in the fortress Sveaborg, near Helsinki.

19 August-3 September: Lenin is in Vyborg; he organises the publication of *Proletarii*, the illegal Bolshevik organ which runs to 50 issues between 1906 and 1909. It is later published in Geneva and Paris.

2 September: Lenin moves to Vasa, a country house in Kuokkala, Finland.

3 September: The first number of *Proletarii* appears in Vyborg. The leading article 'Before the Storm' and three other articles by Lenin are included. (CW 11 pp. 135-69)

Beginning of September: Lenin meets Rosa Luxemburg in Kuokkala.

9 September: Lenin chairs a Party meeting in Terijoki; he asks for the convocation of the 5th Party Congress.

11 September: Lenin's article 'Lessons of the Moscow Uprising' appears in *Proletarii* no 2. Lenin analyses the uprising in Moscow in December 1905, one of the high points of the revolution. He examines partisan tactics and predicts: 'A great mass struggle is approaching. It will be an armed uprising.' (CW 11 pp. 171-8)

21 September: Lenin's article 'Vacillating Tactics', directed against Plekhanov, appears in *Proletarii* no 2. (CW 11 pp. 179-83)

Beginning of November: Lenin writes the pamphlet 'The Social Democrats and Electoral Agreements' and it is published in November. (CW 11 pp. 275-98)

16-20 November: Lenin attends the 2nd Congress of the RSDLP (Ist All-Russian Conference) in Tampere. 18 Mensheviks and Bundists, 6 Bolsheviks, 5 Polish and 3 Latvian social democrats make up the 32 delegates. The Bolsheviks, Polish and Latvian social democrats support Lenin in his opposition to an electoral agreement with the Cadets but Lenin finds himself in the minority. He asks for the convocation of the 5th Party Congress.

Before 29 November: Lenin gives instructions, by letter, to the organisers of the Ist Bolshevik Conference of Military and Combat Organisations in Tampere.

November-December: Lenin edits the Russian translation of Karl Kautsky's pamphlet 'Triebkräfte und Aussichten der russischen Revolution' (The Driving Forces and Prospects of the Russian Revolution) and writes an introduction to it.

20 December: Lenin's article 'The Crisis of Menshevism' appears in *Proletarii* no 9. (CW 11 pp. 341-64)

29 December: Lenin's sister Maria joins him at Kuokkala for the New Year celebrations. Apparently he lives here under the name of Erwin Weykoff. (Gautschi p. 34)

1907

2 January: *Proletarii* no 10 carries three articles by Lenin including 'The Proletariat and its Ally in the Russian Revolution' in which Lenin examines and supports Kautsky's views. (CW 11 pp. 365-75)

13 January: Lenin's article 'The Attitude of the Bourgeois Parties and of the Workers' Party to the Duma Elections' in which he is for fighting the election alone and against all 'blocs' appears in *Ternii Truda* (Thorns of Labour) no 2, the legal Bolshevik St Petersburg weekly newspaper. (CW 11 pp. 414-8)

19 January: Lenin, as Moscow's delegate, attends the Conference of the St Petersburg Party Organisations. He is elected to the presidium and speaks on the question of electoral alliances during the forthcoming Duma elections.

26–27 January: Lenin writes the pamphlet 'Social Democracy and the Duma Elections'. He comments again on the question of an agreement with the (liberal) Cadets during the Duma elections. Lenin opposes such an agreement and writes that democratically organised parties may not in important questions 'dispense without exception with such a canvass of the opinion of every member.' (CW 11 pp. 431–55)

1 or 2 February: Lenin writes the pamphlet 'The St Petersburg Elections and the Hypocrisy of the Thirty One Mensheviks'. (CW 12 pp. 33–44) Lenin speaks of the 'sale of workers' votes to the Cadets' by the Mensheviks, accuses them of bargaining with the Cadets 'against the will of the workers', etc. As a result the CC, Menshevik-dominated, decides to arraign Lenin before a Party tribunal.

7 February: Lenin's article 'The St Petersburg Elections and the Crisis of Opportunism' appears in *Proletarii* no 12. In it Lenin demands that large enterprises be made into bases of revolutionary social democracy and made impregnable to 'opportunism.'

18 February: Lenin writes a preface to the Russian translation of Marx's *Letters to Dr Kugelmann*. (CW 12 pp. 104–12)

24 February: Three articles by Lenin, including 'The Election Results in St Petersburg', an analysis of the Cadet liberals and the defeat of the right appear in *Proletarii* no 13. (CW 12 pp. 119–26)

2 March: Lenin gives an interview to E Avenard, a special correspondent of *L'Humanité*, the Paris socialist paper, and discusses the tactics of the RSDLP during the elections. The interview appears in *L'Humanité* no 1082 on 4 April 1907. (CW 12 pp. 145–51)

6 March: Karl Kautsky and Rosa Luxemburg propose to Lenin that he should contribute to *Neue Zeit* and *Vorwärts*.

14 March: Lenin returns the proofs of his interview for *L'Humanité* to Avenard. He writes that in Russia the revolution is bourgeois and not proletarian. 'And it is only the proletariat together with the peasants . . . who can bring *such* a revolution to victory.' (CW 43 p. 175)

27 March: *Neue Zeit* no 26, the theoretical organ of the SPD, publishes Lenin's article 'The Duma Elections and the Tactics of Russian Social Democracy'. (Signed A Linitsch).

Beginning of April: Lenin is arraigned before a Party tribunal for his article against thirty one Mensheviks (compare 1 or 2 February). The courts consists of three representatives nominated by him, three Mensheviks and three members of the Presidium (representatives of the CC of the Latvian and Polish parties and the Bund). Abramovich is in the chair. Lenin, in his speech defending himself, states that his wording was 'calculated to evoke in the reader hatred, aversion and contempt for people who commit such deeds. Such wording is calculated not to convince but to break up the ranks of the opponent, not to correct the mistakes of the opponent but to destroy him, to wipe his organisation off the face of the earth.' Lenin maintains that such methods are not permissable in a united Party but 'obligatory for sections of a Party that has been split.' He had 'actually succeeded in causing that section of the proletariat, which trusts and follows the Mensheviks, to waver' and would always act so after a split. By 'insulting attacks on the Mensheviks' he had caused their ranks to waver. 'That was my goal.' There are no limits to a struggle stemming from a split but 'only the limits set by criminal law.' Every split is 'a great crime against the Party.' (CW 12 pp. 421-32)

3-7 April: Lenin drafts a speech on the agrarian question which G Aleksinsky, a member of the Duma, is to deliver. (CW pp. 267-99) Aleksinsky speaks on 18 April in the Duma but he only makes partial use of the draft.

7 April: Lenin chairs the St Petersburg City Conference of the RSDLP in Terijoki, Finland, and speaks on the question of organisation.

18 and 20 April: Lenin's article 'The Strength and Weakness of the Russian Revolution' appears in the legal Bolshevik daily newspaper *Nashe Ekho* (Our Echo) nos 10 and 12. He writes that a bourgeois revolution under the leadership of the bourgeoisie can only bring reform. 'It can be a real revolution only under the leadership of the proletariat and the peasantry.' (CW 12 pp. 349-58)

19 April: Lenin writes a preface to the Russian edition of the book *Letters from Johannes Becker, Joseph Dietzen, Friedrich Engels, Karl Marx and others to Friedrich Sorge and others* which appears in St Petersburg in July. (CW 12 pp. 359-78)

21 April: Lenin attends the 2nd Conference of St Petersburg Social Democratic Organisations in Terijoki, Finland.

24 April: Lenin is elected to the Presidium of the St Petersburg committee of the RSDLP.

April: The Party organisation in Verkhne-Kamskaya, in the Urals, elects Lenin as their delegate to the forthcoming Party Congress.

Beginning of May: Lenin sends a telegram to the chairman of the Norwegian Workers' Party, Nilssen, asking him if the Party Congress could take place in Norway. This is not possible. Lenin travels to Copenhagen where the Party Congress is now to take place.

Between 7-11 May: On his way to London to attend the 5th Party Congress Lenin breaks his journey for a few days in Berlin. He meets Rosa Luxemburg and Karl Kautsky and visits the Tiergarten and the theatre with Maxim Gorky. He and Gorky travel together to London and he reads Gorky's novel *Mother* in manuscript form.

11 May: Lenin arrives in London where the 5th Party Congress of the RSDLP takes place between 13 May and 1 June. He visits the British Museum and the theatre with Gorky, who is the guest of the Congress, when the Congress is not in session.

13 May: The Congress opens; 303 delegates with full mandates and 39 with consultative votes represent 150,000 members. There are 106

Bolsheviks and 97 Mensheviks. The Polish and a majority of the Latvian
social democrats usually support the Bolsheviks. Lenin is elected to the
Presidium of the Congress. Lenin's election is contested by the Mensheviks who maintain that he has not carried out Party resolutions since
he has tolerated the so-called expropriations (attacks on banks and
money in transit, especially in the Caucasus, so as to finance revolutionary activity). Gorky describes later Lenin's behaviour at the
Congress: 'His guttural 'r' made him seem a poor speaker, but within a
minute I was as completely engrossed as everyone else. I have never
known one could talk of the most intricate political questions so
simply.' (*About Lenin*, p. 29) Gorky writes about Lenin personally:
'I had not imagined him that way. I felt there was something missing
in him. His 'r's' were guttural and he stood with his thumbs shoved into
the armholes of his waistcoat. He was too plain, there was nothing of
the "leader" in him . . . But the bald, 'r'-rolling, strong, thickset man
who kept wiping his Socratic brow with one hand and jerking mine
with the other began to talk at once, with beaming eyes, of the short-
comings of my book *Mother*.' (Ibid p. 28)

15 May: Three articles by Lenin appear in *Proletarii* no 16, including
'Reorganisation and the End of the Split in St. Petersburg' in which he
calls for 'adherence to consistent democratic centralism.' (CW 12 pp.
395–403)

16 May: Lenin is in the chair for the 6th and 8th sessions of the 5th
Party Congress.

17 May: Lenin addresses the Congress on the report of the activities of
the CC. He criticises the (Menshevik) CC: 'The bankruptcy of our CC
was primarily and above all the bankruptcy of this policy of opportunism.' (CW 12 pp. 442–7)

18 May: Lenin speaks about the expenditure of 60,000 roubles of
Party money at the Congress.

21 May: Lenin chairs the 14th and 15th sessions of the Congress; he
comments on the report of the activities of the Duma group.

23 May: Lenin makes a statement at the 18th session, maintaining
that Martov has incorrectly interpreted his interview with *L'Humanité*
(compare 2 March). (CW 12 pp. 453–4)

25 May: Lenin delivers a major speech on the attitude of the Party
towards bourgeois parties at the 22nd session. (CW 12 pp. 456–68)

26 May: Lenin, Plekhanov, Gorky, Deutsch and other Congress partici-
pants visit Felix Moscheles, the painter, in the hope of securing a
donation to Party funds so that the Congress can continue.

27 May: Lenin adds some concluding remarks to his speech on the
attitude towards bourgeois parties at the 24th session. He declares that
Trotsky 'has come closer to our views.' 'Quite apart from the question
of "permanent revolution" we have here solidarity on fundamental
points in the question of the attitude towards bourgeois parties.' He

opposes Plekhanov, claiming that the liberal bourgeoisie has taken a 'counter-revolutionary turn.' (CW 12 pp. 469–74) Acquiring money for the Congress is discussed at the 25th (closed) session.

28 May: Lenin chairs the 27th session of the Congress.

30 May: Lenin and other delegates sign a pledge to repay a loan which Joseph Fels, a soap manufacturer, has made to permit the Party Congress to continue. After the October Revolution the loan was repaid to Fels' heirs.

1 June: Lenin chairs the 34th and 35th sessions of the Congress. The CC is elected; its members are 6 Bolsheviks (including Zinoviev) and 4 Mensheviks, two Polish and one Latvian social democrat. The candidate members are 12 Bolsheviks (including Lenin, Bogdanov, Krasin and Rykov), 4 Mensheviks (including Martov), three Polish and one Latvian social democrat.

3–7 June: Lenin attends the 2nd Party Congress of the Social Democratic Party of the Latvian Territory and makes a short speech on 6 June.

Between 7–15 June: Lenin returns to Kuokkala from London.

15 June: On the evening before the Duma is dissolved Lenin consults with Bolshevik Duma members.

Before 28 June: Lenin leaves Kuokkala and moves into Knipovich's house near the lighthouse at Styrs Udde, Finland.

8 July: Lenin is elected the CC representative on the International Socialist Bureau.

9 July: Lenin writes the article 'Against the Boycott' which appears in August in the pamphlet 'Concerning the Boycott of the Third Duma.' Lenin explains why he was for a boycott of the Duma in 1905-6 but is now against it. (CW 13 pp. 15–49)

10 July: Lenin writes, in a letter to his mother from Styrs Udde, Finland: 'I came back terribly tired. I have now completely recovered.' Krupskaya writes: 'We have all put on so much weight and it's not decent to show ourselves in public . . . Here there is a pine forest, sea, magnificent weather, in short, everything is excellent.' (CW 37 pp. 365-7)

Mid July: Lenin writes, in a letter to his sister Maria: 'I am having a rest such as I have not had in years.' He opposes the boycott of the Third Duma. Krupskaya writes: 'We are bathing in the sea, cycling . . . Volodya plays chess, fetches water, at one time we had a craze for the English game of "Donkey".' (CW 37 pp. 368-9)

21 July: Lenin attends the St Petersburg City Conference of the RSDLP in Terijoki, Finland. Lenin's resolution opposing a boycott is adopted.

3–5 August: The 3rd Conference of the RSDLP in Kotka, Finland. Lenin speaks on participation in the elections; his resolution, opposing a boycott, is adopted.

Before 14 August: Lenin and I P Goldberg travel together to the International Socialist Congress in Stuttgart.

14 August: Lenin writes to Gorky: 'We arrived here today [presumably Berlin] and tomorrow we are going to Stuttgart.' (CW 34 p. 369)

16–24 August: Lenin attends the daily sessions of the International Socialist Bureau. He receives 5,000 marks for the Duma electoral campaign from the executive committee of the SPD. The Mensheviks receive the same.

18 August: The International Socialist Congress opens in the Liederhalle in Stuttgart. Lenin is elected to the Presidium as the Russian representative. He meets Clara Zetkin for the first time.

20 August: Lenin opposes the participation of the Russian Zionists in the Congress at a meeting of the International Socialist Bureau. A compromise proposal allows them to be admitted with a consultative voice.

22 August: Lenin, Luxemburg and Martov propose four alterations to Bebel's resolution during the fourth session of the commission on conflict and militarism. (*Internationaler Sozialistenkongress* p. 102)

After 24 August: Lenin returns to Vasa, the country house in Kuokkala.

August–December: Lenin prepares the first three volume selection of his works *12 Years* for publication. It appears in December 1907 in St Petersburg.

2 September: The CC elects Lenin editor-in-chief of its central organ, *Sotsial Demokrat* (Social Democrat).

15 September: Lenin reports on the International Socialist Congress in Stuttgart at a Conference of the St Petersburg City Organisation of the RSDLP in Terijoki.

20 September: The CC rescinds the decree appointing Lenin editor-in-chief of the central organ, he is elected to the editorial board.

Beginning of October: Lenin describes an émigré's life, in a letter to G A Aleksinsky: 'For over there you are frightfully out of touch with Russia, and idleness and the state of mind which goes with it, a nervous, hysterical, hissing and spitting mentality, predominate . . . there is no *live* work or an environment for live work to speak of.' He advises him to work with Knunyants and Trotsky. (CW 43 p. 176)

21 October: Lenin's sister Maria writes to her sister Anna from Kuokkala: 'V[olodya] has already recovered and today I went with him for long walks.' (*Vom Alltag der Uljanows* p. 154)

28 October: Lenin writes to his mother: 'Nearly all of us recently paid tribute to autumn with a dose of influenza for a couple of days. Now we are all well or convalescent.' (CW 37 pp. 370–1)

2 November: Two articles by Lenin including 'The International Socialist Congress in Stuttgart' appear in *Proletarii* no 17. Lenin writes: 'Only the proletarian class . . . can bring about the social revolution.' (CW 13 pp. 75–81)

Between 2-11 November: Lenin defends Bebel and criticises Trotsky in a letter to Lunacharsky. He thinks that one should so write 'that criticism will be aimed not at orthodoxy, not at the Germans in general, but at opportunism.' (CW 34 pp. 370-1)

9 November: Lenin speaks on the Duma and co-operation with the bourgeois press at a Conference of the St Petersburg Organisation of the RSDLP, in Terijoki.

18-25 November: At the 4th Conference of the RSDLP, in Helsinki, Lenin delivers the 'Report on the Tactics of the Social Democratic Group in the Third State Duma'; his resolution is adopted. (CW 13 pp. 141-3)

Between 29 November-6 December: The first volume of Lenin's works, including 'One Step Forward . . . Two Tactics . . .' is published by *Zerno* (Grain). The volume is seized soon after its appearance and of the two further volumes only the first part of Volume Two appears — in early 1908.

November-December: Lenin works on his pamphlet 'The Agrarian Programme of Social Democracy in the First Russian Revolution of 1905 to 1907'. (CW 13 pp. 217-429). It is first published in 1917.

Beginning of December: Lenin hides from the police; he moves from Kuokkala to Helsinki.

Before 21 December: The Bolshevik Centre decides to publish *Proletarii* abroad and Lenin, Bogdanov and Dubrovinsky are charged with the task.

December: Lenin travels as Professor Müller, a German geologist, from Oglbu, near Helsinki, abroad. (Wolper *Pseudonyme Lenins* pp. 103-4) Since he was being followed by the secret police he had to cross three kilometres of ice on foot to Sweden. He only just made it over the cracking ice. Lenin related that he had thought to himself: 'Oh what a silly way to die.' (Krupskaya p. 146) He stays a few days in Stockholm and Krupskaya joins him there on 31 December. The second emigration has begun and will last until 1917.

28 December: Lenin, in a letter from Stockholm to Karl Hjalmar Branting, states that he intends to travel to Berlin on 31 December.

1908

3 January: Lenin and Krupskaya travel from Stockholm, via Berlin, to Geneva.

Between 4-6 January: Lenin meets Rosa Luxemburg in Berlin. He and Krupskaya contract food poisoning, through eating fish. Krupskaya writes later: 'A doctor had to be summoned in the night. Vladimir Ilich was registered as a Finnish cook and I as an American citizen. Therefore the chamber maid fetched an American doctor. First he examined

Vladimir Ilich and said it was a very serious business . . . guessing that something was not quite in order, he charged us outrageously for the visit. We hung about for a couple of days and then dragged ourselves on, half ill, to Geneva.' (Krupskaya p. 147)

7 January: Arrival in Geneva; Lenin and Krupskaya rent a room in Rue des deux ponts 17 c/o Küper. (Gauschi p. 66) In Geneva Lenin says: 'I feel just as if I'd come to be buried.' (Krupskaya p. 148)

13 January: Lenin writes to Lunacharsky: 'It is devilishly sad to have to return to this accursed Geneva again but there's no other way out! After the disaster in Finland there was no alternative but to transfer *Proletarii* abroad.' (CW 43 p. 179)

14 January: Lenin writes to his sister Maria in St Petersburg: 'We have been hanging about in this damned Geneva for several days now . . . It is an awful hole but there is nothing we can do. We shall just get used to it. How are you? Are you freezing? Is Mother well? Please kiss her for me.' (CW 37 pp. 372-3)

15 January: Lenin responds to an invitation from Maxim Gorky: 'The idea of dropping in on you in Capri is delightfully tempting, dash it! You have painted such an attractive picture that I have definitely made up my mind to come out and I shall try to bring my wife with me.' (CW 34 pp. 373-4)

22 January: Lenin writes to his mother: 'We are now settling down here and our arrangements, of course, will not be worse than before.' He reports that Gorky has invited them to Capri and he wants to 'accept the invitation . . . but not yet.' (CW 37 p. 374)

2 February: Lenin writes to Gorky that Bogdanov, Dubrovinsky and himself are getting *Proletarii* ready for publication in Geneva. In a preparatory notice Gorky was apparently named as a colleague on the paper.

7 February: Lenin writes to Gorky that the defeatist mood after the revolution must be combated. The intellectuals are 'fleeing' the Party. 'And a good riddance to these scoundrels. The Party is purging itself from petty bourgeois dross. The workers are having a bigger say in things. The role of the worker professionals is increasing.' He is fully aware of his 'unpreparedness' in philosophy but as a 'rank and file Marxist' he attentively reads 'the empirio-monist Bogdanov and the empirio-critics Bazarov, Lunacharsky, etc. and *they* drive me to give *all* my sympathy *to Plekhanov*!' Plekhanov's tactics are the height of ineptitude but 'in philosophy he upholds the right cause. I am for materialism and against "empirio-" etc.' (CW 34 pp. 379-82)

13 February: Lenin writes to Gorky that the editorial board had suddenly decided to invite Trotsky to work on *Proletarii* although there 'had been a big fight with Trotsky, a regular fierce battle in 1903-05 when he was a Menshevik.' Trotsky has refused and is acting as a *poseur*. (CW 34 pp. 385-6)

14 February: Lenin, in a letter to his sister Maria, informs her that he needs his marriage certificate and asks her to get him a copy from Krasnoyarsk.

25 February: Lenin writes to Gorky that the 'long-standing differences in philosophy among the Bolsheviks' have been greatly exacerbated. 'I don't regard myself as competent enough in these questions' and hence he does not rush into print. As a 'rank and file Marxist' as far as philosophy is concerned he is appalled at Bogdanov and the others. 'No, that is not Marxism.' A dispute over philosophy is coming to a head among the Bolsheviks but 'in my opinion it would be an unforgivable piece of stupidity if the dispute over materialism or Machism is permitted to hinder the employment of the tactics of social democracy'. The Bolsheviks, as a group, are not to be affected by the dispute over philosophy. (Briefe II pp. 138–44) On the same day Lenin begins work on his major philosophical treatise *Materialism and Empiriocriticism*.

26 February: Lenin's article 'Political Notes' appears in *Proletarii* no 21, published in Geneva. (CW 13 pp. 440–6) The Party will not lose its head just because of the defeat of the revolution and because of chauvinism. 'Not for nothing do they say that we are as hard as rock'.

2 March: Three articles by Lenin including 'Trade Union Neutrality' (CW 13 pp. 460–9) appear in *Proletarii* no 22. In it Lenin opposes the neutrality of the Russian trade unions and favours the 'close alignment of the trade unions with the socialist society.'

16 March: Lenin writes to Gorky: 'I am neglecting the newspaper because of my hard bout of philosophy. One day I read one of the empirio-critics and swear like a fish-wife, the next I read another and swear still worse.' (CW 34 p. 387)

18 March: Lenin speaks before an audience of 600 in the artisans' hall in Geneva at a meeting commemorating the twenty-fifth anniversary of the death of Karl Marx, the 1848 revolution and the Paris Commune of 1871. Lenin, in a letter to Leon Tyszka (Leo Jogiches), comments on the case initiated by the Party against Litvinov, who had attempted to exchange money which had come from the Tbilisi 'expropriation'.

End of March: Lenin writes to Bogdanov, who like him lives in Geneva, that Tyszka (Jogiches) will visit him. 'In our opinion he does not know anything yet about the *aggravation* of our philosophical differences and it would be very important (for our success in the CC) that he should not know of it.' (CW 43 p. 189)

Beginning of April: Lenin tells Gorky that *Proletarii* is 'an uncared-for waif' as he spends whole days reading the 'accursed Machists' and so the articles for the newspaper have to be written 'in incredible haste.' (CW 34 p. 391)

1 April: Three articles by Lenin, including 'On the Straight Road' in which he analyses the decline of the revolution since the coup d'état of 16 June 1907, appear in *Proletarii* no 26. (CW 15 pp. 15–21)

16 April: Lenin concludes work on the article 'Marxism and Revisionism'. (CW 15 pp. 29–39) Lenin regards revisionism as 'inevitable . . . determined by its class roots in modern society' and he places the struggle between 'the orthodox and the followers of Bernstein' in Germany and the disputes between Bolsheviks and Mensheviks in Russia on a par. The article appears in 1908 in St Petersburg in a volume for Karl Marx. In letters to Gorky and Lunacharsky, Lenin reveals that he is not of like mind. He opposes those who preach the 'union of scientific socialism and religion.' (CW 34 pp. 392–3)

19 April: Lenin writes to Gorky that henceforth the political work of the Bolsheviks should be carried out harmoniously; disputes over philosophy should be conducted 'as a thing apart.' (CW 34 p. 394)

23–30 April: Lenin visits Gorky in Capri. He goes boating, plays chess, visits Naples, Vesuvius and Pompeii with him. He opposes Bogdanov and Lunacharsky. He writes later: 'I was on Capri in April 1908 and told them . . . that my views on philosophy were unconditionally opposed to theirs.' There was no reconciliation. Krupskaya writes later: 'There was a big crowd at Gorky's place, much noise and bustle. Ilich said very little about his trip. He spoke mostly about the beauty of the scene and the quality of the local wine but he was reticent about the discussions on the big question that took place there. It was too painful a subject with him to talk about.' (Krupskaya p. 160)

1 May: Lenin attends a May Day meeting of socialists in Geneva.

7 May: Lenin speaks in Geneva on the Russian revolution and its probable future.

8 or 9 May: Lenin speaks on the Russian revolution in Lausanne en route to London via Paris and Brussels.

10 May: Lenin addresses a meeting in Paris.

14 May: Lenin speaks to the Russian social democratic group in Paris.

16 May: Lenin is in Brussels. In a letter to Camille Huysmans Lenin regrets not having met him in the Maison du Peuple.

16 May–10 June: In London; Lenin works in the British Museum on *Materialism and Empiriocriticism*.

20 June: Lenin writes to his mother from Geneva that he returned from London ill: 'I arrived back . . . with a bout of abdominal catarrh. I am better now and have begun to eat properly and after the diet feel happy all the time. I have begun work again.' (CW 37 p. 384)

June: Bolsheviks of the left, led by Bogdanov, oppose Lenin's tactics. These 'otsovists' (recallists) demand the recall of the Bolshevik members of the Duma.

1 July: Lenin writes to V V Vorovsky that the situation has become serious: 'A split with Bogdanov is imminent.' He had been offended by Lenin's criticism of his philosophy and had linked up with Aleksinsky who 'is kicking up a terrible row and with whom I have been compelled to break off relations.' They had 'made the boycott clear' and had organised the split 'on empirio-monistic and boycott grounds.' A split is probable. 'I shall leave the faction as soon as this policy of the "left" and of true "boycottism" gets the upper hand.' (CW 34 p. 395)

8 July: Lenin writes to T A Rothstein in London that since his return from London he has felt ill all the time.

13 July: Lenin writes to his sister Maria: 'My illness has held up my work on philosophy very badly. I am now almost well again and will most certainly write the book.' He has received 340 roubles. 'So far I do not need money.' (CW 37 pp. 386-7)

15 July: Lenin's article 'Some Features of the Present Collapse' (CW 15 pp. 148-57) appears as the leader in *Proletarii* no 32.

5 August: Three articles by Lenin, including 'Bellicose Militarism and the Anti-Military Tactics of Social Democracy' appear in *Proletarii* no 33. Lenin defines contemporary militarism as 'the product of capitalism' externally as well as internally. The assessment of war, according to Lenin, depends not on 'the defensive or offensive character of the war but the interests of the class struggle of the proletariat.'

9 August: Lenin writes to his sister Maria that he had gone into the mountains to go walking but has returned to Geneva because of the bad weather and hopes to finish his work, *Materialism and Empiriocriticism*, in about a month and a half.

24–26 August: Lenin is elected a member of the editorial board abroad of the central organ at a meeting of the CC of the RSDLP in Geneva.

31 August: On the anniversary of the death of Ferdinand Lassalle, who had died on 31 August 1864, Lenin and some German socialists travel to Mount Salève, where a memorial stands at the foot of the mountain.

8 September: Lenin writes to Camille Huysmans that he has been away three days.

15 September: Lenin receives 500 francs for previous literary work. He rents a three bedroomed flat 'on the second floor of the Rue du Maraîchers 61' after Krupskaya's mother has arrived in Geneva and Maria, Lenin's younger sister, has come to Geneva to study. She, however, rents a separate room. (Gautschi p. 66)

24 September: Lenin's article 'Leo Trotsky as the Mirror of the Russian Revolution' appears in *Proletarii* no 35. (CW 15 pp. 202-9)

30 September: Lenin writes to his mother that his work on philosophy is almost complete. His brother Dmitri should come to Geneva to convalesce, 'we could go for some splendid walks together. I hope I shall now earn a lot.' (CW 37 p. 390)

10–12 October: Lenin attends a meeting of the International Socialist Bureau in Brussels.

27 October: Lenin tells his sister Anna in Moscow that he has finished *Materialism and Empiriocriticism*. In searching for a publisher 'chasing after royalties' is not important and he is 'prepared to make concessions (any you like).' He intends to forward the work in a fortnight. (CW 37 pp. 392-3)

17 November: Lenin informs his mother that he intends moving to Paris.

26 November: Lenin writes to his sister Maria that after posting his manuscript *Materialism and Empiriocriticism* he is rather nervous. 'I am simply scared to death of losing a huge piece of work that took many months.' (CW 37 pp. 398-9) Lenin's articles 'How Plekhanov and Co Defend Revisionism' and 'Two Letters' appear in *Proletarii* no 39. (CW 15 pp. 281-302) In the latter he takes issue with the Recallists.

28 November: Lenin's sister Anna writes to him from Moscow that she is reading *Materialism and Empiriocriticism*. 'The more I read the more interesting it becomes.' However 'a lot of the abuse must be taken out or toned down. Heavens above, Volodek, there is an enormous amount in it comparable to the "Victory of the Cadets"! Especially for a study of philosophy it is stuffed full . . . In between it is very convincing . . . But il ne faut pas outrer [one should not exaggerate] (to use one of your favourite expressions) since, believe me, every exaggeration weakens the argument.' (*Vom Alltag der Uljanows* pp. 165-6)

10 December: Lenin writes to his mother that they have given up their flat in Geneva and will soon be on their way to Paris.

14 December: Lenin, Krupskaya and her mother leave Geneva, arrive in Paris on the 15th and spend four days in an hotel. The editorial office of *Proletarii* has been moved to Paris. Krupskaya writes later: 'We had completely settled down in Geneva. My mother arrived and we set up our little household — we rented a small apartment . . . Maria Ilinichna [Lenin's sister] arrived from Russia . . . Zinoviev and Lilina arrived from Russia . . . Kamenev and his family arrived . . . Finally Lyadov and Zhitomirsky arrived from Paris and began to persuade us to go there . . . In the late autumn we moved to Paris. In Paris we spent the most trying years of exile.' (Krupskaya pp. 165-6)

19 December: Lenin writes to his sister Anna from Paris. He is willing to 'tone down abuse; the same applies to vulgar expressions' in *Materialism and Empiriocriticism*. They have a flat in Rue Beaunier 24, four rooms, 'elegant and expensive.' (CW 37 pp. 402-3) After they settle in they find a more suitable two bedroomed flat in July 1909 in Rue Marie Rose 4.

24 December: Lenin writes to his sister Anna about the corrections to the proofs of *Materialism and Empiriocriticism*.

1909

3–9 January: Lenin attends 5th All-Russian Conference of the RSDLP in Paris.

5 January: Lenin speaks at the conference 'On the Present Moment and the Tasks of the Party' and proposes a draft resolution on the same theme. (CW 15 pp. 320–4)

6 January: Lenin speaks on the organisational question.

9–11 January: Lenin attends a meeting of the CC in Paris.

12 January: Lenin, armed with a letter of recommendation from L Roblen, a member of parliament, submits an application for a reader's ticket to the Bibliothèque Nationale in Paris.

Mid January: Lenin attends a meeting, in Paris, to commemorate the victims of Bloody Sunday in St Petersburg on 9(22) January 1905.

19 January: Lenin forwards Camille Huysmans, secretary of the International Socialist Bureau, 300 francs: 'This is the sum the Party owes the International Socialist Bureau for 1908.' He adds: 'Our entire organisation is at present (at last!) in Paris.' (CW 43 p. 199)

January–February: Lenin lectures to Bolshevik circles in Paris on philosophy.

6 February: Lenin writes to his sister Anna and sends a list of corrections of *Materialism and Empiriocriticism*. 'Regards from all. Manyasha [Maria] and I are just leaving for the theatre to see a Russian play. They are doing Andreev's *Days of Our Life*.'

10 February: Lenin's article 'On the Road' appears in *Sotsial Demokrat*, the illegal central organ of the RSDLP, no 2. Lenin describes the decline of the movement in Russia, 'a year of Party driftage lies behind us', but regards the loss of the 'fellow-travellers' as a gain. (CW 15 pp. 345–55) Lenin publishes 80 articles and notes in the 58 numbers of *Sotsial Demokrat* which appear between February 1908 and January 1917.

14 February: Lenin calls for an open stand against Lunacharsky and his 'God building' at an editorial board meeting of *Proletarii*.

16 February: A worried Lenin asks his sister Anna about the state of health of their sick mother.

23 February: Lenin writes to his sister Anna that he is relieved at the improvement in their mother's health.

25 February: Lenin's note 'On the Article "Questions of the Day"' appears in *Proletarii* no 42. In it he attacks the left 'Otsovists' (Recallists): 'Otsovism is not Bolshevism but the worst political travesty of Bolshevism . . . Is this not obvious renunciation under the flag of revolutionariness" and "leftism" of the fine tradition of the old Bolsheviks?' Lenin invites 'otsovists' and 'orthodox Bolsheviks' alike to state their views in *Proletarii*. (CW 15 pp. 356–9)

26 February: Lenin travels to Nice where he meets his brother-in-law, Mark Elizarov, and relaxes until 8 March.

2 March: Lenin writes to his sister Anna from Nice: 'I am taking a holiday in Nice. The place is wonderful — sunny, warm, dry and a southern sea. I am returning to Paris in a few days.' (CW 37 p. 412)

9 March: Lenin writes to his sister Anna from Paris about corrections to *Materialism and Empiriocriticism*. He states that she is not to tone down the 'places against Bogdanov and against Lunacharsky's *popovshchina*. We have *completely broken off* relations with them. There is no reason for toning them down.' (CW 37 pp. 413–4)

18 March: Lenin speaks on the Paris Commune at a meeting of émigrés in Paris.

21 March: Lenin, in a letter to his sister Anna, repeats that the passages against Bogdanov and Lunacharsky are 'not under any circumstances to be toned down.' (CW 37 pp. 417–8)

22 March: Lenin's article 'The Aim of the Proletarian Struggle in Our Revolution', directed against Martov, appears in *Sotsial Demokrat* no 3 and is continued in no 4 of 3 April. (CW 15 pp. 360–79)

After 5 April: Lenin sends, in the name of the CC of the RSDLP, a letter of protest to the executive committee of the SPD against the 'distorted version' of the nature of the differences among Russian social democrats in *Vorwärts* of 3 April 1909. (CW 15 pp. 379–82)

6 April: Lenin writes to his sister Anna: 'As far as money is concerned — please send it on to me all at once (I am now in need of money).' (CW 37 pp. 424–5)

8 April: Lenin writes to sister Anna about *Materialism and Empiriocriticism*. 'It is *hellishly* important to me for the book to appear sooner. I have not only literary but also serious political commitments that are linked up with the publication of the book.' (CW 37 pp. 426–7)

21 April: Two articles by Lenin appear in *Proletarii* no 44, including 'A Caricature of Bolshevism' in which he again attacks 'otsovism' and 'ultimatumism' because these would lead the 'Duma group and the Party' into 'a bog.' (CW 15 pp. 383–94)

29 April: Lenin writes to I F Dubrovinsky: 'We here have found the struggle against this stupid, petty, underhand, disgusting squabble utterly nerve racking [with the Bolshevik left opposition].' (CW 43 p. 206)

5 May: Lenin tells Dubrovinsky: 'The Paris group [of Bolsheviks] met today. The Geneva group announced its break with the Bolshevik Centre and urged the Paris one to follow suit.' Shantser spoke for the left opposition (otsovists) and Rykov for the Lenin group. (CW 34 pp. 208–9)

Between 12–17 May: Lenin's treatise *Materialism and Empiriocriticism: Critical Comments on a Reactionary Philosophy* is published by the *Zveno* (Link) publishing house in Moscow. (CW 14 pp. 17–361) Lenin's chief work in philosophy is a polemic against the followers of Mach and Avenarius, above all against those who belong to the recallists, the Bolshevik minority faction. Lenin sets out to provide a philosophical base for political action and to develop the Marxist theory of knowledge. Lenin defines knowledge as a reflection of the real existing world which is independent of the human brain and human consciousness. Through a process of progressive approximation to the 'image' of the real world, perception contains, given the imperfections of time and relativity, elements of absolute truth. Philosophical materialism for Lenin means the recognition of an objective reality independent of our consciousness. The polemical tone of the treatise reflects the factional struggle against Bogdanov and the others.

18 May: Lenin informs Rosa Luxemburg that the previous day he had forwarded her a copy of his treatise *Materialism and Empiriocriticism* 'in memory of our conversations about Mach when we last met.' He praises her article against the 'otsovists' and takes it that Leo Jogiches had briefed her on the internal struggle among the Bolsheviks. 'It is a pity you write *so rarely* in Russian; you prefer the rich Social Democratic Party of the Germans to the poor Social Democratic Party of the Russians.' (CW 34 p. 397)

21 May: Lenin speaks on religion and the workers' party in the editorial club of *Proletarii* in Paris. Lenin confirms, in a letter to his mother, the receipt of *Materialism and Empiriocriticism*. 'It has been beautifully published – everyone grumbles about the price (2 roubles 60 kopeks) but that, apparently, is the publisher's fault.' (CW 37 pp. 428-9)

26 May: Lenin's article 'The Attitude of the Workers' Party to Religion' appears in *Proletarii* no 45. (CW 15 pp. 402-13) Lenin explains that Marxism means materialism. 'We must combat religion – that is the ABC of *all* materialism.' But the social roots have to be explained and the class nature of the church revealed. Atheistic propaganda must be subordinated to the chief task, the class struggle. Lenin writes to his sister Anna: 'Things are bad here – *Spaltung* (split) or rather, there will be one.' He asks for pressure to be put on the publisher to pay the royalties due. 'I am beginning to be afraid that he will swindle us.' [This did not occur; see 25 October.] (CW 37 pp. 430-1)

10 June: Lenin receives a letter from Rosa Luxemburg in which she acknowledges receipt of *Materialism and Empiriocriticism*.

17 June: Lenin's article 'Classes and Parties in Their Attitude to Religion and the Church' appears in *Sotsial Demokrat* no 6. (CW 15 pp. 414-23)

21-30 June: Lenin attends a meeting of the extended editorial board of *Proletarii* in Paris. Bogdanov and another member of the left opposition are present. Lenin sharply criticises Bogdanov during a speech on the tasks of the Bolsheviks in the Party. He says that since he (Bogdanov) refuses to fight openly but continues his 'intrigues within the Party', he must be removed from the section (but not from the Party). The meeting passes the appropriate resolution. After a hard struggle Lenin wins

over the majority of the Bolsheviks to his point of view. He demands
that 'Bolshevism must now be strictly Marxist.' (CW 15 pp. 425-51)

19 July: Lenin writes to his mother that his sister Maria who is living
with him in Paris has had her appendix removed but is well again.

24 July: Three articles by Lenin, including 'The Liquidation of Liquidationism' appear in *Proletarii* no 46. (CW 15 pp. 452-60) Lenin opposes
the attempts of the Mensheviks to restrict illegal work. This is liquidationism to Lenin and he concentrates his main attacks on it in the
coming weeks.

Summer: Lenin and Krupskaya visit Paul Lafargue and his wife Laura,
a daughter of Karl Marx, in Draveil, near Paris and they discuss philosophy. Krupskaya goes walking with Laura Lafargue: 'I was a little
excited — I was actually walking with Marx's daughter.' (Krupskaya
p. 178)

3 August: Krupskaya, her mother, Lenin and his sister Maria travel to
Bombon, a village 50 kilometres from Paris, for a holiday. They remain
until 14 September. Lenin does not work during the holiday 'and we
tried to refrain from discussing Party affairs. We went for walks every
day and almost every day we cycled to the Clamart forest, fifteen kilometres away.' (Krupskaya p. 173)

18 August: Lenin writes from Bombon to the organisers of the Party
school in Capri. (Krupskaya p. 174)

24 August: Lenin writes to his mother from Bombon: 'We are having
a good holiday here . . . Our rooms here are good and the board is
good and not expensive.' (CW 37 pp. 436-7) Lenin writes to Zinoviev:
'After three weeks' holiday, I am beginning to come round.' He vehemently attacks the 'vile' polemics of the Mensheviks, the 'lies' of the
'scoundrels' around Bogdanov and the 'scoundrel' and 'swindler'
Trotsky. (CW 34 pp. 399-400)

30 August: Lenin repeats his refusal to speak in a letter to the students
of the Party school in Capri. He regards the school as the work of the
otsovist faction and God-builders. But 'Trotsky, who is not linked to
any faction' has perceived immediately that the school was linked to
the new faction. (Briefe II pp. 197-8)

Beginning of September: Lenin, in a letter to A I Lyubimov, writes
about 'the company of offended writers, unrecognised philosophers
and ridiculed God builders who have hidden away their so-called
"school" from the Party.' He speaks of Bogdanov and his 'gang of
scoundrels.' 'There is nothing more harmful now than sentimentalising.
A *complete break* and war, *more determined than that against the
Mensheviks*.' (CW 34 pp. 401-2)

14 September: Return to Paris from Bombon.

19 September: Lenin writes to Tomsky that 'the Trotsky business,
regrettably, will not work out.' Although he was offered a bloc he
only wanted to form his own faction. 'By means of "his" faction he

will win over some people from the Mensheviks, a few from us, but in the end he will inevitably lead the workers to Bolshevism.' (CW 43 pp. 211-2)

24 September: Lenin's long article 'The Faction of Supporters of Otsovism and God Building' appears in a supplement to *Proletarii* nos 47-48. (CW 16 pp. 29-61) In it he labels the left Bolsheviks 'otsovist chatterboxes' and accuses them of 'deceit' and 'hypocrisy.' 'Now we declare the most ruthless and irreconcilable war on the liquidators, both of the right and of the left, who are corrupting the workers' party by theoretical revisionism and petty bourgeois methods of policy and tactics.'

17 or 18 October: Lenin and Krupskaya witness the demonstrations in protest against the sentence passed on the Spanish anarchist Francisco Ferrer.

25 October: Lenin writes to his mother that he has received the money (for *Materialism and Empiriocriticism*) from the publisher.

28 October: Lenin addresses social democratic groups in Liège on the situation in the Party.

29 October: Lenin speaks on the ideology of the counter revolutionary bourgeoisie at an open meeting in Liège.

October: Lenin, in a letter to the economic commission of the Bolshevik Centre in Russia, favours a reduction and systematic supervision of expenditure. He argues for monthly breakdowns of expenditure and forwards a table containing a breakdown of expenditure between June and September. (CW 43 pp. 226-8)

3-4 November: Lenin introduces, at an editorial board meeting of *Sotsial Demokrat*, a draft resolution on Party unity, but it is rejected by the majority. Lenin then announces his resignation from the editorial board and demands the publication of his resignation and his draft resolution.

5 November: Lenin travels to Brussels to attend a meeting of the International Socialist Bureau.

6 November: Lenin informs the editorial board of *Sotsial Demokrat*, from Brussels, that he is withdrawing his resignation.

7 November: Lenin speaks at the meeting of the International Socialist Bureau in Brussels on the split in Dutch social democracy.

After 8 November: Lenin returns to Paris from Brussels.

16 November: After a talk with N I Vilonov, Lenin writes to Gorky that he had believed until then that he and Gorky were 'the most hardened factionalists in the new faction' and any friendly conversation was silly. After their talk he has changed his mind; above all he now knows that Gorky was 'taking things hard' but he must learn about this side of the labour movement. Gorky's artistic talent has been 'of such tremendous service to the whole labour movement, not only that of Russia, that he must not fall victim to such moods of depression.

Struggles, splits and so on are not to be seen as the expression of the weakness of the labour movement which is being forged. (CW 34 pp. 403–4)

After 20 November: Lenin writes to Gorky that he wrote his letter of the 16th 'at once, in the heat of the moment without even reading through the letter', but that was right and contact has been reestablished. The split is inevitable 'but it does not come anywhere near the split between the Bolsheviks and Mensheviks.' (CW 34 pp. 405–6)

2 December: Lenin writes to I I Skvortsov-Stepanov: 'With the so called "Lefts" we have a complete split, which was made good in the spring of 1909.' Plekhanov had left the liquidators. 'Things are moving towards an alignment with the Plekhanovite Mensheviks with the aim of strengthening the Party.' The 'general democratic' movement must be led in such a way as to produce 'a real French scrimmage' and not 'the German way' (1848, 1871). 'There are no historical laws to prevent a rotten crisis from turning into a real scrimmage.' (CW 34 pp. 407–10)

4 December: Lenin speaks on the International Socialist Bureau session at a meeting of the Paris group for the support of the RSDLP.

11 December: Five articles by Lenin, including 'Methods of the Liquidators and Party Tasks of the Bolsheviks' appear in *Proletarii* no 50. (CW 16 pp. 95–102) Lenin calls the left 'otsovism-ultimatumism' the 'liquidationism of the Mensheviks'; the Bolsheviks have to fight 'on two flanks.'

16 December: Lenin once again analyses the capitalist development of Russia in a letter in reply to I I Skvortsov-Stepanov. A peculiarity of Russian opportunism, for Lenin, is that 'it is associated with a doctrinarist simplification, vulgarisation and distortion of the letter of Marxism – a betrayal of its spirit.' (CW 16 pp. 117–22)

End of December: Krupskaya writes to Lenin's mother that he is working a lot at home. 'He has been working a lot this winter and he always feels better when he is working. For over a week now he has been getting up at eight in the morning to go to the library; he returns from there at 2 o'clock. At first he found it difficult to get up so early . . . Recently we went to a little theatre near here and enjoyed it. The audience was pure working class, mothers with babies, hatless, lively and talkative.' (CW 37 pp. 607–8)

24–25 December: Lenin attends a reunion of old students of the school in Capri and speaks on the current situation.

1909–1910: Lenin becomes acquainted with Inessa Armand (1874–1920) who arrives in Brussels in 1909 from Russian exile. She moves in 1910 to Paris and becomes good friends with the Lenin household. 'She had two little children, a boy and a girl. She was a very ardent Bolshevik and soon gathered our Paris crowd around her.' (Krupskaya p. 185) Inessa Armand was 'a very attractive woman. Lenin felt the attraction.' (Louis Fischer *The Life of Lenin* p. 75) Everything points to the fact that Lenin and she were on intimate terms and that they loved one another.

1910

2 January: Lenin writes to his sister Maria who is again in Moscow with their mother that they have made 'good use' of the holidays. They had been to museums, the theatre and to the Musée Grévin (a French Madame Tussaud's) 'which gave us great pleasure.' (CW 37 pp. 445-6)

Beginning of January: Lenin watches an air display at Juvisy, near Paris. On the way home a motor car runs into him and smashes his bicycle, but he is able to jump clear in time. Lenin writes to his sister Maria: 'People helped and took the number and acted as witnesses. I have found out who the owner of the car is (a viscount, the devil take him!) and now I have taken him to court.' (CW 37 p. 447)

6 January: Two articles by Lenin, including a report on the session of the International Socialist Bureau in November 1909 (on the split in the Dutch party) appears in *Sotsial Demokrat* no 10. (CW 16 pp. 140-4)

First half of January: Lenin writes the note 'The *Vperyod* Group: A Conspectus'; it is first published in 1933. He makes clear his opposition to the left Bolsheviks under Bogdanov who publish their own organ, *Vperyod*, during 1910 and 1911. The dispute between Lenin and his supporters and the *Vperyod* group, the otsovists, becomes physical at times. Once Aleksinsky and his supporters burst into a Bolshevik meeting in a Parisian café: 'With an insolent air Aleksinsky sat down at a table and demanded to be allowed to speak, and when this was refused he began to create an uproar. The *Vperyod*-ists who came in threw themselves upon our comrades to attack them.' (Krupskaya p. 180)

12 January: Lenin writes to his sister Maria: 'I have begun to pay more attention to the theatre. I have seen Bourget's new play *La Barricade*. Reactionary but interesting.' (CW 37 p. 448)

15 January-5 February: Lenin attends the plenary session of the CC, RSDLP in Paris. The various groups engage in violent arguments. Lenin writes later: 'Its merit was the rejection of the ideas of liquidationism and otsovism, its mistake was the agreement concluded indiscriminately with persons and groups.' (CW 17 p. 266) Lenin is partly successful in pushing through his political theses but because of the 'conciliatory' attitude of the majority of his supporters the compromise is reached to cease publication of *Proletarii*, to support Trotsky's *Pravda* with Kamenev joining as an editor and liquidators being elected to the CC. Lenin writes to Gorky about the 'long plenum.' Three 'weeks of agony, all nerves were on edge, the devil to pay!' (CW 34 p. 420)

22 January: Lenin writes to Gustav Mayer, who is to write on the Russian social democratic movement for the *Pocket Dictionary of Political Science*, that he is 'well aware of the scientific character of the dictionary' but could not help him, due to lack of time. He refers to articles by Trotsky and Cherevanin. (CW 43 pp. 231-2 Khr. II p. 535)

30-31 January: Lenin informs his sister Maria: 'My bicycle case ended in my favour.' (CW 37 p. 450)

1 February: Lenin tells his sister Maria: 'We have closed down the factional newspaper [*Proletarii*] and are trying harder to promote unity.' Paris is 'in many respects a rotten hole'; after a year there he has been unable to adapt himself completely to it. (CW 37 p. 451)

13 February: Lenin writes to his mother that he has received the chess set but has few opportunities to play.

22 February: Lenin and Krupskaya translate Rosa Luxemburg's article 'August Bebel'.

26 February: Lenin's article 'Towards Unity' appears in *Sotsial Demokrat* no 11. (CW 16 pp. 147-55) In it he analyses the resolutions of the January plenum.

19 March: The first part of Lenin's article 'Notes of a Publicist' appears in *Diskussionny Listok* (Discussion Sheet) no 1, the supplement to *Sotsial Demokrat*. The second part is printed in no 2 dated 7 June. In the first part Lenin takes issue with the 'platform' of the *Vperyod* Bolsheviks and the otsovists, and also provides a critical analysis of the literary and political activity of Maxim Gorky. (CW 16 pp. 195-259)

20 March: At a meeting of the Bolshevik group in Paris Lenin supports unification with the 'Party faithful' Mensheviks around Plekhanov.

29 March: Lenin writes to Plekhanov in San Remo that he agrees with him that there is a need 'for a close and sincere alignment of all genuinely social democratic elements in the struggle against liquidationism and otsovism'; he proposes a meeting and is willing to travel down to San Remo. (CW 34 p. 416)

6 April: Lenin writes to Kamenev in Vienna that a 'Party core' is necessary, one that is not built 'on the cheap *phrases* of Trotsky and Co but on *genuine* ideological rapprochement between the Plekhanovites and the Bolsheviks.' (CW 43 pp. 243-4)

11 April: Lenin writes to Maxim Gorky about the January plenum of the CC. Scandals and squabbles are loathsome. 'But one should not allow oneself to succumb to the mood. Life in exile is now a hundred times harder than it was before the revolution. Life in exile and squabbling are inseparable.' But squabbling is only an accessory feature of the 'purging' of the Party. (CW 34 pp. 419-22)

2 May: Lenin informs his sister Anna that he has again taken to cycling and goes from time to time from his home in the suburbs to the countryside around Paris. Lenin writes to the CC that his situation on the editorial board of *Sotsial Demokrat*, to which Martov and Dan also belong, is 'intolerable' and he describes the altercations. (Briefe II pp. 250-3)

9 May: Four articles by Lenin appear in *Sotsial Demokrat* no 13.

18 June: Lenin and Krupskaya send greetings to their relatives in Moscow during a Sunday outing on their bicycles in the Bois de Meudon.

28 June: Lenin travels from Paris to Capri to see Gorky. He travels to Naples by steamer from Marseilles.

1 July: Lenin sends his mother greetings from Naples; the steamer from Marseilles was 'cheap and pleasant. It was like travelling on the Volga. I am going to Capri from here for a brief visit.' (CW 37 p. 462) In Capri Lenin stays with Gorky in the villa Blaesus and meets Bogdanov, Lunacharsky and Bazarov as well. 'Lenin arrives at lunch time . . . I come back for tea . . . Lenin and A M [Gorky] are talking . . . I return at 3 am and they are still arguing.' (K Pyatnitsky in *Lenin und Gorki* p. 403)

14 July: Lenin and Gorky leave Capri together.

22 July–23 August: Lenin, Krupskaya and her mother holiday in Pornic, France on the Bay of Biscay. 'My mother and I rented two small rooms from the coast guard. Soon Ilich arrived. He bathed in the sea a good deal, cycled — he loved the sea and the sea breezes — chatted cheerfully on all sorts of subjects with the Kostytsins, and enjoyed eating the crabs which the coast guard caught for us. In fact, our landlord and his wife took a great liking to Ilich. The stout, loud-voiced landlady — she was a laundress — would tell us of the conflicts she had with the priests . . . the priests tried to persuade the mother to allow the boy to be educated in a monastery . . . but the laundress indignantly showed the priests the door . . . And this is why Ilich praised the crabs so highly.' (Krupskaya pp. 181-2)

28 July: Lenin writes to his mother from Pornic that he is having a wonderful holiday.

16 August: Lenin books his rail and sea tickets for the journey to Copenhagen and Stockholm via Hamburg.

23 August: Lenin leaves Pornic to attend the International Socialist Congress in Copenhagen.

24 August: En route to Copenhagen Lenin meets Plekhanov in Paris for a talk.

26 August: Lenin arrives in Copenhagen to attend the sessions of the Congress Bureau.

28 August–3 September: Lenin participates in the discussions at the Congress of the Socialist International in Copenhagen. Since many Russian Party leaders are present (Plekhanov, Zinoviev, Kamenev, Martov, Martynov, Trotsky, Lunacharsky and others) there are discussions about the situation in Russia. They decide to establish a popular organ *Rabochaya Gazeta* (Workers' Newspaper). Lenin also takes part in the commission on co-operation.

4 September: Lenin writes to his mother that he intends to stay in Copenhagen until 15 September. 'On 17 September (New Style) I shall be waiting for you on the wharf in Stockholm.' (CW 37 p. 464)

11 September: Lenin travels from Copenhagen to Stockholm.

12 September: Lenin arrives in Stockholm. His article 'The *Vperyod* Faction' appears in *Sotsial Demokrat* no 15-16. (CW 16 pp. 268-74)

13 September: Lenin's 75-year-old mother and his sister Maria arrive in Stockholm and stay until 25 September with him.

15 September: Lenin speaks in Stockholm; his sister Maria is present.

24 September: Lenin speaks in Stockholm on the socialist Congress in Copenhagen. About sixty persons are present. Lenin's mother hears him speaking in public for the first time. Lenin's sister Maria writes: 'She listened quite attentively to Vladimir Ilich and apparently became very excited. He spoke well, "so impressively and skilfully," she then said to me, "but why does he exert himself so much, why does he speak so loudly, that is so harmful. He is not looking after himself!"' (*Vom Alltag der Uljanows* p. 356)

25 September: Lenin says goodbye to his mother and sister as they leave Stockholm by ship. 'This was the last time he saw his mother. He had a premonition of that and it was with sad and wistful eyes that he followed the departing steamer. When he returned to Russia seven years later, in 1917, she was already dead.' (Krupskaya p. 182)

26 September: Lenin speaks in Copenhagen to Russian émigrés on the International Socialist Congress.

27 September: He returns to Paris from Copenhagen.

30 September: Lenin writes to Karl Radek about the latter's leading article in the *Leipziger Volkszeitung*, 'Critical Remarks About Copenhagen'.

8 October: Two articles by Lenin, 'The Question of Co-operative Societies at the International Socialist Congress in Copenhagen' and 'How Certain Social Democrats Inform the International About the State of Affairs in the RSDLP' appear in *Sotsial Demokrat* no 17. (CW 16 pp. 275-88) In the latter article Lenin takes issue with Trotsky on his presentation of Party differences in *Vorwärts*.

9 October: Lenin writes to Radek that he 'cannot leave unanswered Martov's and Trotsky's most incredible absurdities and distortions' and intends eventually to write on factional struggles in the *Leipziger Volkzeitung*. (CW 34 pp. 174-5)

14 October: Lenin writes to G L Shklovsky: 'Since 1909 I have been *wholly* in favour of a rapprochement with the Plekhanovites. And even more so now. We can and should build the Party only with the Plekhanovites.' He fully agrees with Plekhanov that 'nothing can be done with Trotsky.' (CW 34 pp. 430-1)

12 November: The first number of the newspaper *Rabochaya Gazeta*, an illegal Bolshevik organ, appears in Paris. Nine numbers, edited by

Lenin, appear by August 1912. Lenin's article 'The Lessons of the Revolution' appears in no 1. (CW 16 pp. 296-304)

14 November: Lenin writes to Gorky that he is involved with Plekhanov in publishing 'a small legal periodical.' (CW 34 pp. 432-3) He has *Mysl* in mind. Gorky sends 500 francs for *Rabochaya Gazeta* before 12 December.

29 November: Four articles by Lenin appear in *Sotsial Demokrat* no 18 including 'Two Worlds' in which he reports on the SPD Congress in Magdeburg and writes: 'Opportunism is opportunism for the very reason that it sacrifices the *fundamental* interests of the movement to momentary advantages or considerations based on the most short-sighted, superficial calculations.' (CW 16 pp. 305-13)

3 December: Lenin writes to students of the school in Bologna that he is unable to accept their invitation. 'Both the trend and the methods of the group which has organised the school on the island of Capri and in Bologna I consider harmful to the Party and unsocial democratic.' (CW 16 pp. 328-9)

11 December: Lenin's article 'L N Trotsky and the Modern Labour Movement' appears in *Nash Put* (Our Way). (CW 16 pp. 330-2)

29 December: The first number of the legal Bolshevik newspaper *Zvezda* (The Star) appears in St Petersburg. Sixty-nine numbers appear by May 1912. Almost simultaneously the first number of *Mysl* (Thought), the legal Bolshevik journal on philosophy and economics, appears in Moscow. Five numbers appear by April 1911. Over 50 articles and notes by Lenin appear in these two publications. Lenin's article 'Differences in the European Labour Movement' appears in *Zvezda* no 1. (CW 16 pp. 347-52) In it Lenin attacks revisionism and anarcho-syndicalism as both are departures 'from Marxist theory and Marxist tactics that are dominant in the labour movement.' The first part of Lenin's 'Strike Statistics in Russia' appears in *Mysl* no 1. (CW 16 pp. 393-421)

1911

3 January: Lenin writes to his brother-in-law, Mark Elizarov, that he feels cut off and longs for the Volga. Finances do not permit long trips, such as to Italy. 'Yesterday I received *Zvezda* no 1 from Russia and today *Mysl* no 1. That is something to cheer one up! I hope you have seen it! It really is a pleasure.' (CW 37 pp. 465-6) Lenin writes to Gorky that only through the growth of capitalism is there a guarantee of victory over it. 'Marxists do not defend a single reactionary *measure*, such as banning trusts, restricting trade etc. *Resistance* to colonial policy . . . *by means* of organising the proletariat . . . *does not retard* the development of capitalism but *accelerates* it, forcing it to resort to more civilised, technically higher methods of capitalism.' (CW 34 pp. 437–40)

5 January: Lenin's article 'Certain Features of the Historical Development of Marxism' appears in *Zvezda* no 2. In it he refers to the statement by Engels that Marxism is not a dogma. (CW 17 pp. 39–44)

5 or 6 January: Lenin's pamphlet 'The State of Affairs in the Party' appears in a supplement to *Sotsial Demokrat*. (CW 17 pp. 23–38) It is directed against articles by Martov and Trotsky. Trotsky is pursuing 'an anti-Party policy' and is embarking on the path of 'adventurism and a split.'

19 January: Lenin writes to his mother that she need not send any money. 'I beg you, my dear, not to send anything and not to try to save anything from your pension. If things get bad I will write quite frankly.' He continues to receive the 'salary' about which he told her in Stockholm — a salary paid by the Party since he has no other source of income. (CW 37 pp. 467–8)

31 January: Lenin writes to Kautsky that he is sending him his article against Trotsky and Martov 'not for publication but to ask your advice.' (CW 43 p. 263)

January–February: Lenin's article 'Those Who Would Liquidate Us', directed against Potresov and Bazarov, appears in *Mysl* nos 2 and 3. (CW 17 pp. 60–81)

3 February: Lenin writes to Plekhanov that the liquidators have started a new offensive. He is suffering from slight influenza.

Before 9 February: Lenin prepares four lectures on the Foundations of Political Economy. He delivers the lectures on 9–10 February in Paris to an audience of about one hundred.

21 February: Lenin's article 'The Fiftieth Anniversary of the Fall of Serfdom' appears in *Rabochaya Gazeta* no 3. An obituary of the SPD leader Paul Singer who had died on 31 January is also included. (CW 17 pp. 87–95)

25 February: Lenin writes to A I Rykov in Berlin and warns him against a conciliatory attitude by the CC towards the *Vperyod* group. 'The Vperyodists are very strong. They have a school = conference = agents. We (and the CC) have *not*. They have money — some 80,000 roubles. You think they will give it to you? Are you really so naive?' (CW 34 pp. 441–5)

7 March: Lenin replies to N G Poletaev in St Petersburg who had written to him asking if people in Paris were not aware of the effects of the 'squabble' on the Party in Russia. Lenin writes that the liquidators were perfectly well aware of what they were doing. 'It is a pity that among you in St Petersburg there are people who *do not understand* what they are doing and what they read. A great pity! Such people are fated always to be led by the nose.' (CW 43 pp. 269–71)

March: In a letter to Berlin, presumably to Rykov, Lenin writes that money is urgently needed for *Zvezda*. 'There is only one source — the

Germans. Apply to the Vorstand [the executive committee of the SPD] through Pfannkuch. Ask for 5,000 marks (they'll give you 3,000).' (CW 43. 276)

Not later than 26 March: Lenin travels to Berlin to obtain money for the newspaper *Zvezda*. Poletaev, a member of the editorial board, travels with him. In 1908 the Bolsheviks had received a large legacy from the furniture manufacturer Nikolai Shmidt, who had died in a tsarist prison, a nephew of the Russian textile magnate Morozov. It may have amounted to 280,000 roubles. Since the RSDLP was formally a united Party with the CC at its head, the Mensheviks demanded their share. In 1910 the CC plenum had decided to hand part of the money over to the CC and the other part to three German trustees, Franz Mehring, Clara Zetkin and Karl Kautsky. Lenin is now trying to get some of the money back from the trustees.

March: Lenin's articles 'The Social Structure of State Power, the Prospects and Liquidationism' and 'Polemical Notes' appear in *Mysl* no 4. (CW 17 pp. 144-67)

Between 4-19 April: Lenin and Gorky meet in Paris.

8 April: Lenin writes to his mother that on the whole he is living quietly.

Before 19 April: Lenin travels to Berlin to negotiate about the publication of the report of the faction in the Third State Duma. In a letter he outlines the form of the report.

21-22 April: Lenin writes the article 'Conference of the British Social Democratic Party'; he comes to the conclusions that in Britain too 'the spirit of proletarian struggle is gaining the upper hand' over opportunism in the Independent Labour Party. (CW 17 pp. 173-8)

28 April: Lenin's article 'In Memory of the Commune' appears in *Rabochaya Gazeta* no 4-5 commemorating the 40th anniversary of the Paris Commune. (CW 17 pp. 139-43)

30 April: Lenin writes to the CC Bureau Abroad of the RSDLP on the results of the negotiations in Berlin. Zinoviev, Steklov and Semashko are to be members of the editorial commission to publish the report; the faction is to provide at least 500 roubles. He puts total costs at 2,100-2,200 roubles. Lenin asks for the rest of the money, 1,600 roubles, to be paid from Party resources (trustees' money). The representatives of the Bolshevik faction are agreeable to this. (CW 43 pp. 277-8)

12 May: Lenin's article 'The Historical Meaning of the Inner Party Struggle in Russia', which was written in 1910 against Martov and Trotsky, appears in *Diskussionny Listok* no 3. (CW 16 pp. 374-92)

Mid May: Lenin asks, in a letter, for Gorky's help in finding a new publisher in St Petersburg after the seizure of *Mysl* no 5.

27 May: Lenin writes to Gorky that he has heard that he is working on a plan to unite the Social Democratic Party. 'Our unity with Mensheviks like Martov is *absolutely* hopeless, as I told you here. If we start arranging a meeting for such a hopeless plan — the result will be nothing but a disgrace (personally I would not go even to a meeting with Martov).' He counsels Gorky against the meeting; 'we should not be uniting now but dissociating.' (CW 34 pp. 446-7)

May: A Bolshevik Party school is established at Longjumeau, near Paris. The eighteen students, mostly Russian workers, live in the village. Inessa Armand has rented a house so that the students can have their lunch there. Lenin, Krupskaya and the Zinoviev family move into the village as well. Lenin speaks on the Communist Manifesto at the opening of the school and during the course, which lasts three months, he delivers more than fifty lectures (on political economy, the agrarian question, history, the position of the Party and so on). 'The students worked very hard, but some evenings they would go out into the field where they would sing or lie near a haystack and talk about all sorts of things. Ilich would sometimes accompany them.' (Krupskaya p. 194)

Between 1-5 June: Lenin protests, in a letter to the CC members of the RSDLP who live abroad, against the intention of the (Menshevik) majority of the Bureau Abroad to postpone the CC plenum. Four Bolshevik members of the CC have in the meanwhile been arrested in Russia (Goldenberg, Nogin, Leiteisen and Dubrovinsky) and Lenin accuses the Mensheviks of living 'for the day when *all* the Bolsheviks have been arrested' so as to achieve a majority with 'fictitious' CC members. (CW 17 pp. 197-9)

6 June: Lenin writes to Karl Kautsky about the money which the trustees hold.

10-17 June: Lenin leads CC discussions but the meeting is boycotted by the Mensheviks. Since Lenin has accused the Mensheviks of being liquidators he demands the whole Shmidt legacy for the Bolsheviks (compare 26 March). His representative has already obtained money from the CC; the session supports Lenin's stand but the German trustees, after this arbitrary act, are not willing to hand the money over to Lenin.

24 June: Lenin's article 'Old Troubles that Are Ever New' appears in *Zvezda* no 25. (CW 17 pp. 211-5) Lenin writes that every capitalist country passes through an epoch of bourgeois capitalism during which 'a definite degree of democracy' or a parliamentary regime appears but its form depends on whether the bourgeoisie or the 'lower classes' exercises hegemony. Lenin writes a letter on financial affairs to the editorial board of *Zvezda*.

27 June: Lenin travels to Stuttgart to see Clara Zetkin to negotiate with her about the money. She is one of the trustees of the Shmidt legacy.

5 July: Lenin writes from Longjumeau to Clara Zetkin in Stuttgart about his visit to a Paris bank to which she has forwarded some money.

30 July: Lenin and Zinoviev sign a letter of protest to the technical commission which has refused to provide funds for the school in

Longjumeau. This commission was set up at the June plenum of the rump CC (one representative each from the Bolsheviks, the conciliators and the Polish social democrats) to look after publications, etc. The commission holds back funds to the Bolshevik organ *Zvezda* and provides no money for the school. Lenin and Zinoviev label this 'illegal' in their declaration (PSS 20 p. 294). The commission attacks Lenin and the Bolsheviks and opposes their policies. Eventually, in November, the Bolshevik representative Vladimirsky withdraws from the commission.

July: Lenin writes the article 'The State of Affairs in the Party', first published in 1956. He speaks of a 'crisis in the Party centres' and writes: 'In January 1910 the Bolsheviks dissolved their group *on condition* that all the other factions would also be dissolved. This condition has not been carried out, as everyone knows. *Golos*, *Vperyod*, and Trotsky and Co have *intensified* their factional activity. And on December 5, 1910 we Bolsheviks publicly declared that the stipulation had been *violated*, and that our agreement on the dissolution of all factions had been *broken*, and demanded a return of our group's funds.' Lenin concedes that after the revolution the Bolsheviks have committed two mistakes: '1) otsovism-Vperyodism and 2) conciliationism (wobbling in the direction of the liquidators).' He opposes 'conciliatory mistakes' and any wavering 'to the left or to the right.' (CW 36 pp. 180-4)

2 August: Lenin writes a preface to Lev Kamenev's pamphlet 'Two Parties'. (CW 17 pp. 225-8)

20 August: Lenin and Krupskaya send greetings to Lenin's mother in Berdyansk, Russia, during a visit to Fontainebleau.

14 September: Three articles by Lenin, including 'Reformism and the Russian Social Democratic Movement' appear in *Sotsial Demokrat* no 23. (CW 17 pp. 229-41)

15 September: Lenin writes to Gorky and asks him to send an article for *Zvezda*. 'Our Party affairs are in a pretty mess but still, things are coming to a head.' (CW 36 pp. 185-6)

20 September: Lenin receives a telegram inviting him to a meeting of the International Socialist Bureau in Zürich from Camille Huysmans.

21 September: Krupskaya writes to Lenin's sister Maria in Moscow: 'Today, at long last, we moved back to town [from Longjumeau to Paris] . . . Volodya is going away for a few days.' (CW 37 pp. 611-2)

22 September: Lenin writes to Clara Zetkin and asks for the payments of the '10,000 francs of Party money' which the trustees are holding into the account of the organisation commission for the preparation of the Party Conference. (Khr. II p. 624)

23-24 September: Lenin attends the meeting of the International Socialist Bureau in Zürich.

25 September: Lenin speaks to the Zürich group of the RSDLP on the position of the Party.

26 September: Lenin addresses a meeting in the Volkshaus in Zürich on Stolypin and the revolution.

28 September: Lenin writes to his mother from Lucerne: 'I came to Switzerland quite unexpectedly (on account of the meeting of the International Socialist Bureau in Zürich). I am travelling around lecturing. Yesterday I went out climbing on the Pilatus — 2,122 metres. The weather is wonderful so far and I am having an excellent holiday.' (CW 37 p. 472)

28 September: Lenin speaks in Berne on Stolypin and the revolution. He writes to G L Shklovsky about his preparations: 'What I meant was a *public* lecture . . . with the admission fees to go for the benefit of *Rabochaya Gazeta* . . . The presiding committee (or the chairman) at the meeting must be from among local *Bolsheviks* and by no means "elected" (to avoid intrigues and scandals).' (CW 36 p. 188)

2 October: Lenin addresses an audience of 150 in the Maison du Peuple in Geneva on Stolypin and the revolution.

18 October: Lenin is visited in Paris by his sister Anna and she stays two weeks. On 22 October she writes to her mother in Saratov that Lenin is 'well and goes continually to the library; he is working on an article.' (*Vom Alltag der Uljanows* p. 209)

31 October: Four articles by Lenin, including 'Stolypin and the Revolution' appear in *Sotsial Demokrat* no 24. (CW 17 pp. 247–56) Lenin sees in the murder of Stolypin, 'the arch hangman', the end of the 'first stage of the Russian counter revolution.' The 'Stolypin period' is 'characterised specifically by the fact that the liberal bourgeoisie has been turning its back on democracy.' Lenin sees 'symptoms of a gathering new revolution.' In his article 'The New Faction of Conciliators or the Virtuous' (CW 17 pp. 257–77) Lenin takes issue with the conciliators (Lyubimov, Vladimirov, Leiteisen, Nogin and so on) who as 'pro-Party Bolsheviks' oppose the 'Leninist Bolsheviks.' 'As regards the expression "Leninist" it is merely a clumsy attempt at sarcasm intended to insinuate that it is only a question of the supporters of a *single* person. In reality, everybody knows perfectly well that it is not a question of people sharing my view on this or that aspect of Bolshevism.'

1 November: Lenin, in a letter to Antonin Némec, the representative of the Czech social democrats, enquires if a conference of the RSDLP can be held in Prague. (CW 34 p. 448)

2 November: Lenin writes to Karl Kautsky and asks for the money held by the trustees to be forwarded.

5 or 6 November: Lenin travels to Brussels and speaks to an audience of about 100 on Stolypin and the revolution.

7 November: Lenin speaks in Antwerp to an audience of 200 on Stolypin and the revolution. He also visits the museum and the harbour and travels, on 7 or 8 November, on to London.

10 November: Lenin writes to Lev Kamenev from London: 'I am sitting in the British Museum.' (CW 43 p. 282)

11 November: Lenin speaks in the New King's Hall in London on Stolypin and revolution.

20 November: Lenin travels from London to Liège and speaks on Stolypin and the revolution.

27 November: Lenin speaks on the manifesto of the Liberal Labour Party.

3 December: Lenin delivers the oration at the funeral of Paul and Laura Lafargue. (CW 17 pp. 304-5) The suicide of the daughter and son-in-law of Karl Marx made a 'deep impression' on Lenin. 'We recalled our visits to them. Ilich said: "If we cannot work for the Party any longer, we must be able to look truth in the face and die like the Lafargues" . . . I remember with what deep emotion he delivered the speech . . . in the name of the RSDLP.' (Krupskaya p. 197)

21 December: Six articles by Lenin, including 'The Climax of the Party Crisis' appear in *Sotsial Demokrat* no 25. (CW 17 pp. 343-53) Lenin defends the Russian organisation commission for the preparation of the Party Conference against the conciliators and the Polish social democrats, especially against Tyszka (Leo Jogiches) whom he brands 'an intriguer.' He states in the article 'The Results of the Arbitration of the "Trustees"' (CW 17 pp. 365-7), which is signed by Lenin, Zinoviev and Kamenev, that the trustees Mehring and Kautsky had resigned in October 1911 and that Zetkin, after some hesitation, had also resigned. Hence the Bolshevik faction was now 'taking possession of its other property.' If 'the former trustees now attempted to hold up the Bolshevik funds that would be an unlawful act.'

27-30 December: Bolshevik groups abroad meet in Paris. Lenin opens the Conference with a report on the state of affairs in the Party and proposes draft resolutions on the situation in the Party and on the Russian organisation commission for the preparation of the Conference. (CW 17 pp. 393-6)

Before 30 December: Three articles by Lenin, including Part One of 'Fundamental Problems of the Election Campaign' appear in *Prosveshchenie* (Enlightenment) no 1, a legal Bolshevik theoretical monthly which appears until June 1914 in St Petersburg. Lenin publishes twenty-six articles in it. (CW 17 pp. 397-423)

1912

Before 18 January: Lenin arrives in Prague and stays in the Hotel Belvedere.

18 January: The Prague Conference of the Bolsheviks opens. Eighteen Bolsheviks and two 'pro-Party' Mensheviks confer until 30 January.

If the 2nd Party Congress in 1903 produced the ideological split in the RSDLP and the founding of Bolshevism, then the split was healed at the Prague Conference; the Bolsheviks finally form an organisationally independent Party. Lenin speaks on the calling of the Conference, on the current situation and on the tasks of the Party and proposes some draft resolutions. (CW 17 pp. 451-86)

20 January: Lenin speaks several times during the 5th and 6th sessions of the Prague Conference. He reports on the work of the International Socialist Bureau and says that in the SPD there are 'two different trends' and the hegemony of German Social Democracy is on the 'decline.' (CW 41 pp. 247-8)

21 January: Lenin speaks on the struggle against famine at the 8th session. (CW 41 p. 249)

24 January: Lenin addresses himself to the organisational question at the 12th session. He favours 'organisations' flexibility'; the foundation should be 'illegal cells surrounded by a network of legal cells.' (CW 41 pp. 250-1)

Between 25-30 January: The Prague Conference elects Lenin as its representative on the International Socialist Bureau, a member of the central organ and of the new Bolshevik CC — Lenin, Zinoviev, Ordzhonikidze, Shvartsman, Goloshchokin, Spandaryan and the Okhrana (secret police) agent Malinovsky.

30 January: Lenin closes the Prague Conference and his resolutions are adopted.

31 January: Lenin travels from Prague to Leipzig and speaks there to the RSDLP group on Tolstoy.

1 February: Lenin meets Poletaev and Shurkanov, RSDLP members of the Duma, in Leipzig.

Beginning of February: Lenin travels to Berlin. In accordance with a resolution at the Prague Conference he attempts to obtain the money held by the trustees. He returns to Paris from Berlin.

25 February: Lenin writes to A S Enukidze from Paris: 'I am living as before; I have recently been a little tired but on the whole I feel well and am very satisfied.' (Briefe III p. 48)

26 February: Lenin explains his position on the money held by the trustees in a letter to Karl Zraggen in Berne. Until January 1910 Lenin had had the money but in July 1911 he handed it over to Clara Zetkin. 'I held the money from June 1910 to July 1911 not as a representative of the Bolsheviks but as a member of the CC.' It was said that Lenin's right to the money had been contested before 1910. 'That is absolutely of no importance. Everyone has the right to disagree but I have the right to the money.' Lenin calls Tyszka (Leo Jogiches) an 'intriguer.' (Haas pp. 36-7 Khr. II p. 657)

February: Lenin writes to Gorky about the Prague Conference: 'We have finally succeeded — in spite of the liquidationist scroundels —

in reviving the Party and its Central Committee. I hope you will be as glad of this as we are.' (CW 35 p. 23)

8 or 9 March: Lenin writes to his mother: 'A few days ago we received another present from you; fish, caviare and smoked sturgeon fillets. A big *merci*. We are greatly enjoying these delicacies and thinking of the Volga as we eat them. You really have been plying us with dainties from home this year!' Lenin has got his 'bicycle out again' and has been to the countryside. (CW 37 p. 473)

9 March: Krupskaya writes to Lenin's sister Anna: 'Life goes on so monotonously here that I don't know what to write about . . . We went to the theatre, the play was idiotic . . . Today we are going to see Sophocles' *Electra*.' (CW 37 pp. 612-3)

After 15 March: Lenin writes the article 'Against Unity with the Liquidators' and it appears in *Prosveshchenie* no 3-4 in March 1912. (CW 17 pp. 491-6)

18 March: The International Socialist Bureau distributes *Rundschreiben* no 4 with Lenin's article 'Report to the International Socialist Bureau on the All-Russian Conference of the RSDLP' in it. (CW 17 pp. 503-6) Lenin provides information on the Prague Conference and writes: 'All relations with the RSDLP must be carried on solely through the Central Committee whose address abroad is: Wladimir Oulianoff, 4 Rue Marie Rose, Paris XIV.'

24 March: Lenin writes to his sister Anna from Paris: 'Among our people here . . . there is more bickering and abuse of each other than there has been for a long time . . . All the groups and sub-groups have joined forces against the last Conference and those who organised it, so that matters even went as far as fisticuffs at meetings here.' (CW 37 p. 474)

Between 26 March-1 April: Lenin writes the pamphlet 'The Anonymous Writer in *Vorwärts* and the State of Affairs in the RSDLP' (CW 17 pp. 533-46) and it is published in German in Paris. Lenin takes issue with the article on the Prague Conference which appeared in *Vorwärts*, the SPD organ, on 26 March. Lenin describes the differences from his point of view and writes that the otsovists were joined 'by a section of the Bolsheviks, on whom Lenin, Zinoviev, Kamenev and others declared implacable war.' It is clear, 'of course, to every Marxist' that both liquidationism and otsovism are petty bourgeois tendencies which attract the bourgeois fellow-travellers of the Social Democratic Party. 'Peace' or 'conciliation' with these tendencies is something excluded *a priori*.

28 March: Lenin writes to G K Ordzhonikdze, S S Spandaryan and E Stasova in Tbilisi that his contacts with Russia have been completely disorganised. 'There is a great battle over the [Prague] Conference – but Russia is silent . . . this is collapse and disorganisation. A round of visits and contacts. Precise correspondence. Reprinting of the announcement even by hectograph, otherwise it's all boasting.' (CW 35 pp. 28-30)

16 April: Lenin writes to the CC Bureau in Kiev: 'For God's sake give
us more contacts. Contacts, contacts, contacts, that's what we haven't
got . . . As regards money, it is time to stop being naive about the
Germans. Trotsky is now in full command there and carrying on a
furious struggle. You must send is a mandate to take the matter to the
courts otherwise we shall get nothing.' CW 35 pp. 34-5)

5 May: The first number of *Pravda* (Truth), the legal Bolshevik newspaper, appears in St Petersburg in a print of 60,000 copies. Lenin
played a considerable role in getting it published. 636 numbers appear
by June 1914, from July 1913 under various names. Over 280 articles
by Lenin appear in the newspaper.

9 May: Lenin speaks at a session of the Paris group of the RSDLP, on
the massacre by the tsarist police of the Lena gold miners in Siberia,
the strikes in Russia, and the tactics which should be adopted.

21-22 May: Lenin's article 'The Trudoviks and the Worker Democrats'
appears in *Pravda* nos 13 and 14. (CW 18 pp. 36-43)

23 May: Lenin's article 'Political Parties in Russia' appears in *Nevskaya
Zvezda* (The Neva Star) (CW 18 pp. 44-55) Lenin opposes the view that
parliaments are dangerous. 'In the absence of representative institutions
there is *much more* deception, political lying and fradulent trickery of
all kinds . . . The greater the degree of political liberty in a country, the
more stable and democratic its representative institutions, the easier it
is for the mass of the people to find its bearings in the fight between
the parties and to *learn politics.*'

Between 23-26 May: Lenin travels from Paris to Germany for a few
days and in Berlin, among other things, visits the archives of Russian
social democracy.

27 May: Lenin writes to his mother in Saratov. He comforts her after
the arrest of his sisters. 'Have you any acquaintances, my dear? Does
anyone visit you? Sudden loneliness is the worst thing that can happen
at such times.' (CW 37 p. 476)

1 June: Lenin writes to the French lawyer Georges Ducos de la Haille
and forwards documents on the matter of the money held by the
trustees.

2 June: Lenin writes to his mother: 'Perhaps you will feel a little less
miserable if we write to one another more often.' (CW 37 p. 477)

10 June: Lenin writes again to Ducos about the money held by the
trustees.

13 June: Lenin speaks to the Paris group of the RSDLP on the revolutionary upswing of the Russian proletariat. Lenin's article 'Economic
and Political Strikes' appears in *Nevskaya Zvezda* no 10. (CW 18
pp. 83-90)

15 June: Lenin writes once again to Ducos and asks for an interview
before he leaves Paris.

17 June: Lenin, Krupskaya and her mother leave Paris for Krakow. Four articles by Lenin, including 'The Revolutionary Upswing' appear in *Sotsial Demokrat* no 27. (CW 18 pp. 102-9) Lenin writes of the revolutionary upsurge of the masses but 'organisation and again organisation' is necessary to extend it. Only an illegal Party can carry out this work. 'Without a victorious revolution there will be no freedom in Russia. Without the overthrow of the Tsarist monarchy by a proletarian and peasant uprising there will be no victorious revolution in Russia.'

Between 17-22 June: Lenin spends a few days in Leipzig en route to Krakow. He speaks on the revolutionary upsurge in Russia.

22 June: Lenin, Krupskaya and her mother arrive in Krakow and stay in the Hotel Victoria.

22 or 23 June: Lenin meets J Hanecki and other Polish social democrats. At Lenin's request, Otto Hörsing, the German social democrat comes from Beuthen to Krakow to discuss with him possibilities of influencing developments in Russia.

24 June: Lenin, Krupskaya and her mother move into Ulica Zwierzyniecka, in a suburb of Krakow. 'We rented a house together with the Zinovievs. The streets in this district were unpaved and exceedingly muddy. But the river Vistula was quite near in which we were able to bathe and about 5 kilometres away there was the 'Volsky Lyas', a beautiful wood which Ilich and I frequently visited on our bicycles. In the autumn we moved to the other end of town, a newly built section. Bagozki and the Zinovievs moved there with us. Ilich liked Krakow very much; it reminded him of Russia. The change of environment and the absence of émigré squabbles soothed our nerves somewhat.' (Krupskaya p. 206) As a foreigner Lenin has to submit to questioning by the police in Krakow, Austria-Hungary: 'I am a correspondent of *Pravda*, the Russian democratic newspaper published in St Petersburg, and of *Sotsial Demokrat*, the Russian newspaper which appears in Paris; these are my sources of income.' (Biographie p. 291)

1 July: Lenin writes to his mother: 'This summer we have moved a long way from Paris — to Krakow. Almost in Russia! Even the Jews are like Russians and the Russian frontier is 8 versts away.' (CW 37 pp. 479-80)

16 July: Lenin's article 'The Situation in the RSDLP and the Immediate Tasks of the Party' appears in the Warsaw newspaper *Gazeta Rabotnicza*. (Workers' Newspaper) (CW 18 pp. 150-7) Lenin attacks the chief executive committee of the Polish Social Democratic Party under Tyszka (Leo Jogiches); they are 'deceiving' the workers.

Before 23 July: Lenin writes a report on the origin of the money held by the trustees, 'The Behaviour of the Arbitration Court' (Mehring, Kautsky and Zetkin) and its breaking of the agreement. (Khr. III p. 16) Inessa Armand, who stops two days in Krakow en route from Paris to Russia, translates the text and it is then forwarded to Ducos de la Haille, the French lawyer.

24 July: Lenin tells the editor of *Nevskaya Zvezda* that 'by avoiding "painful questions", *Zvezda* and *Pravda make themselves* dry and monotonous, uninteresting, uncombative organs. A socialist newspaper must carry on polemics; our times are times of desperate confusion and we can't do without polemics.' (CW 35 pp. 42-4)

28 July: Lenin's article 'Democracy and Narodism in China' appears in *Nevskaya Zvezda* no 17 (CW 18 pp. 163-9) In it he takes issue with Sun Yat-sen. He predicts the founding 'of some kind of Chinese social democratic labour party' which 'while criticising the petty bourgeois utopias and reactionary views of Sun Yat-sen will certainly take care to single out, defend and develop the revolutionary democratic core of his political and agrarian programme.'

1 August: Lenin writes to V M Molotov, secretary of *Pravda*, asking why if the editorial board in principle considers his, Lenin's, article 'fully acceptable *including the attitude to the liquidators* ... why then does *Pravda* stubbornly and systematically cut out any mention of the liquidators both in my articles and in the articles of other colleagues?' (CW 35 pp. 47-9) Lenin writes to Maxim Gorky: 'It's a bad, philistine, bourgeois style you have adopted, to wave us away with a "you're all squabblers".' (CW 35 pp. 50-1)

7 August: Lenin's article 'Liberals and Clericals' appears in *Pravda* no 74. (CW 18 pp. 227-8) 'We are opposed, not to the priests taking part in the election campaign, in the Duma, etc., but *solely* to the medieval privileges of the priesthood. We are not afraid of clericalism and will readily join issue with it on a free platform on which all will be on equal footing.'

12 August: Three articles by Lenin, including 'Revolts in the Army and Navy' appear in *Rabochaya Gazeta* no 9. (CW 18 pp. 233-6) 'Appeals for an uprising are most unwise now. An uprising would be *premature*. Only a *combined* onslaught by the mass of the workers, by the peasantry and the best sections of the armed forces can create conditions for a *victorious*, i.e. *timely* uprising.'

Before 25 August: Lenin writes to Gorky: 'You ask why I am in Austria. The CC has organised a Bureau here (between ourselves); the frontier is close by, we make use of it, it's nearer to St Petersburg, we get the papers from there on the third day, it's become far easier to write to the papers there, co-operation with them goes better. There is less squabbling here, which is an advantage. There isn't a good library which is a disadvantage. It's hard without books.' (CW 35 pp. 54-5) Lenin writes to Kamenev: 'I received today from Trotsky an invitation to "their" conference (on 25 April). So they have organised it after all! We, of course, are not going.' (CW 43 p. 296)

August: Lenin travels to Makuw, a village near Krakow, and goes for walks and trips into the Tatras with S Bagozki.

2 September: Lenin moves into Ulica Lubomirskiego 17 in Krakow. The rent is 40 crowns a month.

6 September: Lenin writes to L B Kamenev that he should attend the SPD Party Congress in Chemnitz (now Karl-Marx-Stadt). Lenin is for making closer contact with Pannekoek; 'Kautsky replied to him on some cardinal issues in an extremely *opportunist* way.' (CW 43 p. 297)

11 September: Lenin's article 'The Workers and *Pravda*' appears in *Pravda* no 103. (CW 18 pp. 299-301) Lenin writes that it is necessary to cover Russia with a 'network of workers' organisations with workers' newspapers.'

Between 14-17 September: Lenin writes the article 'Rosa Luxemburg and the Polish "Partei" Vorstand in Martov's Wake'. (CW 41 pp. 255-9) He takes issue with an article in *Vorwärts* of 14 September 1912 by Rosa Luxemburg criticising Karl Radek. He calls Luxemburg's complaints against Radek slander, 'a malicious bit of gossip'. She and her 'Partei' Vorstand are conducting 'an unprecedentedly fierce fight against their own party's best workers.'

17 September: Lenin writes to Kamenev and congratulates him on his speech at the SPD Party Congress in Chemnitz (Karl-Marx-Stadt). Lenin states that he is not simply 'for Radek' but 'against Rosa and for our Party.' (CW 43 p. 301)

Autumn: Lenin writes to his sister Anna: 'Here we feel much better than we did in Paris — our nerves are at rest and there are more literary work and less squabbling. I hope it will be easier for us to meet too — as long as there is no war; I do not greatly believe there will be one.' (CW 37 p. 482)

After 3 October: Lenin complains, in a letter to the editorial board of *Pravda*, that it is behaving during the elections 'like a sleepy old maid. *Pravda* doesn't know how to fight.' (CW 36 pp. 197-8)

9 October: Lenin's article 'Reply to the Liquidators' Article in the *Leipziger Volkszeitung*' appears in the *Leipziger Volkszeitung* no 235 signed by the CC, RSDLP. (CW 41 pp. 260-2)

21 October: Lenin, Krupskaya and their visitor V G Shumkin from Moscow attend a meeting in Krakow.

26 October: The appeal of the CC, RSDLP 'To All the Citizens of Russia', written by Lenin, appears in the *Leipziger Volkszeitung* no 250. It appears also in *Vorwärts* no 252, of 27 October 1912, in Berlin. (CW 41 pp. 262-6)

October: Lenin writes the article 'Two Utopias' against liberal and Narodnik utopias. (CW 18 pp. 355-9) He states that Marxists are 'opposed to all utopias.'

17 November: Lenin writes to Plekhanov that Kautsky has abandoned 'the *revolutionary* mass strike' and that this is inadmissable. He informs Plekhanov that Kamenev will represent the Bolsheviks on the International Socialist Bureau at the meeting in Basle. (CW 36 pp. 202-3)

18 November: Two articles by Lenin, including 'The Illegal Party and Legal Work' appears in *Sotsial Demokrat* no 28-29. (CW 18 pp. 387-

96) According to Lenin a revolution is 'necessary' and is coming. 'The *forms* of the development leading to the revolution have changed but the *old tasks* of the revolution remain.'

22 November: *Pravda* no 164 carries Lenin's article 'The Result and Significance of the US Presidential Elections' (the election of Woodrow Wilson). (CW 18 pp. 402–4) Lenin writes that the Roosevelt 'progressives' have been hired by . . . astute multimillionaires.'

25 or 26 November: Lenin chairs a meeting of the CC in Krakow.

End of November: Lenin writes to his sister Maria: 'This place is full of rumours of war . . . But I do not believe there will be a war.' If there is, Lenin will have to move to Vienna or Stockholm. (CW 37 p. 481)

6 December: Lenin writes to Stalin in St Petersburg: 'Write more often and in greater detail.' (CW 18 pp. 430–1)

8 December: Lenin writes a long letter to Lev Kamenev in Paris: 'I simply cannot understand you — although we have been working together so long — when you now begin making "domestic scenes".' (CW 43 pp. 312–6)

13 December: Lenin's article 'Impoverishment and Capitalist Society' appears in *Pravda* no 181. (CW 18 pp. 435–6) 'The worker is becoming impoverished *absolutely*, i.e. he is actually becoming poorer than before . . . But the relative impoverishment of the workers, i.e. the diminution of their share in the national income, is still more striking.'

21 or 22 December: Lenin writes to his mother: 'We are not thinking of moving unless the war chases us away, but I do not greatly believe in the war. We shall wait and see.' (CW 37 pp. 483–4)

22 or 23 December: Lenin writes to Gorky: 'Probably there will be no war and we shall remain here for the time being, "taking advantage" of the desperate hatred of the Poles towards tsarism.' (CW 35 pp. 67–8)

28 December: Lenin's article 'The "Reconciliation" of the Nationalists and Cadets' appears in *Pravda* no 194. (CW 18 pp. 439–40) In all Lenin publishes 45 articles in *Pravda* between July and December 1912. (Compare volume 18)

1913

3 January: Lenin writes to his mother and sends New Year's greetings. 'We intend to celebrate the Russian festivals more than the local ones.' (CW 37 p. 488)

8 January: Lenin writes to Gorky. He sends New Year's greetings and asks how Malinovsky can find him in St Petersburg or Moscow. 'Malinovsky, Petrovsky and Badaev send you warm greetings and good wishes.' On Gorky's hope that the *Vperyod* people will return, Lenin writes that this is possible providing they have drawn the correct conclusions. 'Have they understood that *Marxism* is a more serious and profound thing than it seemed to them, that one cannot scoff at it, as Aleksinsky used to do, or dismiss it as something dead, as the others did? *If* they have understood this — a thousand greetings to them, and everything personal (inevitably brought on by the sharpness of the struggle) will in one moment be thrown on to the scrapheap.' Otherwise there will be no unity. 'Against attempts to abuse Marxism or to confuse the policy of the workers' party we shall fight without sparing our lives.' (CW 35 pp. 69-71)

8-14 January: Lenin chairs in Krakow the so-called February Conference of the CC, the Duma representatives and representatives of illegal Russian groups. Fourteen persons attend. Lenin's seven draft resolutions are adopted. (CW 18 pp. 447-66) In a resolution on the reorganisation of the Party it is also decided to act very 'circumspect[ly]' towards the *Vperyod* people so as not to make the rapprochement more difficult. (CW 41 pp. 272-3) Krupskaya writes on the conference: 'Malinovsky [the police agent] arrived first. He seemed to be very excited about something . . . Malinovsky gave one the impression of being a very intelligent and influential worker. Badaev and Petrovsky were shy but it was quite obvious that they were good, reliable proletarians. At this conference the plan of work was drawn up.' (Krupskaya p. 211)

10 January: Lenin writes to L B Kamenev: 'The meeting here is in full swing . . . Things are going better.' (CW 43 pp. 326-7)

12 January: Lenin writes to Kamenev: 'I am writing at the meeting. It's going wonderfully. It will be no less significant than the 1912 January Conference . . . All the resolutions are being adopted unanimously.' (CW 43 pp. 327-8)

After 16 January: Lenin writes the article 'The Development of Workers' Choirs in Germany'. (CW 36 pp. 225-6) He points out that Lassalle attached great importance to the organisation of workers' choirs and writes that 'the singing of the hearty proletarian song about mankind's coming emancipation' (the Internationale) can be heard more and more often.

24 January: Lenin writes to the editorial board of the *Bremer Bürgerzeitung* and asks for two copies of the issue in which a review of Rosa Luxemburg's book *Accumulation of Capital* appeared. 'The "dialectics" of Luxemburg seem to me . . . to be *electicism*.' (CW 43 pp. 332-3)

25 January: Lenin writes a letter to the editors of *Pravda* and proposes a reorganisation of the board. Lenin's article 'The Split Among the Polish Social Democrats' appears in *Sotsial Demokrat* no 30 (CW 18 pp. 479-84) It is directed against the executive committee (Tyszka (Leo Jogiches) and Luxemburg).

Not before 25 January: Lenin writes the article 'On Bolshevism' for the volume *Among Books* edited by N A Rubakin. (CW 18 pp. 485-6) According to Lenin the most important Bolshevik writers are G Zinoviev, V Ilyin (V I Lenin), L Kamenev and P Orlovsky (V V Vorovsky).

January: Lenin writes 'Results of the Elections' (CW 18 pp. 493–518), an analysis of the Duma elections. The article appears in January in *Prosveshchenie* no 1.

13 or 14 February: Lenin chairs a meeting of the CC in Krakow. Stalin also attends the meeting. Krupskaya writes later: 'Ilich had long discussions with Stalin on the national question. He was glad to meet a man who was seriously interested in this question and who was well informed on it.' (Krupskaya p. 226)

14 February: Lenin protests to the editorial board of *Pravda* about the publication of a letter by Bogdanov.

21 February: Lenin proposes to the editorial board of *Pravda* that a special edition should appear on 14 March to mark the 30th anniversary of Marx's death.

24 February: Lenin writes to his mother and sister Anna in Saratov that the winter weather in Krakow is wonderful. 'I have bought some skates and skate with great enthusiasm – it brings back Simbirsk and Siberia. I have never before skated abroad.' (CW 37 pp. 489–90)

14 March: Lenin's article 'The Historical Destiny of the Doctrine of Karl Marx' appears in *Pravda* no 50. (CW 18 pp. 582–5) Lenin divides world history after 1848 into three periods: from 1848 to the Paris Commune of 1871; from the Paris Commune to the Russian Revolution of 1905; and the period from 1905 to the present. Marxism proved victorious in the labour movement during the second period. 'The dialectics of history were such that the theoretical victory of Marxism compelled its enemies to *disguise themselves* as Marxists.'

15 March: Lenin writes to the executive committee of the SPD. (CW 41 pp. 274–7) He rejects, in the name of the CC, a proposal for a Conference of Russian groups. He stresses: 'We Russian revolutionary social democrats have a very great respect for the party of the German revolutionary proletariat.' They desire the 'most fraternal relations' but, notwithstanding, the proposal is unacceptable.

18 March: Krupskaya writes to Lenin's mother: 'Life here goes on like clockwork . . . We live as we lived in Shushenskoe, from one post to the next. Until eleven we fill in the time somehow; at eleven the first postman comes and then we impatiently await the six o'clock post.' (CW 37 pp. 615–6)

23–26 March: Lenin chairs a meeting of the CC in Krakow.

26 March: Lenin's article 'A "Scientific" System of Sweating' appears in *Pravda* no 60. (CW 18 pp. 594–5) Lenin writes about Taylorism; Europe must keep up with the 'Yankees' but the European bourgeoisie is not borrowing 'democratic institutions' or 'political liberty' but 'the latest methods of exploiting the workers.' Lenin's conclusion is: 'In capitalist society, progress in science and technology means progress in the art of sweating.'

Before 29 March: Lenin writes to Lev Kamenev that Karl Radek had written a pamphlet against Tyszka (Leo Jogiches) and has given him a 'terrific lambasting.' Lenin has read Rosa Luxemburg's new book *The Accumulation of Capital*. 'She has got into a shocking muddle. She has distorted Marx. I am very glad that Pannekoek and Eckstein and O Bauer have all with one accord condemned her and said against her what I said in 1899 against the Narodniks.' (CW 35 pp. 93-4)

5 April: Lenin writes to the editorial board of *Pravda* in St Petersburg about how the 'six' (Bolsheviks) are to be helped in their struggle with the 'seven' (Menshevik) members of the Duma. 'One can't in any way talk about unity with the liquidators: one cannot unite the Party with the destroyers of the Party.' (CW 35 pp. 95-6)

Before 7 April: Lenin rents a house near Zakopane.

7 April: Lenin writes to Kamenev: 'And so we shall be seeing each other in the summer. Welcome. We have rented a summer place at Zakopane . . . from 1 V to 1 X; there is a room for you. The Zinovievs are near neighbours.' (CW 43 pp. 339-40)

10 April: Krupskaya writes to Lenin's sister Maria that they are moving to the country. 'It's lovely there — forest, mushrooms, mountains and a stream. All that I am afraid of is that we shall get bored.' (CW 37 p. 617)

18 April: Lenin delivers a lecture on present day Russia and the labour movement at the People's University in Krakow.

19 April: Lenin's article 'Three Sources and Three Component Parts of Marxism' appears in *Prosveshchenie* no 3. (CW 19 pp. 23-8) Lenin attempts to analyse Marxist theory and its origins very succinctly. He repeats Engels' statement that Marxism is derived from classical German philosophy, English political economy and French socialism. As a result Lenin divides Marxism into philosophy, economics and the theory of socialism.

26 April: Lenin delivers a lecture on the social upswing in Russia and the tasks facing social democrats.

1 May: Lenin takes part in a workers' meeting to commemorate May Day.

3 May: Lenin writes to his mother that they are going to Poronin in three days' time. They are looking for a maid during the summer so as to have less work to do.

6-7 May: Lenin and Krupskaya move to Poronin, near Zakopane, for the summer. 'Zakopane was too overcrowded and expensive; Poronin was simpler and less expensive. We . . . rented a large bungalow . . . This bungalow was situated 700 metres above sea level at the foot of the Tatra mountains. The air was wonderful and although there were frequent mists and drizzle, the view of the mountains during the clear intervals was extremely beautiful. We would climb up to the plateau which was quite close to our bungalow and watch the snow-capped peaks of the Tatra mountains.' (Krupskaya p. 228)

8 May: Lenin writes to G L Shklovsky in Berne that they have moved for 'a mountain air cure . . . for Nad. Konst.'s goitre.' The surge on Kocher in Berne is first-class and Shklovsky is to make enquiries. (CW 43 pp. 343-4)

After 9 May: Lenin writes to Gorky: 'Things are not too well with me. My wife is down with goitre. Nerves! My nerves are also playing me up a little. We are spending the summer in the village of Poronin . . . Suppose you took it into your head to pay us a visit?' (CW 35 pp. 97-8)

12-13 May: Lenin writes to his sister Maria that they have moved; the house is too big. The inhabitants are Polish peasants 'with whom I converse in incredibly broken Polish (I prefer talking to Jews — in German).' (CW 37 pp. 495-6)

16 May: Lenin's article 'The Struggle of Parties in China' appears in *Pravda* no 100. (CW 41 pp. 281-3) Lenin writes that 'Sun Yat-sen's party' is becoming 'a great factor of progress in Asia and of mankind's progress.'

20 May: Lenin's article 'The Awakening of Asia' appears in *Pravda* no 103. (CW 19 pp. 85-6) Lenin analyses the troubles in Java and states that the workers of the advanced countries 'follow with interest and inspiration this powerful growth of the liberation movement, in all its various forms, in every part of the world . . . The awakening of Asia and the beginning of the struggle for power by the advanced proletariat of Europe are a symbol of the new phase in world history.'

25 May: Krupskaya writes to Lenin's mother: 'This is the real summer cottage routine . . . Fortunately you cannot do a lot of cycling. Volodya used to abuse that amusement and overtire himself.' (CW 37 pp. 497-8)

31 May: Lenin's article 'Backward Europe and Advanced Asia' appears in *Pravda* no 113. (CW 19 pp. 99-100) Lenin writes that civilised and developed Europe is ruled by the bourgeoisie which supports everything backward. Europe 'is plundering China and helping the foes of democracy.'

End of May: Lenin writes to the editorial board of *Pravda* and gives advice on how to gain an extra 100,000 readers. Write 'kindly and mildly' to Plekhanov; he is valuable now, since he is fighting the enemies of the working class. Regarding Demyan Bedny: 'Don't find faults, friends, with human failings. Talent is rare. It should be systematically and carefully supported.' (CW 35 pp. 93-100)

16 June: Lenin writes to Kamenev: 'Some time after the 20th I am going to *Berne* with N K. I shall be there on 27 VI. There will probably be an operation.' (CW 43 pp. 353-4)

Before 22 June: Lenin writes to Plekhanov: 'I invite you to come for a few weeks to Zakopane in the summer to deliver lectures on such questions of Marxism and the social democratic movement as you may select.' (CW 35 pp. 103-4)

22 June: Lenin travels with Krupskaya to Berne. Professor Kocher, a Nobel Prize winner, is to operate on her. She is suffering from goitre. (Basedow's disease).

24 June: They break their journey in Vienna. They visit the Bukharins. 'Nadezhda Mikhailovna, Bukharin's wife, was very sick and Bukharin had to look after the house. Putting sugar instead of salt into the soup, he talked animately with Ilich about questions which interested Ilich and about our people who lived in Vienna. We met some of the Viennese comrades and rode about the town with them. Vienna has a charm of its own. It is a large capital city and in contrast with Krakow we were greatly impressed by it.' (Krupskaya p. 228) Lenin writes to his mother: 'Nadya and I have reached Vienna and today we are continuing our journey.' (CW 27 p. 500)

25 June: Lenin and Krupskaya arrive in Berne and stay first with the Shklovksys. They 'lived in a little detached cottage with a garden. Ilich joked with the younger girls and teased Jenorka. I stayed in the hospital about three weeks. Ilich would stay with me one half of the day and spend the rest of the day in the libraries. He read a great deal; he even read a number of medical books on my disease.' (Krupskaya p. 228)

After 25 June: Lenin writes from Berne to the editorial board of *Pravda* and asks for his fees for May and June, 100 roubles, to be sent. 'I shall have to stay here for about a month as my wife is going to have an operation. I need the money badly.' (CW 43 p. 356) Lenin's mother writes later to her daughter-in-law: 'The treatment, the operation, the journey and so on cost V[olodya] quite a lot of money; the clinic alone cost 25 francs a day. V[olodya] had booked a single room, of course.' (*Vom Alltag der Uljanows* p. 255)

29 June: Lenin writes to Kamenev that 'Kocher is a great bother — capricious. He still hasn't received us. We shall have to wait.' Plekhanov has not yet answered his invitation (compare before 22 June). 'The sly boots, Ignatius Loyola, the master shuffler. All the worse for him. We shall have a school. Gorky has as good as consented.' (CW 43 p. 357)

June: Lenin writes 'The Theses on the National Question'. (CW 19 pp. 243-51)

3 July: Lenin writes to Karl Kautsky about the money held by the trustees.

9 July: Lenin travels to Zürich and speaks on the national question.

10 July: Lenin speaks in Geneva on social democracy and the national question.

11 July: Lenin speaks in Lausanne on the national question.

13 July: Again in Berne, Lenin also speaks on the national question.

18 July: Lenin's article 'The Adjourned Duma and the Embarrassed Liberals' appears in *Pravda* no 151 (CW 19 pp. 258-9) This is the last issue before it is banned; from now on it appears mostly under other names. Lenin has published 76 articles in *Pravda* since the beginning of 1913.

23 July: Krupskaya undergoes surgery.

25 July: Lenin informs Gorky that Krupskaya has undergone an operation 'and things are now on the mend. The operation proved rather a difficult one; I am very glad indeed that we managed to get Kocher to operate.' (CW 35 pp. 107–8)

26 July: Lenin writes to his mother: 'The operation seems to have been successful because she looked quite well yesterday and began to drink willingly. It seems to have been a rather difficult operation; they tormented Nadya for about three hours without an anaesthetic, but she bore it bravely.' (CW 37 pp. 502–3) Lenin's article 'Fifth International Congress Against Prostitution' appears in *Rabochaya Pravda* (Workers' Truth) no 1. (CW 19 pp. 260–1) He exposes the hypocrisy of the Congress which prevented a delegate from speaking because 'he tried to raise the question of the social causes of prostitution.'

29 July: Four articles by Lenin, including 'Fresh Data on German Political Parties' appear in *Rabochaya Pravda* no 3. (CW 19 pp. 268–71)

2 August: Lenin meets Shklovsky and discusses the latter's visit to August Bebel concerning the money held by the trustees. Lenin sends Stalin, in exile, 120 francs.

3 August: Lenin attends the Conference of the RSDLP organisations abroad in Berne and speaks on the situation in the Party. Lenin's article 'A "Fashionable" Branch of Industry' appears in *Rabochaya Pravda* no 8. (CW 19 pp. 283–4) It is on the automobile industry. Lenin writes that under capitalism motorcars 'are available only to a relatively narrow circle of rich people.' Industry could produce 'hundreds of thousands of motor vehicles but the poverty of the *masses* hampers development.' Motor vehicles would be of great significance if they served the people. 'A large number of draught animals in farming and carting' could be replaced by them.

4 August: Lenin and Krupskaya leave Berne for Poronin.

5–6 August: They break their journey in Munich. A planned stay has to be abandoned because of lack of time. 'We stayed there only for several hours until we got the train. Boris [Knipovich] and his wife came to meet us. We spent the time in the restaurant which was famous for its Hofbrau beer.' (Krupskaya p. 230) The journey is also broken in Vienna where Lenin meets A V Shotman.

9 August: Lenin chairs a meeting of CC members in Poronin. Key items are the Party school and the publication of a Bolshevik newspaper in Moscow.

Between 13–21 August: After the death of August Bebel Lenin writes an obituary 'August Bebel'. (CW 19 pp. 296–301) and calls him a 'model workers' leader.'

10 September: Lenin's article 'The Russian Bourgeoisie and Russian Reformism' appears in *Nash Put* (Our Way) no 3, a legal Bolshevik daily newspaper. It had already appeared in *Severnaya Pravda* (Northern

Truth) on 9 September. (CW 19 pp. 325-7) Lenin publishes ten articles in the sixteen issues of *Nash Put* which appeared in September 1913.

Before 13 September: Lenin asks Shklovsky to try again for some money (the money held by the trustees). 'We haven't got a penny.' It is Clara Zetkin who is difficult but 'she was in Tyszka's [Leo Jogiches's] pocket.' (Haas pp. 65-6)

25 September: Lenin's article 'Marxism and Reformism' appears in *Pravda Truda* (Labour Truth) no 2. (CW 19 pp. 372-5) In contrast to the anarchists, Marxists 'recognise struggle for reforms, i.e. for measures that improve the conditions of the working people without destroying the power of the ruling class.' But it is necessary to combat the reformists who wish to restrict the struggle to reform. Reformism means 'abandoning Marxism and replacing it by bourgeois social policy.'

30 September: Lenin writes to Gorky that he is concerned about his pulmonary disease and recommends a German sanitorium to him. 'Because to squander official property, i.e. to go on being ill and undermining your working capacity, is something quite intolerable in every respect.' (CW 35 pp. 112-3)

3 October: Lenin congratulates the SPD publisher J Dietz on his 70th birthday and thanks him for his 'fraternal assistance.' (CW 43 p. 360)

6-14 October: Lenin leads the so-called Poronin summer Conference of Party functionaries. Twenty-two persons attend. He drafts resolutions, (CW 19 pp. 417-31) delivers the report of the CC, speaks on the national question and on the International Socialist Congress as well. 'While the Conference was in progress Inessa arrived. She was arrested in September 1912 with a false passport. Conditions in prison were very hard and undermined her health; she showed symptoms of tuberculosis but she had not lost any of her energy. We were all very glad that she had arrived.' (Krupskaya p. 231)

20 October: Lenin and Krupskaya return to Krakow from Poronin.

Beginning of November: Lenin writes to Gorky that he is worried that the latter is being given a new kind of treatment by a former Bolshevik doctor. 'The saints preserve us from comrade doctors in general and Bolshevik doctors in particular! Really and truly in 99 cases out of a 100 the comrade doctors are "asses", as a *good* doctor once said to me.' (CW 36 p. 265)

10 November: Lenin writes to Shklovsky about the money held by the trustees: 'I have received a copy of Zetkin's letter. It is an insolent lie.' (Haas p. 73)

11 November: Two articles by Lenin, including 'Capitalism and Workers' Immigration' appear in *Za Pravdy* (For the Truth) no 22. (CW 19 pp. 454-7) 'Capitalism has given rise to a special form of migration of nations. The rapidly developing countries . . . raise wages at home above the average rate and thus attract workers from the backward countries . . . There can be no doubt that dire poverty alone compels people to abandon their native land and that the capitalists exploit the immigrant workers in the most shameless manner. But only reactionaries can shut their eyes to the progressive significance of this modern immigration of nations . . . And it is into this struggle that capitalism is drawing the masses of the working people of the *whole* world, breaking down the musty, fusty habits of local life, breaking down national barriers and prejudices, uniting workers from all countries in huge factories and mines in America, Germany and so forth.'

13 or 14 November: In a letter to his sister Maria, Lenin reports that he has completed reading the four volumes of the Marx-Engels correspondence. 'There is much of interest. It is a pity the publishers — those Bosches — charge such a price for it — 40 marks!' (CW 37 pp. 504-5)

13-15 November: In two letters Lenin opposes Gorky's views on 'God-building' which is precisely the 'fond self-contemplation of the thick-witted philistines.' In the second letter he is not so violent. 'Don't be angry that I lost my temper. Perhaps I did not understand you *aright*?' (CW 35 pp. 121-4) and CW 36 p. 266)

22 November: Lenin writes to Shklovksy: 'I have read today in *Vorwärts* the silly attack on us in the International Socialist Bureau by Rosa Luxemburg.' Since 'Rosa = Zetkin' quick action has to be taken about the money held by the trustees and the option of the court case kept open. (Haas pp. 74-5)

Between 4-13 December: Lenin writes several letters about the money held by the trustees.

21 December: Lenin writes to his sister Maria: 'I have already got thoroughly used to the Krakow way of life — narrow, quiet, sleepy, but in some respects more convenient than in Paris.' (CW 37 p. 506)

26 December: Lenin's article 'A Good Resolution and a Bad Speech' appears in *Proletarskaya Pravda* (Proletarian Truth) no 6. (CW 19 pp. 528-30) It is directed against Rosa Luxemburg and Karl Kautsky who had said in the International Socialist Bureau meeting that the Russian Party was dead. Krupskaya writes to Lenin's mother that Volodya has become 'a great fiction lover' and an 'out-and-out nationalist' since he does not want to know anything about Polish artists. He is always burying himself in a catalogue of the Tretyakov Gallery. 'Volodya takes a cold shower every day, goes for walks and does not suffer from insomnia.' (CW 37 pp. 507-8)

End of December: Lenin writes to Inessa Armand: 'People for the most part (99 per cent of the bourgeoisie, 98 per cent of the liquidators, about 60-70 per cent of the Bolsheviks) don't know how to think they only *learn words by heart*.' (CW 35 p. 131) In the article 'On the Question of the Bureau's Next Steps' (CW 41 pp. 299-300) Lenin attacks small and tiny groups 'who have no support in Russia (like Rosa Luxemburg and the Tyszka people . . .) and who are keen for "unity".'

1914

7 January: Lenin and Krupskaya send New Year's greetings to his mother and complain: 'We do not seem to be able to make acquaintances among the local inhabitants.' (CW 37 pp. 509–10)

9–11 January: Lenin has discussions with CC members in Krakow.

12 January: Lenin criticises German Social Democracy in a letter sent from Krakow to David Wijnkoop in Amsterdam.

Before 15 January: Lenin informs Inessa Armand of his intention to come to Paris to take part in a meeting to commemorate Bloody Sunday (9 (22) January).

Between 15–18 January: Lenin arrives in Paris. (He is in Berlin on 15 January.)

20 January: Lenin attends a lecture by Malinovsky in Paris.

22 January: Lenin speaks in Paris at two social democratic meetings to commemorate Bloody Sunday.

23 January: Lenin speaks on the national question in the Grande Salle of the Geographical Society in Paris.

25 January: Lenin arrives in Brussels and meets Emile Vandervelde, leader of the Belgian Workers' Party and chairman of the International Socialist Bureau. In the evening, the eve of the opening of the 4th Congress of the Social Democratic Party of the Latvian Territory, Lenin addresses delegates on the theory and tactics of Bolshevism on the national question at a large meeting in the Golden Cock. Beforehand he meets two sailors who have been recruited for conspiratorial work in Russia. He writes to his friend Inessa Armand in Paris, in English: 'Dear Friend, I am writing you briefly – business. Victory!! Hurrah! The majority are for us. I shall stay here about a week and shall probably have a lot of work to do. I am delighted that we have won. Sincerely yours, V I. (CW 43 p. 377) In another letter to Inessa Armand, headed 'No 2' Lenin reports that the post has arrived. 'Again nothing from you.' (CW 37 pp. 377–9)

26 January: Lenin attends the 4th Congress of the Latvian social democrats in Brussels. It remains in session until 8 February. He delivers the report to the CC, RSDLP. (CW 41 pp. 324–7) He writes to Inessa Armand: 'Dear Friend, I was terribly glad to receive your nice, friendly, warm, charming letter. I am inexpressibly grateful to you for it. Things here have gone worse. One has already deserted to the conciliators – so now we have no majority and the conciliators will have it all their own rotten way . . . My new address: Oulianoff, Rue Souveraine 18 (Ixelles) Bruxelles. My very, very, very best regards, my dear friend. Excuse the haste and brevity. I have no time. Yours, V U.' (CW 43 pp. 379–80)

28 January: Lenin writes to Inessa Armand: '*We must publish*. But we have *neither* money nor any printing facilities outside of Paris. Therefore it is of *primary* importance for the Party to *arrange* publication [of the Bulletin] in Paris. I beg you to *do* this both as a duty and a favour.' (CW 43 pp. 381-3)

31 January and 1 February: Lenin writes, in Brussels, a short report on the chief points at issue among Russian social democrats for Camille Huysmans, the secretary of the International Socialist Bureau. (CW 20 pp. 74-81)

January-February: Lenin receives information, from the Banque du Nord in Paris, that on 31 December 1913 there were 399 francs 25 centimes in his account no 2444. (Khr. III p. 187)

2 February: Lenin travels to Liège from Brussels and speaks on the national question.

After 2 February: Lenin travels to Leipzig; he stays with V M Zagorsky at Elisenstrasse 45.

4 February: Lenin speaks in Leipzig to Russian social democrats, mostly students, in the Sieben-Männer-Haus, Arthur Hoffmann Strasse 1.

6 February: Lenin returns to Krakow.

13 February: Lenin's article 'The Liberals' Corruption of the Workers' and his 'Letter to the Editor', in which he attacks Bogdanov, appear in *Put Pravdy* (The Way of Truth) no 9. (CW 20 pp. 90-4)

Mid February: Lenin sends F N Samoilov, a Bolshevik Duma member who is ill, to Shklovsky in Berne and writes to him: 'For God's sake take care of him as quickly as possible ... The most important thing is to find a *first class* sanitorium (from the medical point of view) for him.' (Haas p. 76)

16 February: Lenin writes to his sister Maria that he has just returned to Krakow; 'amongst other things I lectured on the question of nationalities in Paris ... There have been no changes here. We still live modestly. Nadya seems to be in for a relapse of her thyroid trouble — the symptoms are still mild but they are there ... I am quite well.' (CW 37 p. 513)

21 February: Lenin writes to his mother that his trip to Paris has cheered him up.

27 February: Lenin writes to L B Kamenev in St Petersburg: 'Bogdanov's depature [from *Pravda*] is said to have caused displeasure (among the intelligentsia riff-raff, apparently).' (CW 43 pp. 385-6) Lenin writes to his sister Anna, on the editorial board of *Prosveshchenie* Bogdanov is 'a minus (and not a 0).' No workers support him. 'These are fairy tales from soft-headed muddleheads from among the intelligentsia.' (CW 43 pp. 386-7)

February: Lenin writes to the sick Samoilov in Montreux: 'Now — quiet, sunshine, sleep, *food*. Take care of all this. Do they give you enough to eat? *You should drink more milk*. Do you? You should weigh yourself once a week and make a note of it each time.' (CW 43 pp. 387-8)

2 March: Lenin writes to Inessa Armand in Paris that he is concerned about Samoilov in Montreux and wonders where 'a good doctor' can be found to 'look after him there (nervous complaint).' (CW 43 pp. 388-9)
5 March: Lenin's articles 'More About "Nationalism"' and 'The Peasantry and Hired Labour' appear in *Put Pravdy* no 17. (CW 20 pp. 109-13) On the national question in multi-national states, the working class, writes Lenin, 'is opposed to *all* privileges, that is why it upholds the *right* of all nations to self-determination. The class conscious workers do not advocate *secession*. They know the advantages of large states and the amalgamation of large masses of workers. But large states can be democratic only if there is complete equality among the nations; that equality implies the *right* to secede.'
7 March: Lenin writes to Camille Huysmans in Brussels that he has writeen the report he promised on the RSDLP (compare 31 January). 'The expressions you use in your letter ("tergiversation", "policy of procrastination", etc.) are insulting and you have no right to employ them towards a comrade. I must ask you therefore to take back these expressions without reserve. Unless you do so, this letter to you will be my last.' (CW 43 pp. 390-1)
10 March: Lenin's article 'Concerning A Bogdanov' appears in *Put Pravdy* no 21. (CW 20 pp. 121-4) On the protest of thirteen 'left Bolsheviks' against the termination of Bogdanov's association with *Pravda*, Lenin writes that such an association is impossible because 'A Bogdanov is not a Marxist.' It was a mistake to print his previous articles.
15 March: Lenin, in a letter to the secretary of the editorial board of the Granat Bros' Encyclopaedic Dictionary, accepts an invitation to 'write an article on Marx for the Dictionary.' (CW 43 pp. 392-3) Lenin writes to Camille Huysmans that he is very pleased that after receiving his 'witty and friendly letter', he can 'consider the incident definitely closed.' (compare 7 March) (CW 43 p. 393)
16 March: Krupskaya and Lenin write to his mother: 'We are very lonely here — there is really only one family in the whole town with whom we are acquainted . . . Nor do we get many letters. We live mostly on newspapers.' (CW 37 pp. 515-6)
After 15 March: Lenin writes to Inessa Armand. He discusses the case of 'Mme Caillaux', the wife of a French politician who shot dead the nationalist editor Calmette because he had been waging a campaign against her husband. 'I can't get rid of a certain feeling of sympathy. I thought only venality, cowardice and meanness were rife in those circles. And suddenly this plucky woman goes and delivers a resolute leçon!!' (CW 43 p. 394)
21 March: Lenin speaks to Spojnia, the student society, in Krakow, on social democratic Russia and the national question.
24 March: Lenin's article 'A Liberal Professor on Equality' appears in

Put Pravdy no 33. (CW 20 pp. 144-7) Lenin states that social democrats mean by political equality 'equal rights and by economic equality
. . . they mean the abolition of classes.' When 'socialists speak of
equality they always mean *social* equality, the equality of social status
and not by any means the physical and mental equality of individuals.'

28 March: Lenin's article 'The Breaking of the "August" Bloc' appears
in *Put Pravda* no 37. (CW 20 pp. 158-61) He writes that the bloc
formed in August 1912 with 'tremendous ballyhoo' from 'liquidators,
Trotsky, the Latvians, the Bundists and the Caucasians' has disinte-
grated. 'Under cover of high-sounding, empty and obscure phrases that
confuse the non-class-conscious workers', Trotsky is defending the
liquidators.

1 April: Lenin writes to Inesssa Armand in Paris that he is sending her
a Ukrainian Appeal which he cannot publish under his own name. 'I
have received your story of Stepanyuk's report and the speech by
Yurkevich; frankly speaking I was angry with you — you didn't understand what the *essence* of Yurkevich's position was. And I again — I'm
sorry — called you the Holy Virgin. Please don't be angry, it was
because I'm fond of you, because we're friends, but I can't help being
angry when I see "something that recalls the Holy Virgin".' (CW 35
pp. 135-6)

3 April: Lenin writes about the money held by the trustees to Shklovsky and tells him, through Karl Zraggen, to engage Vinck, a Belgian
lawyer. It should be possible to 'get the money back without going to a
bourgeois court, which doubtlessly Zetkin and Kautsky would
condemn and which is undesirable for us all.' (Haas p. 73 Khr. III p. 203)

Before 8 April: Lenin writes to Inessa Armand: 'The Germans virtually
have *2 parties* and this has to be borne in mind without trying to shield
the opportunists (*the way* Neue Zeit *and Kautsky* are now doing). But
it is incorrect to say that the German *party* is the most opportunistic
party in Europe. It is nonetheless the best party and our task is to
adopt from the Germans *all* that is most valuable (the mass of newspapers, the large party membership, the mass membership of the trade
unions, the systematic subscription to the newspapers, strict control
over MPs).' (CW 43 pp. 396-7)

10 April: Lenin writes to his mother: 'In these last few days I have
caught a slight cold (that has to happen every spring!) but am now
quite well. Very soon, early in May, we are going to Poronin again.'
(CW 37 p. 517)

11 April: Lenin writes to Inessa Armand and hopes that she has finished
with Aleksinsky. 'The *only* remedy in such cases (I speak from my own
long, over 15 years, experience) is an absolute boycott by the *entire*
section . . . I am awfully glad that your children are coming to see you
and that you will soon go off to spend the summer with them.' (CW 43
p. 398).

15-17 April: Lenin chairs a meeting of the Bolshevik CC in Krakow. His resolution, on the establishment of an organisational section of the CC to direct illegal work, is adopted. (CW 41 pp. 330-1) The St Petersburg committee is to appoint 3-5 persons, co-ordinate all legal organisations and adopt conspiratorial means to cover up the illegal work.

22 April: Lenin writes from Krakow to his sister Anna in Vologda: 'The weather here is wonderful and I frequently go cycling. No matter how provincial and barbarous this town of ours may be, by and large I am better off here than I was in Paris. The hurly-burly of life in the émigré colony there was incredible; one's nerves got worn down badly and for no reason at all. Paris is an inconvenient place to work in, the Bibliothèque Nationale is badly organised – we often thought of Geneva, where work was better, the library was convenient and life was less nerve-racking and time-wasting. Of all the places I have been in my wanderings I would select London or Geneva, if those two places were not so far away.' (CW 37 pp. 518-9)

Before 5 May: Lenin telegraphs the editor of *Put Pravdy* on the occasion of its second anniversary and encloses 6 roubles 68 kopeks, 'the one day earnings of two Pravdists.' (CW 43 p. 399)

5 May: Lenin's article 'What should Not be Copied from the German Labour Movement' appears in *Prosveshchenie* no 4. (CW 20 pp. 254-8) It is directed against Carl Legien, as is the beginning of the pamphlet 'The Right of Nations to Self-Determination'. (CW 20 pp. 393-454) Lenin criticises Rosa Luxemburg's theses on the national question and defends the right to self-determination of all nations. First and foremost he quotes Marx in opposing Rosa Luxemburg's view that independence for Poland is utopia.

5 or 6 May: Lenin, Krupskaya and her mother travel from Krakow to Poronin. They stay in T Skupen's house.

7 May: Lenin writes to F N Samoilov, already from Poronin, that the summer is wet. 'We have "political troubles" as well, troubles which someone ill with neurasthenia should *not be party to*. However I am planning that you come here (or to Zakopane, 7 versts away, where there is a clinic, etc.) when you are completely well again. At present you should have treatment and you should have treatment.' (Haas pp. 78-9)

Before 9 May: Lenin chairs a meeting of the CC which is preparing a Congress to coincide with the opening of the Congress of the Second International in Vienna (the outbreak of war prevents it).

First half of May: Lenin writes from Poronin to Inessa Armand in Paris that 'all kinds of petty affairs' have prevented him from answering Vinnichenko in 1911 or 1912. 'Oh, these "petty affairs", these apologies for business, imitative products of business, a hindrance to business, how I hate fuss and bustle and petty affairs, and how tied I am to them inseparably and for all time!! *That's a sign that I am lazy* *and tired and badly humoured. Generally I like my profession and now I almost hate it.* (These last two sentences are in English in the original.) (CW 43 pp. 400-1)

17 May: Lenin's article 'The Ideological struggle in the Working Class Movement' appears in *Put Pravdy* no 77. (CW 20 pp. 277-80) Lenin speaks of the 'twenty-year history of Marxism's ties with the mass working class movement in Russia' but only now the foundations of a Marxist Party have been laid; the 'overwhelming majority' of 'class-conscious workers' are 'Pravdists.'

25 May: Lenin writes to Inessa Armand: 'The Malinovsky affair is warming up.' He is not in Poronin. Malinovsky, a member of the Bolshevik CC since 1912 had resigned his Duma seat and had disappeared. 'It looks like "flight". Naturally this gives food for the worst thoughts. Alexei wires from Paris that the Russian newspapers are wiring Burtsev that Malinovsky is accused of being a provocateur. You can imagine what it means!! Very improbable, but we are obliged to control all "oui-dire" . . . You can easily imagine how much I am worried.' (The last three sentences are in English in the original.) (CW 43 pp. 402-3) On the other hand he writes to Shklovsky: 'The Malinovsky affair is an adventure and due to nerves. The rumours about provocation are a mean trick and a piece of stupidity on the part of the liquidators.' (Haas p. 83) (compare also 13 August) Lenin writes to Petrovsky in St Petersburg: 'A wish − that you bear the irresponsible departure of Malinovsky more firmly and stop worrying. No need to expel him. He has removed himself. Condemned. Political suicide. What other punishment can there be? Of what use?' (CW 43 pp. 403-4)

4 June: Lenin's article 'The Liquidators and Malinovsky's Biography' appears in *Rabochii*, the cover name for *Pravda*, illegal at that time, no 2. (CW 20 pp. 302-5) Lenin takes issue with the 'liquidators' who claim that only the 'splitting activities' of the Bolsheviks secured such a prominent position for Malinovsky. Malinovsky, because of his 'political background and talents could have played an important political role in any political group.'

Before 5 June: Lenin writes to Inessa Armand and criticises Vinnichenko's novel *Paternal Testaments* as a poor imitation of Dostoevsky. 'Once I had to spend a night with a sick comrade (delirium tremens) and once I had to "talk round" a comrade who had attempted suicide (after the attempt) and who some years later did commit suicide. Both recollections à la Vinnichenko. But in both cases they were small fragments of the lives of both comrades. But this pretentious, crass idiot Vinnichenko in self-admiration, has from such things compiled a collection that is nothing but horrors . . . Muck, nonsense, pity I spent so much time reading it!' (CW 35 pp. 144-5)

12 June: Lenin's article 'Unity' appears in *Trudovaya Pravda* (Truth about Labour) no 2. (CW 20 pp. 319-21) This can only be achieved through struggle. 'Unity without organisation is impossible. Organisation is impossible unless the minority bows to the majority.' These are incontestable truths. The majority of workers are behind 'the Pravdists'; this is 'unity in deed', unity of workers and not 'unity of intellectual groups.'

14 June: Four articles by Lenin, including the continuation of 'The Right of Nations to Self-Determination' and 'Disruption of Unity Under Cover of Outcries for Unity' appear in *Prosveshchenie* no 5. (CW 35 pp. 325–47)

24 June: Lenin receives a letter from M F Vladimirsky who informs him about a conversation with a relative of N P Shmidt concerning the Shmidt legacy.

Beginning of July: Lenin writes three letters to Inessa Armand. In one letter, not later than 4 July, he asks her to go as a delegate to the 'unity Conference' of all Russian groups, called by the International Socialist Bureau, in Brussels from 16–18 July. 'I don't want to go "on principle". Apparently the Germans (the resentful Kautsky and Co.) are out to annoy us. Soit. We shall calmly (I am no good for that), on behalf of the eight tenths majority, propose our conditions in the most polite (I am no good for that either) French. You . . . could carry this through splendidly!' (CW 43 pp. 406–7) In a second letter, not later than 3 July, Lenin reports that he had gone for 'a walk in the mountains' the day before. (CW 43 p. 408 Khr. III p. 242) In a third letter, not later than 6 July, Lenin writes: 'Dear Friend [these words are in English in the original], I am terribly afraid that you will refuse to go to Brussels and thus place us in an *absolutely impossible position* . . . Besides excellent French, of course, an *understanding of essentials* and proper tact are required. You are the *only suitable person*. So please — I beg you most earnestly — consent, if only for one day.' (CW 43 pp. 409–10)

Before 6 July: In a letter to S G Shaumyan, Lenin writes: 'It is shameful to stand for an official language. It is a police regime idea. But there is not a shadow of police regime practice in *advocating* Russian for small nations.' (CW 43 pp. 410–11)

Before 9 July: Lenin writes two letters to Inessa Armand about the Brussels Conference. In the second he states: 'I have just settled with Grigory [Zinoviev] that he is not going (Zina, [Zinoviev's wife] is still ill) (I am not going either) — and that *you and Popov* . . . have been *endorsed by the Central Committee*.' (CW 43 pp. 412–3)

Before 10 July: In letters to Inessa Armand and I F Popov, Lenin gives precise instructions about tactics at the 'unity Conference.'

Between 10–16 July: Lenin writes a long letter to Inessa Armand: 'I am sure you are one of those people who develop, grow stronger, become more vigorous and bold when they are alone in a responsible position . . . You will manage splendidly! . . . The essential thing, in my opinion, is to prove that only we are the Party . . . Argument against Rosa Luxemburg: *what is real is not her party* but the "opposition" . . . If there is talk of the money held by the former trustee, refer to the resolution of January 1912 and refuse to say any more. We, that is, don't renounce the right!!' (CW 35 pp. 146-9)

11 July: Three articles by Lenin, including 'The Bourgeois Intelligentsia Methods of Struggle Against the Workers' (CW 20 pp. 455-86) and the concluding part of 'The Right of Nations to Self-Determination' appear in *Prosveshchenie* no 6.

Between 12-19 July: Lenin chairs, in Poronin, a meeting of the CC to prepare the planned Party Congress.

Before 13 July: Lenin writes to Inessa Armand: 'I am extremely grateful to you for giving your agreement. I am positive you will carry off our important role with flying colours and give a fitting answer to Plekhanov, Rosa Luxemburg and Kautsky.' He gives 'occasional advice' to make her 'difficult task easier.' (CW 43 pp. 417-20)

13 July: Lenin sends off his 'Report of the CC of the RSDLP to the Brussels Conference and Instructions to the CC delegates' (written between 6-13 July). (CW 20 pp. 495-535) The report consists of four parts: 1) the main differences among social democrats 2) the mass working class movement in Russia 3) the position of his opponents 4) practical proposals for unity. Lenin declares, in reply to Rosa Luxemburg, that there is no 'chaos of factional strife' in Russia, but there is a 'struggle against the liquidators.' The class-conscious workers are behind *Pravda*. He also complains about the 'personal campaign against several members of our Party' and says: 'Our Central Committee declared that it vouched for Malinovsky, had investigated the rumours and was convinced that Dan and Martov were indulging in base slander.'

19 July: Lenin writes two letters to Inessa Armand: 'You handled the matter better then I could have done . . . Language apart I would probably have *gone up in the air*. I would not have been able to stand the hypocrisy and would have called them scoundrels . . . that's what they were trying to provoke. But you and the others carried it off calmly and firmly. Extremely thankful & greeting you . . . [This sentence is in English in the original]. I greet you a thousand times!! Your task was heavy & . . . You have rendered a very great service to our Party! I am especially thankful because you have replaced me. (These four sentences are in English in the original.) Write — are you very tired, very angry? Are you wild with me for persuading you to go?' (CW 43 pp. 423-5)

21 July: Lenin's 'Reply to the Article in the *Leipziger Volkszeitung*', signed editor of *Pravda*, appears in the *Leipziger Volkszeitung* (CW 20 pp. 558-9)

Before 24 July: Lenin writes to Inessa Armand, in English, that Kautsky is a 'mean creature, totally without character, under private influences, always changing position according to secret influence and angry against me because of "money story" . . . Kautsky is a victim of intrigues from Rosa L., Plekh. & Co. Plekhanov is a *mean turncoat, as always* [these italicised words are in Russian in the original]. Popov writes me that you were ill, your voice was feeble. What is this illness? Please write me more details!! I cannot be quiet otherwise.' (CW 43 pp. 425-6)

26 July: Lenin writes to I Rudis-Gipslis: 'It would be important to make clear our attitude in principle towards federation. We are *against* it in *principle*. We are for democratic centralism.' (CW 36 pp. 288-9)

1 August: Lenin learns in Poronin of the German declaration of war on Russia. Zinoviev says to Lenin: 'You will see that the German social democrats will not dare to speak against the war, they will abstain. Lenin replies: 'No, despite everything they are not such rascals. Certainly they will not struggle against the war, they will just vote against it as is their custom, so that the working class does not rise up against them.' (Zinoviev *N Lenin* p. 25)

5 August: Lenin learns of the unanimous vote for war credits by the SPD in the Reichstag. When Zinoviev brings him the SPD newspaper *Vorwärts* with the information Lenin at first refuses to believe it. 'That isn't possible, this is perhaps a forged edition of *Vorwärts*, these miserable German bourgeois have published it to deceive us and to force us to betray the International.' (Zinoviev *N Lenin* p. 25) After he learns that it is not a forged number he is said to have commented to S Bagozki: 'This is the end of the Second International.' (Khr. III p. 266)

7 August: The Austrian authorities search Lenin's house in Poronin. The same evening Lenin tells J Hanecki, who also lives in Poronin: 'My house has just been searched. The head of the local police was in charge . . . the blockhead left all the Party correspondence but took my manuscript on the agrarian situation. He thought the statistical tables in it were a secret code.' (Briefe IV p. 424) Lenin sends a telegram to the chief of police in Krakow: 'The local police suspect me of espionage. I lived in Krakow for two years, in Zwierzyniec and 51 Ulica Lubormirskiego. I personally gave information about myself to the commissary of police in Zwierzyniec. I am an emigrant, a social democrat. Please wire Poronin and mayor of Nowy Targ to avoid misunderstanding.' (CW 43 pp. 430-1)

8 August: Lenin is arrested and held in prison in Nowy Targ (Neumarkt) in Galicia until 19 August.

9 August: Krupskaya visits Lenin in prison; she visits him daily during his imprisonment.

11 August: Krupskaya sends Victor Adler a letter and asks him to arrange for Lenin's release from prison.

14 August: Krupskaya sends a telegram to Victor Adler in Vienna asking him to help Lenin. She also writes to Hermann Diamand, a Socialist Party member of parliament, and asks him to vouch for Lenin.

20 August: Lenin and Krupskaya thank Adler and Diamand for helping to get Lenin released.

26 August: They return to Krakow. Lenin receives papers to leave the country for himself, his wife and mother-in-law.

29 August: They leave Krakow. They stay in Vienna until 3 September while Victor Adler obtains papers for them to enter Switzerland. 'In Vienna, Ryazanov took Vladimir Ilich to see Victor Adler who had helped to secure Ilich's release. Adler told us of his conversation with the Minister. The latter had asked: "Are you certain that Ulyanov is an enemy of the Tsarist government?" — "Oh yes," Adler replied, "a more implacable enemy than your Excellency".' (Krupskaya p. 244) Lenin sends a telegram to Hermann Greulich, a Swiss social democrat, and asks him to vouch for him so that he can enter Switzerland.

3 September: They leave Vienna for Switzerland.

5 September: Lenin, Krupskaya and her mother arrive in Zürich and then on to Berne. Lenin writes to Victor Adler: 'Your help was therefore extremely useful to me. Passports are required for entry into Switzerland but I was allowed in without a passport when I mentioned Greulich. Very best regards and deepest gratitude.' (CW 36 p. 291) Lenin lives after 5 September at Donnerbühlweg 11a, Berne.

6 September: Lenin writes from Berne to V A Karpinsky in Geneva: 'I arrived here safely yesterday with my whole family, after a brief captivity in Austria. Zinoviev will also be coming . . . Can one now publish a leaflet, etc.? In Russian? . . . (against the war, of course, and against the new type of nationalists, from Haase to Vandervelde and Guesde — they've all played false!' (CW 36 p. 292)

6–8 September: Lenin holds discussions with Bolsheviks (Samoilov, Shklovsky, Safarov, etc.); he speaks on the attitude to be adopted towards the war. His theses 'The Tasks of Revolutionary Social Democracy in the European War' (CW 21 pp. 15–19) are adopted. Lenin calls it a 'bourgeois, imperialist, dynastic war', and condemns the support of the leading social democrats as a 'betrayal of socialism.' For Russia he states that the 'destruction of the tsarist monarchy' during the war is a 'lesser evil.' He proposes 'For the Socialist Revolution' as the slogan for social democracy, 'a republican United States of Europe' as the immediate goal.

After 27 September: Lenin writes to Inessa Armand in Les Avants, Switzerland: 'I am extremely anxious & angry with the position of the European socialists in the present war [this sentence is in English in the original] . . . Grigory [Zinoviev] has arrived with his family. We are remaining in Berne. A dull little town but . . . better than Geneva . . . I am poking around the libraries — I have missed them.' (CW 43 pp. 432–3)

September (until May 1915): In Berne library Lenin reads works by Feuerbach, Hegel, Aristotle, Lassalle and other philosophers; he makes excerpts and notes, etc. for his *Philosophical Notebooks* (CW 38 pp. 85-339) Also during this time Lenin begins 'The Question of the Dialectic' (CW 38 pp. 355-63), his own systematic philosophical point of view. Lenin writes that the dialectic is inherent in the whole of human knowledge; the dialectic is the Marxist theory of knowledge. Plekhanov and other Marxists have paid no attention to this 'essence' of the matter.

After September: Lenin writes on the war: 'The only correct proletarian slogan is to transform the present imperialist war into a civil war . . . These are the only kind of tactics that will be truly revolutionary.' (CW 41 p. 337)

7 October: Inessa Armand, who has also moved to Berne, reports to the police in Berne that she lives in Drosselweg 23 and is therefore 'a neighbour of the Ulyanovs.' (Gautschi p. 158)

Before 11 October: Lenin writes 'The War and Russian Social Democracy' and it is published in *Sotsial Demokrat* no 33 on 1 November. (CW 21 pp. 25-34) He states: 'It must be the primary task of social democrats in every country to combat that country's chauvinism.'

11 October: In Lausanne Lenin speaks against Plekhanov (CW 36 pp. 294-6) after the latter's lecture 'The Attitude of the Socialists to the War.' Lenin writes to V A Karpinsky: 'I spoke here today at Plekhanov's lecture, against his chauvinism.' (CW 35 p. 158)

14 October: Lenin speaks in Lausanne on the proletariat and the war. (CW 36 pp. 297-302) He states that the attitude of socialists to war must be based on the real situation; the present war is an 'imperialist war', the epoch of national wars is over. He refers to Marx's thesis that the proletariat has no fatherland. Lenin praises Martov: 'The more frequently and the more violently I differed from Martov before, the more definitely I must say now that that writer is doing precisely what a social democrat should do. He is criticising his own government.'

15 October: Lenin speaks in Geneva on the European war and socialism.

17 October: After returning to Berne, on 16 October, Lenin moves to Distelweg 11. Krupskaya writes: 'We lived in Berne on Distelweg, a small, tidy, quiet street adjoining the Berne forest which extended for several kilometres. Across the road lived Inessa [Armand], five minutes' walk — the Zinovievs, ten minutes' walk — the Shklovksys. We could wander for hours along the forest roads, bestrewn with fallen yellow leaves. On most occasions the three of us went together on these walks, Vladimir Ilich, Inessa and myself. Vladimir Ilich would develop his plans of the international struggle. Inessa took it all very much to heart. In this unfolding struggle she began to take a most direct part, conducting correspondence . . . sometimes we would sit for hours on the sunlit wooded mountain side while Ilich jotted down

outlines of his speeches and articles and polished his formulations.'
(Krupskaya p. 252) Lenin writes a detailed letter to A G Shlyapnikov in
Stockholm. The most important thing is a 'consistent and organised
struggle against chauvinism . . The German "Centre", headed by
Kautsky, is a concealed evil.' The slogan of peace is wrong at present;
the slogan 'should be the transformation of the national war into a
civil war.' (CW 35 pp. 161-3)

27 October: Lenin speaks in Zürich on the war and social democracy.
He writes to Shlyapnikov: 'I hate and despise Kautsky now more than
anyone, with his vile, dirty, self-satisfied hypocrisy.' (CW 35 pp. 167-
9)

31 October: Lenin writes to Shlyapnikov: 'Pannekoek is right: the
Second International is dead for ever. It was killed by the opportunists
(and not by "parliamentarism" as the slow-witted Pannekeok put it).'
(CW 35 pp. 170-2)

1 November: After a break of a year, *Sotsial Demokrat* (no 33) re-
appears, edited by Lenin. It carries Lenin's articles 'The War and Russian
Social Democracy' and 'The Position and Tasks of the Socialist International.' (CW 21 pp. 25-41) In the latter article Lenin states: 'The
Second International is dead, overcome by opportunism . . . To the
Third International falls the task of organising the proletarian forces for
a revolutionary onslaught against the capitalist governments, for civil
war against the bourgeoisie of all countries for the capture of political
power, for the triumph of socialism.'

14 November: Lenin writes to Shlyapnikov: 'The epoch of the *bayonet*
has begun. This is a fact; consequently we have to fight *with such a
weapon too* . . . We must stand for the watchword of the *revolutionary
proletariat*, capable of *fighting* for *its own* aims — and that is civil war.'
Lenin opposes the peace slogan since this does not now serve the propa-
gandist ideals of the revolutionary proletariat; the war must be used
to 'hasten the collapse of capitalism.' (CW 36 pp. 306-7) Lenin writes
to his sister Anna: 'I do not need any money at present. My incarcera-
tion was a very brief one, only 12 days, and I was soon granted certain
privileges so that the "time" I did was very easy, the conditions and the
treatment were good. Now I have had time to look round and settle
down here. We are living in two furnished rooms, very good ones, and
we eat in a neighbouring dining room. Nadya feels quite well, so does
E V [Krupskaya's mother], although she has aged badly. I have finished
my article for the Granat Encyclopaedia (about Marx).' (CW 37 pp.
520-1)

17 November: Lenin sends off the manuscript of his essay on Karl
Marx, on which he has been working since July, to the Granat publishing
house. (CW 21 pp. 43-91) The essay is typical of Lenin's understanding
of Marx. He defines Marxism as the 'system of Marx's views and teachings.' Marx was the 'genius who continued and consummated the three

main ideological currents of the nineteenth century, as represented by the three most advanced countries of mankind: classical German philosophy, classical English political economy, and French socialism combined with French revolutionary doctrine in general.' Out of the 'remarkable consistency and integrity' of the totality of Marx's views is constituted 'modern materialism and modern scientific socialism, as the theory and programme of the working class movement in all the civilised countries of the world.' In a letter to the secretary of the editorial board of the Granat publishing house, Lenin writes: 'Send the fee due to me as soon as possible' to his brother-in-law Mark Elizarov in Petrograd (the former St Petersburg). (CW 35 pp. 173-4)

28 November: Lenin writes to A G Shlyapnikov: 'Times are difficult but . . . we shall get through.' (CW 35 pp. 175-6)

12 December: Lenin's articles 'Dead Chauvinism and Living Socialism' and 'On the National Pride of the Great Russians' appear in *Sotsial Demokrat* no 35. (CW 21 pp. 94-106) The latter article may serve as a short summary of Lenin's concept of the role of the nation; it presents Lenin's attitude to Russian tradition and makes clear that the overcoming of Russian backwardness is one of the goals of the Party. 'Is a sense of national pride alien to us, Great Russian class-conscious proletarians? Certainly not! We love our language and our country . . . We are all full of a sense of national pride and for that very reason we *particularly* hate our slavish past . . . and our slavish present.'

Between 8-16 December: Lenin, in a letter to A M Kollontai in Copenhagen, signed V Ilyin, N Lenin, writes: 'The European war has brought this great benefit to international socialism, that it has exposed for all to see the utter rottenness, baseness and meanness of opportunism, thereby giving a splendid impetus to the cleansing of the working-class movement from the dung accumulated during decades of peace.' (CW 35 pp. 177-8)

16 December: Lenin speaks out in Berne against Martov's lecture 'The War and the Crisis of Socialism.'

22 December: Lenin writes to his sister Maria in Moscow: 'We are living fairly well, quietly and peacefully in sleeply Berne. The libraries here are good . . . It is even pleasant to read after my daily newspaper work.' (CW 37 pp. 522-3)

1915

3 January: Lenin writes to A G Shlyapnikov that his arguments have convinced him. 'If I have offended you, I am prepared to tender my voluble apologies and earnestly ask you to forget it.' (CW 43 pp. 443-4)

9 January: Lenin's article 'What Next?' appears in *Sotsial Demokrat* no 36. (CW 21 pp. 107-14) He states: 'Typical of the socialist parties of the epoch of the Second International was one that tolerated in its midst an opportunism . . . adapting itself to the revolutionary workers, *borrowing* their Marxist terminology and evading any clear cleavage of principles. This type has outlived itself.'

17 January: Lenin, in a letter to Inessa Armand, gives advice on a planned pamphlet. 'I advise you to throw out altogether paragraph 3 — the "demand (women's) for freedom of love". That is really not a proletarian but a bourgeois demand.' (CW 35 pp. 180-1)

24 January: In a letter to Inessa Armand, Lenin continues his discussion on her planned pamphlet on love. He asks if it would not be better for a popular pamphlet to 'contrast philistine — intellectual-peasant . . . vulgar and dirty marriage without love to proletarian civil marriage with love' so as to arrive at 'class *types*.' (CW 35 pp. 182-5)

1 February: Two articles by Lenin 'The Kind of "Unity" Larin Proclaimed at the Swedish Congress' and 'The Russian Brand of Südekum' appear in *Sotsial Demokrat* no 37. (CW 21 pp. 115-24) Lenin calls Plekhanov 'the Russian Südekum', a type of 'smug and unscrupulous opportunist and social chauvinist.'

9 February: Lenin writes to his sister Maria: 'There is a growth in the anti-chauvinist mood among the Germans; there has been a split in Stuttgart and in Frankfurt-am-Main. An anti-chauvinist publication *Lichtstrahlen* (Light Rays) is appearing in Berlin.' (CW 37 pp. 524-5)

11 February: Lenin writes to Shlyapnikov that a new grouping is coming into existence within social democracy. 'The chauvinists ("social patriots") and their friends, their defenders — and the anti-chauvinists. In the main, this division corresponds to the division between the opportunists and the revolutionary social democrats.' (CW 35 pp. 186-8)

20 February: At a meeting in Berne Lenin protests against the arrest in Russia of the Bolshevik members of the Duma.

27 February-4 March: Lenin chairs a Conference of the RSDLP groups abroad in Berne and speaks on the main theme: 'on the Character of the War' and his draft resolutions are adopted. (CW 21 pp. 158-64) No agreement is reached on the slogan of the United States of Europe.

3 March: Two articles by Lenin, including 'How the Police and the Reactionaries Protect the Unity of German Social Democracy' appear in *Sotsial Demokrat* no 39. (CW 21 pp. 129-31) Lenin writes: 'The workers can advance towards their world wide revolution only through a series of defects and errors, failures and weaknesses, but they are advancing towards it.'

9 March: Accompanied by Carl Moor Lenin goes to the Amtsschaffnerei in Berne and pays 100 francs for his Toleranzbewilligung, his residence permit. (Gautschi p. 99)

20 March: Krupskaya's mother dies and is cremated and buried in

Berne on 23 March. 'Our landlady, a pious old laundress asked us to look for another room explaining that she wanted to rent her room to believers. We moved to another room.' (Krupskaya p. 262)

26-28 March: At the International Socialist Women's Conference in Berne, chaired by Clara Zetkin, Lenin is in charge of the work of the Bolshevik delegation (Krupskaya, Inessa Armand, Lilina Zinoviev). He drafts a resolution (CW 41 pp. 346-8) which is rejected by a majority at the Conference as too extreme. 'A feeling of panic seized the delegates; agreement was out of the question since the [Bolshevik] minority declared that it would not budge from its resolution. The Conference was interrupted. Clara Zetkin, deeply shaken and trembling all over, accompanied the minority delegates to an adjacent room. After an hour she returned. She had after all found a way out; the minority declared themselves prepared to vote for the general resolution if their declaration was entered in the minutes. This saved the situation.' (Angelica Balabanoff *Erinnerungen und Erlebnisse* p. 101)

5-7 April: The International Socialist Youth Conference meets in Berne with fourteen delegates present. The Conference had been organised by Willi Münzenberg. Once again the Bolsheviks and their views are in the minority. 'Not being at the conference himself, he [Lenin] led the representatives of his faction from the Volkshaus Café. They came in turns out to him.' (Balabanoff *Erinnerungen und Erlebnisse* p. 102) 'But one sensed how difficult he found the role of a leader, one who stood apart and remained behind the scenes when a matter of extraordinary importance was at stake, and his whole being was straining to take an active part in it.' (Krupskaya *Erinnerungen an Lenin* II p. 149)

14 April: Lenin and Krupskaya move to a new flat, Waldheimstrasse 66 Parterre.

1 May: Three articles by Lenin, including 'The Question of the Unity of Internationalists' and 'Bourgeois philanthropists and Revolutionary Social Democracy' appear in *Sotsial Demokrat* no 41. (CW 21 pp. 188-93) In the former article Lenin declares that the 'old divisions and groupings' among social democrats are being transformed, the fundamental question now is 'internationalist' or 'social patriot.' In the latter article he states that the '*only* road towards democracy and socialism' is 'mass revolutionary action against the bourgeoisie and the governments of their respective countries.'

5 May: Writing to Hermann Gorter, Lenin welcomes the plan of Dutch left socialists to found an 'international social democratic journal . . . under the editorship of Pannekoek' against the 'opportunist traitors (including Kautsky).' (CW 43 pp. 453-4)

22 May: Lenin writes to A M Kollontai in Oslo and criticises the 'Scandanavian petty bourgeois (who) tucked themselves away in their little countries' and who 'on the eve of the social revolution' are '*against* the arming of the people . . . How can one "recognise" the class struggle without understanding its inevitable transformation at certain moments into civil war?' (CW 35 pp. 198-90)

Beginning of June: Lenin and Krupskaya move to the little village of Sörenberg; they stay in the Hotel Marienthal and return only at the beginning of October to Berne. 'We were quite comfortable at Sörenberg; all around there were woods, high mountains and there was even snow on the peak of the Rothorn . . . It was possible to obtain free of charge any book from the Berne or Zürich libraries . . . Ilich had nothing but praise for the Swiss culture. It was very comfortable to work at Sörenberg.' (Krupskaya p. 264)

After 4 June: Lenin writes two letters to Inessa Armand from Sörenberg. He sends her instructions about how to get there and also wants to invite Karl Radek. Inessa Armand arrives in Sörenberg in June.

Between 19 June-5 July: Lenin, in a letter to Karl Radek, expresses his views on the appeal 'The Need of the Moment' by Kautsky, Bernstein and Haase: 'My opinion is that the "swing" by Kautsky + Bernstein + Co (+500+1, 000+??) is a swing of shit who have sensed the masses won't stand for it any longer, that it's "necessary" to make a turn to the left, in order to continue *swindling* the masses.' (CW 36 pp. 329-31) Lenin writes in the same vein to David Wijnkoop, the Dutch social democrat, and adds: 'And the truth is this: either one supports the revolutionary ferment which is beginning and assists it (for this one needs the watchword of revolution, of civil war, of illegal organisation, etc.) or one stifles it (for this one needs the watchword of peace, the "condemnation" of "annexation", maybe disarmament, etc., etc.). History will show that it is we who were right, i.e., the revolutionaries in general, not necessarily A or B.' (CW 35 pp. 191-2)

About 24 June: Lenin sends two letters to Zinoviev and addresses him as 'Dear Friend' and enquires whether he is coming to climb the Rothorn. (CW 43 pp. 456-7)

Before 4 July: G L Pyatakov, E F Rozmirovich and E B Bosh visit Lenin in Sörenberg; they discuss the publication of the journal *Kommunist*. He is greatly surprised that Zinoviev 'for no apparent reason' has not come to the meeting. (CW 43 pp. 458-9)

Between 11-26 July: Lenin writes to A M Kollontai that the left should make a common declaration, '1) unquestionably condemning the social chauvinists and opportunists 2) giving a programme of revolutionary action (whether to say civil war or revolutionary mass action, is not so important) 3) against the watchword of "defence of the fatherland", etc. A declaration of principle by the "left", in the name of several countries, would have a gigantic significance (of course not in the spirit of Zetkin philistinism which she got adopted at the Women's Conference at Berne).' (CW 35 pp. 193-4)

15 July: Lenin writes to Karl Radek: 'Either the German left will not unite (if only for a statement of *principle* on behalf of the *anonymous*

Stern group or whatever you like: the workers will later *join* this group) or we shall have to dismiss them from our minds.' (CW 36 pp. 332-3) In a letter to David Wijnkoop Lenin complains about the 'strange (to put it mildly) role of . . . Frau Clara Zetkin.' (CW 43 pp. 465-6)

After 24 July: Lenin writes to Zinoviev: 'Do you remember *Koba's* surname?' (CW 43 p. 469) Hence he has forgotten Stalin's name (Dzhugashvili). Lenin writes to David Wijnkoop: 'An exploited class which did not *strive* to possess arms, to know how to use them and to master the military art would be a class of lackeys.' Lenin sharply criticises Henriette Roland-Holst, the Dutch socialist. He does not seek the immediate split in this or that party; it is very possible that the time for this will be more favourable . . . somewhat later. He adds: 'But in *principle* we must unquestionably demand a complete break with opportunism.' (CW 35 pp. 195-7)

26 July: Two articles by Lenin, including 'The Defeat of One's Own Government in the Imperialist War' appears in *Sotsial Demokrat* no 43. (CW 21 pp. 275-80) Lenin makes it an 'axiom' that a revolutionary class during a reactionary war should hope for the defeat of its own government.

30 July: Lenin writes to David Wijnkoop: 'I am very glad that we agree on essentials. What we need is not the solemn declaration of leaders (against which Pannekoek has written so well), but the consistent, revolutionary declaration of principles to help the workers find the correct path. This is most essential.' (CW 43 p. 478)

Before 4 August: Lenin writes to Karl Radek and informs him that for him (Lenin) the *Lichtstrahlen* group around Julian Borchardt in Germany is 'more important' than 'Zetkin's [group].' The Borchardt group 'will play an outstanding part in world history.' (CW 35 pp. 334-6)

After 4 August: Lenin writes to Alexandra Kollontai: 'The essence of the thing today is the struggle between the Great Powers for the redivision of the colonies and the subjugation of the smaller powers.' (CW 35 pp. 200-1)

20 August: Lenin receives a mandate for the forthcoming Zimmerwald Conference from the Social Democratic Party of the Latvian Territory.

23 August: Lenin's article 'On the Slogan for a United States of Europe' appears in *Sotsial Demokrat* no 44. (CW 21 pp. 339-43) Lenin again takes up this theme because no agreement was reached on it at the Conference from 27 February–4 March. He states that the slogan is invulnerable, if accompanied by the overthrow of reactionary monarchies, but under present economic conditions a 'United States of Europe, under capitalism, is either impossible or reactionary . . . Uneven economic and political development is an absolute law of capitalism.' Therefore the 'victory of socialism is possible first in several or even in one capitalist country alone. After expropriating the capitalists and organising their own socialist production, the victorious proletariat of that country will rise *against* the rest of the world — the capitalist world — attracting to its cause the oppressed classes of other countries, stirring uprisings in those countries against the capitalists and in case of need using even armed force against the exploiting classes and their states.' The political forces of the victory of the proletariat 'will be a democratic republic'; the abolition of classes is impossible 'without a dictatorship of the oppressed class, of the proletariat.'

August: Lenin and Zinoviev writes the pamphlet 'Socialism and War (The Attitude of the RSDLP to the War)' and it is published in German in Geneva in September. (CW 21 pp. 295-338 — no mention is made here of Zinoviev as the co-author) First the attitude of socialists to war, ('barbarous and brutal'), is examined, the war is defined as 'imperialist' and 'social chauvinism' and 'Kautskyism' condemned. Finally the Russian situation is analysed and the creation of a 'Third International' on a 'revolutionary basis' is advocated.

3-4 September: Lenin travels from Sörenberg via Berne to Zimmerwald.

5-8 September: An International Conference, called on the initiative of the Socialist Party of Italy, meets at Zimmerwald. Among the 38 delegates from eleven countries, Lenin and Zinoviev represent the Bolsheviks, Axelrod and Martov the Mensheviks, and Trotsky is also present. German opponents of the war, including Ernst Meyer and Bertha Thalheimer of the Gruppe Internationale, make up the largest delegation. Lenin rallies around himself the Zimmerwald Left (Lenin, Zinoviev, Berzin, Radek, Borchardt, Höglund, Nerman, Platten). He proposes a draft resolution (CW 21 pp. 345-8) but it is rejected by 19 votes to 12. In it Lenin declares that the task is to 'turn the imperialist war between peoples into a civil war.' The Conference elects the International Socialist Commission (ISC) with headquarters in Berne. The left set up their own Bureau, headed by Lenin. Lenin gets through an immense amount of work at the Conference; he speaks on several questions and holds discussions with delegates. (CW 41 pp. 349-55)

8 or 9 September: Lenin returns to Sörenberg from Zimmerwald. 'The day after Ilich's arrival from Zimmerwald we climbed the Rothorn. We climbed with a "glorious appetite", but when we reached the summit, Ilich suddenly lay down on the ground, in an uncomfortable position almost in the snow, and fell asleep . . . Apparently Zimmerwald had frayed his nerves a good deal and had taken much strength out of him. It required several days of roaming over the mountains and the atmosphere of Sörenberg before Ilich was himself again.' (Krupskaya p. 267)

Between 8-13 September: Lenin writes to Alexandra Kollontai: 'We are very short of cash! That is the *main* trouble!' (CW 36 pp. 346-7)

11-12 September: Three articles by Lenin, including 'The Collapse of the Second International' appear in *Kommunist* (Communist) nos

1-2 in Geneva. (CW 21 pp. 205-59) He states that 'flagrant betrayal of their convictions and of the solemn Stuttgart and Basle resolutions by the majority of the official social democratic parties of Europe . . . signifies the complete victory of opportunism, the transformation of the social democratic parties into national liberal labour parties.' Lenin also defines a revolutionary situation, which exists when a crisis of the upper classes coincides with the 'suffering and want of the lower classes' and the crisis increases the activity of the masses.

Between 17-24 September: Lenin and Krupskaya go walking in the mountains, including the Rothorn.

19 September: Lenin writes to V A Karpinsky in Geneva and to M M Kharitonov in Zürich that he intends in October to give lectures to earn a little money. 'I am devilishly hard up.' (CW 43 p. 492) 'If the slogans are correct, if the tactics are the right ones, the mass of the working class, at a given stage of development of its revolutionary movement, is bound to *come round* to these slogans.' (CW 43 pp. 493-4)

24 September: Krupskaya writes to Lenin's mother: 'There are no changes here. We shall soon be returning to town. The mountains do one a lot of good. The thyroid trouble seems to have gone altogether. This last week we have been having magnificent weather and Volodya and I have been up all the nearby mountains.' (CW 37 pp. 622-3)

End of September–Beginning of October: Lenin writes the article 'The Defeat of Russia and the Revolutionary Crisis' (CW 21 pp. 378-82) first published in 1928. He states that the crisis in Russia, stemming from the bourgeois revolution, is linked to the socialist revolution of the West. 'This link is so direct that no individual solution of revolutionary [problems] is possible in any single country — the Russian bourgeois-democratic revolution is now not only a prologue to, but an indivisible part of, the socialist revolution in the West.'

Beginning of October: Lenin and Krupskaya return to Berne from Sörenberg.

7 October: Lenin writes to his mother: 'Nadya and I moved a few days ago to Berne.' They have returned earlier than planned because of the cold and the snow. 'We have found a nice room here with electricity and bath for 30 francs.' The new address is: Seidenweg 4a, Berne. (CW 37 pp. 526-7)

10 October: Lenin writes to A G Shlyapnikov: 'News from Russia testifies to the growing revolutionary mood and movement, though to all appearances this is not yet the beginning of the revolution.' (CW 35 pp. 208-9)

11 October: Lenin's articles 'The First Step' and 'Revolutionary Marxists and the International Socialist Conference, September 5-8, 1915' appear in *Sotsial Demokrat* no 45-46. (CW 21 pp. 383-93) These are analyses of the Zimmerwald Conference.

12 October: Lenin discusses with Karl Radek a plan to publish a theoretical organ of the Zimmerwald Left in Geneva.

18 October: Lenin and the Bureau of the Zimmerwald Left sign a circular, *Tsirkulyar* no 1. (Khr. III p. 401)

18 or 19 October: Lenin speaks in the Maison du Peuple in Lausanne on the International Socialist Conference in Zimmerwàld.

20 or 22 October: Lenin speaks in Geneva on the Zimmerwald Conference.

23 October: Lenin speaks in Zürich on the Zimmerwald Conference.

28 October: Lenin speaks in Geneva on imperialism and the sovereign rights of nations.

Before 9 November: Lenin speaks in Basle to students and émigrés on the war situation and the future of Russia.

20 November: Lenin's article 'On the Two Lines in the Revolution', directed against Plekhanov, and 'At the Uttermost Limit' appear in *Sotsial Demokrat* no 48. (CW 21 pp. 415-22) In the latter article, directed against Parvus, he states that the war has also its 'useful aspect.' Not 'only are its quick firing guns killing opportunism and anarchism but the war itself is stripping the mask off the adventurers and renegades of socialism.'

12 December: Lenin chairs a meeting called to prepare the 2nd International Conference at an unknown location. (Khr. III p. 417).

14 December: Krupskaya writes to Lenin's sister Maria: 'We shall soon be coming to the end of our former means of subsistence and the question of earning money will become a serious one. It is difficult to find anything here . . . I have to think about a literary income. I don't want that side of our affairs to be Volodya's worry alone. He works a lot as it is. The question of an income troubles him greatly.' Krupskaya asks Maria to find a publisher for her pamphlet 'The Elementary School and Democracy.' (CW 37 pp. 624-5)

1916

Beginning of January: Lenin writes a preface to Bukharin's pamphlet 'Imperialism and the World Economy'. (CW 22 pp. 103-7)

11 January: Lenin writes to Gorky in Petrograd that he is just beginning work 'on a pamphlet about imperialism.' Owing to wartime conditions he is 'in extreme need of earnings' and is sending a pamphlet 'New Data on the Laws Governing the Development of Capitalism in Agriculture'. (CW 22 pp. 13-102) He asks Gorky to 'speed up' its publication. (CW 35 p. 212)

15 January: Lenin discusses with the Bureau of the Zimmerwald Left and with Dutch left socialists the publication of the journal *Vorbote* (Herald). Lenin writes to Inessa Armand who is staying in Paris at his behest: 'After influenza my wife and I took our first walk along the road to Frauen-Kapellen where the three of us – you remember? – had that lovely stroll one day. I keep thinking about it and was sorry you were not here.' (CW 43 pp. 504-5)

Mid January: Lenin applies in Berne for an extension of his residence permit without having to pay the usual 200 francs. He refers to the 'abnormally poor rate of exchange' of the Russian rouble. 'One is happy in such circumstances to be able to get through each day decently and there is just no money over to make such a payment.' (Gautschi p. 100)

19 January: Lenin writes to Inessa Armand: 'As a matter of fact I have been worrying for several days now at the absence of any news from you. The weather is wonderful. Last Sunday we went for a lovely walk up "our" little mountain. The view of the Alps was very beautiful. I was so sorry you were not there with us.' (CW 43 pp. 505-6)

21 January: Lenin writes, in a letter to Inessa Armand, that he has finally received her letter. Trotsky does not want to write for *Vorbote*. 'It looks like there is no avoiding a fight with Trotsky even on this question.' (CW 43 p. 507)

After 25 January: Lenin's article, written in Geneva, 'Opportunism and the Collapse of the Second International' appears in *Vorbote* no 1, the organ of the Zimmerwald Left. (CW 22 pp. 108-20) To Lenin the war is 'imperialist', defence of the fatherland is 'social chauvinism' and 'opportunism in its finished form.' He condemns 'prostituted "Marxism" à la Kautsky.'

27 January: Lenin writes to M M Kharitonov in Zürich that he and Krupskaya wish to spend 2-3 weeks working in Zürich libraries and are looking for cheap accommodation. He enquires what 'net income can there be (i.e. for me) from a lecture?' (CW 36 p. 365)

After 1 February: Lenin writes to Karl Radek that he considers that 'our joint struggle in Russia and Polish affairs is *ruled out*' but 'joint actions in Switzerland' are possible. (CW 43 p. 509)

5-9 February: A meeting of the International Socialist Commission takes place in Berne during which a new Conference of the Zimmerwald Left is prepared. Lenin attends the meeting in the Volkshaus on 6 February.

Before 8 February: Lenin writes to Maxim Gorky and asks him to help get Krupskaya's pamphlet 'The Elementary School and Democracy' published. (CW 36 p. 367)

8 February: Lenin speaks in the Volkshaus in Berne at an international meeting on the imperialist war and the tasks of the proletariat. (CW 22 pp. 123-6) It is Lenin's first speech at a public meeting in Switzerland. He states that the sacrifices are not in vain; the strikes and demonstrations are an earnest of the 'proletarian revolution against capitalism that is bound to follow the European war.'

10 or 11 February: Lenin and Krupskaya move from Berne to Zürich and rent a room from Frau Prelog, Geigergasse 7 where for a time after they leave they have their meals. 'Ilich liked the simplicity of the service, the fact that coffee was served in a cup with a broken handle, that we ate in the kitchen, that the conversation was simple. We very soon realised that we had hit upon a peculiar environment, the very "lower depths" of Zürich.' (Krupskaya p. 271) Lenin works in the Zürich libraries on his pamphlet on imperialism. Originally he had intended to spend only a few weeks, then return to Berne, but it turned out quite differently.

After 11 February: Lenin meets Willi Münzenberg in Zürich; he gives Münzenberg advice concerning his work for the journals *Freie Jugend* (Free Youth) and *Jugendinternationale* (Youth International).

13 February: Lenin writes to S N Ravich in Geneva: 'Please write and tell me when it will be possible to give a lecture in Geneva and whether the cost can be covered. How much will it yield net, as a minimum? I have to know this because I am very short of money.' (CW 36 p. 368)

After 16 February: Lenin and Krupskaya move to another flat in the house of a shoemaker called Kammerer, Spiegelgasse 14. They live here until April 1917. Lenin visits Fritz Platten and Frida Rubiner, among others.

17 February: Lenin speaks in the building of the social democratic club in Zürich, before an audience of 130, on the two Internationals.

20 February: Lenin writes to his sister Maria in Moscow: 'Nadya and I are very pleased with Zürich; there are good libraries here.' (CW 37 p. 528)

26 February: Lenin writes to Inessa Armand in Paris that only Otto Rühle and the 'international socialists of Germany' are unequivocally for a split, the majority of the Gruppe Internationale (Spartakus) are 'clearly turning back to the marsh.' (CW 43 pp. 510–11)

1 March: Lenin lectures in Geneva to an audience of 200 on the peace conditions in connection with the national question.

8 March: Lenin writes to Henriette Roland-Holst that the Gruppe Internationale wishes to come to an agreement with the Kautskyites. 'We are not pacifists, are we? We cannot count on a victory simultaneously all over the world (without civil wars? without wars?)! . . . The labour movement needs clear views on the necessity of breaking with the social chauvinists and Kautskyites, on the illegal organisation.' (CW 43 pp. 513–6)

After 11 March: Lenin writes to A G Shlyapnikov that the split is now the 'basic question'; any compromise here would be a 'crime.' Lenin proposes to stop publication of the journal *Kommunist* since Pyatakov and Bukharin are unstable. (CW 35 pp. 213–7)

12 March: Lenin writes to his mother in Petrograd: 'We like the lake here very much and the libraries are much better than those in Berne so we shall probably stay here longer than we had intended.' (CW 37 p. 529)

After 19 March: Lenin writes to Alexandra Kollontai in Oslo: 'I am very distressed that we do not see eye to eye on self-determination. Let's try to argue this out in detail *without a squabble*.' (CW 36 pp. 375-6)

25 March: Lenin's article 'The Peace Programme' appears in *Sotsial Demokrat* no 52. (CW 22 pp. 161-8) He writes: 'War is the continuation, by violent means, of the policies pursued by the ruling classes of the belligerent powers long before the outbreak of war.' Those who promise the nations a 'democratic' peace 'without at the same time preaching the socialist revolution' deceive the proletariat.

5 April: Lenin lectures in Zürich on the immediate tasks of Russian social democrats.

7 April: Lenin attends Wagner's *Die Walküre* in the Stadttheater in Zürich.

Before 18 April: Lenin writes to Grigory Zinoviev in Berne that he is a 'bit uncertain' whether he should go to the Conference (Kienthal) since he has no mandate. 'I may be turned away for all I know.' He concerns himself with the security of Paul Frölich, the German social democrat, in Berne, and states that meetings of the left are needed. Lenin thinks that the supporters of Georg Ledebour (SPD) would 'probably mess up the *whole* Conference.' (CW 43 pp. 531-2)

18 April: Lenin, in a letter to Grigory Zinoviev, writes: 'My present finances are not altogether hopeless: whence these "false rumours"??' (CW 43 pp. 533-4)

24-30 April: The 2nd International Socialist Conference meets in Kienthal. The Zimmerwald Left, led by Lenin, accounts for 12 delegates, including the Bolshevik delegation of Lenin, Zinoviev and Inessa Armand, out of 43. Ernst Meyer and Bertha Thalheimer represent the Gruppe Internationale and Paul Frölich the Bremen left radicals. There are violent disputes and Lenin speaks eight times but does not succeed in winning over the majority to his point of view. (compare CW 22 pp. 169-79, CW 36 377-87 and CW 41 pp. 369-80). In a letter to A G Shlyapnikov, written between 6-13 May, Lenin analyses the Conference. 'After all, a manifesto was adopted; that is a step forward . . . On the whole, this is *none the less*, despute the mass of defects, a step towards a break with the social patriots. This time the Left was stronger: a Serb, three Swiss and a Frenchman . . . reinforced our Left. Then there were two Germans [from the Gruppe Internationale] who supported us on the main questions.' (CW 36 pp. 390-1)

Beginning of May: *Vorbote* no 2 appears containing Lenin's article 'The Socialist Revolution and the Right of Nations to Self-Determination'. (CW 22 pp. 143-56) The theses are directed at Karl Radek, Nikolai Bukharin and others who reject the right of national self-determination, something that Lenin defends. He links the socialist revolution with democracy: 'The socialist revolution is not a single act . . . but a whole

epoch of the acute class conflicts . . . there can be no victorious socialism that does not practise full democracy, so the proletariat cannot
prepare for its victory over the bourgeoisie without an all-round,
consistent and revolutionary struggle for democracy.' Lenin underlines
the significance of national self-determination and quotes Marx: 'No
nation can be free if it oppresses other nations.'

11 May: Lenin writes to Shklovsky: 'I have a slight attack of the flu but
it is passing.' (Briefe IV p. 218)

21 May: In a long letter to Grigory Zinoviev in Berne, Lenin continues
his correspondence with him on co-operation with other groups,
especially Bukharin–Pyatakov. 'I don't want to turn our correspondence into an altercation.' He points out that 'at Kienthal Radek
wanted to build up a majority against us among the Left, at the meeting
of the Left, making use of Frölich, the Robmann woman, etc. and that
an *ultimatum* was required to force him to recognise the *independence*
of our Central Committee.' (CW 35 pp. 218–22)

21–22 May: An official of the Zürich police administration confirms in
a report the 'recipt of the request of V Ulyanov dated 18 April' for a
residence permit to allow him and his wife to work on a book in the
local library. Oskar Lange and Fritz Platten, both city councillors, stand
surety. Permission is granted. (Khr. III p. 503)

After 24 May: Lenin, in a letter to N I Bukharin, asks if the Stockholm
police have any interest in him.

31 May or 1 June: Lenin leaves Zürich to lecture in Lausanne and
Geneva. He speaks on two currents in the international labour movement.

4 June: Lenin, in a letter to V A Karpinsky and S N Ravich, writes: 'I
received a lot of money for my previous lecture, less for this one; but
nevertheless I have received *more* money that I need for normal day-
to-day expenses.' He insists that the two comrades accept the money
that he wants to give them for lunches and so on. (Briefe IV p. 238)
In a letter to A G Shlyapnikov Lenin pillories the 'Japanese', i.e. Radek,
Bukharin, Bosh; they are engaging in 'intrigue' and their 'purse is full.'
(CW 36 pp. 401–2)

Mid June: Lenin writes to Inessa Armand in Berne that 'it would be
extremely useful for the cause if you could spend a few months in
Sweden or Norway.' (Briefe IV p. 241)

27 June: Lenin writes to Sophia Ravich and asks her to get a passport
for Inessa Armand. On 4 July he writes to Inessa Armand: 'Nadya says
none of her passports is any good.' (CW 43 pp. 544–5)

2 July: Lenin finishes work on 'Imperialism, the Highest Stage of
Capitalism: A Popular Outline'. (CW 22 pp. 185–304) In his chief work
on political economy Lenin attempts to develop further the Marxist
analysis of capitalism. His theory of imperialism originates in his
research on the capitalist world economy and its interrelation before

the First World War. When Lenin analyses economic development or imperialism he bases himself on the work of Hobson and Hilferding but his conclusions go much further. Lenin defines the capitalism of the twentieth century, because of its internal structure, as monopoly capitalism and because of its external political effect as imperialism, and historically as decaying capitalism, as 'capitalism in transition, as moribund capitalism.' On 2 July he sends the manuscript to M N Pokrovsky and the first edition of the pamphlet is published in a very truncated form in mid-1917 by the *Parus* (Sail) publishing house. He writes to Pokrovsky: 'I strove with all my might to adapt myself to the "restrictions". It's terribly difficult for me and I feel there is a great deal of unevenness on account of this. But it can't be helped!' (CW 35 pp. 226-7)

4 July: Lenin writes to Inessa Armand that 'nobody now is allowed passage' through Germany. 'Very sad!' (CW 43 pp. 545-6)

7 July: Lenin writes to Inessa Armand that Krupskaya's health 'is poor.' He tells her that he 'wrote to Malinovsky once.' The former CC member and police agent (compare May 1914) is now a prisoner-of-war, held by the Germans. (CW 43 p. 547)

21 July: Lenin and Krupskaya have moved to the Pension Tschudiwiese on Mount Flums. Lenin writes to Grigory Zinoviev: 'There is only one thing bad about this place; the post is only brought by donkey and even then only once a day.' (Briefe IV p. 260) According to Maurice Pianzola *Lenin in der Schweiz* p. 118 Lenin and Krupskaya arrive at Tschudiwiese only on 14 August; before that they stay in Bex, in the Waadtländer Alps, in a wooden hut. Since letters are sent from Flums from 21 July this appears to be improbable. Krupskaya writes later: 'We went for six weeks to the canton of St Gallen, not far from Zürich, to the Tschudiwiese rest home amidst wild mountains, very high up and not far from the snow peaks. The pension was quite inexpensive, two and a half francs a day per person. It is true, it was a resort where they kept one on a milk diet. In the morning they served coffee with milk, bread and butter and cheese, but they gave us no sugar; for lunch — milk soup, sometimes made of cheese curds and milk . . . During the first first days we positively howled against this milk cure, then we began to supplement it by eating raspberries and blackberries which grew in the vicinity in great quantities. Our room was clean, with electric light, but without service; we had to tidy up the room ourselves and clean our own shoes. The latter function was assumed, emulating the Swiss, by Vladimir Ilich, and every morning he would take my mountain shoes and go to the shed set aside for the purpose, exchanging pleasantries with the other boot-blacks and displaying such zeal that he once knocked down a wicker basket full of empty beer bottles, to the accompaniment of general laughter . . . Among the visitors in the house was a soldier . . . Vladimir Ilich hovered about him like a cat after lard, tried several times to engage him in a conversation about the predatory nature of the war; the fellow was ... clearly not interested ... No one came to visit us ... and we were detached from all affairs, roaming the mountain for days on end. In Tschudiwiese Ilich did not work at all. During our walks in the mountains he spoke a good deal about the questions that occupied his mind at that time, about the role of democracy.' (Krupskaya pp. 278-9)

25 July: Lenin's mother, Maria Aleksandrovna Ulyanova, dies in Petrograd.

After 26 July: Lenin writes to Zinoviev in Hertenstein, Switzerland and sends him his article on the Junius pamphlet, written by Rosa Luxemburg.

5 August: Lenin writes from Flums to Shklovsky in Berne telling him to request after all the return of the 100 francs caution money from the police.

Between 5-31 August: Lenin writes to M N Pokrovsky that the ridiculous and incredible loss' of the manuscript of his pamphlet on imperialism had made him very 'scared'. However printing takes place later from another copy. (CW 43 p. 557)

23 August: Lenin writes from Flums to Grigory Zinoviev in Hertenstein that the *Leipziger Volkszeitung* has been banned (it appears a few days later), 'now I am without a German newspaper ... Could you perhaps send me every other day ... the *Hamburger Echo* when you have finished reading it?' Lenin also writes that he is waiting for 'a letter from Malinovsky.' (Briefe IV p. 279)

Between 27-31 August: Lenin writes to Zinoviev: 'May one print the material on the prisoners-of-war? Will it not harm them? (compare Malinovsky's letter).' Hence he has received mail from Malinovsky (compare 7 July). (Briefe IV p. 279)

End of August–Beginning of September: Lenin writes from Flums to N I Bukharin in Oslo that the latter's article 'On the Theory of the Imperialist State' cannot be printed. (In letters to Zinoviev Lenin attacks the article vehemently). Lenin takes umbrage at Bukharin's definition of Marxism as 'a "sociological" (???) "theory of the state".' The question marks are Lenin's. He states that Bukharin has incorrectly defined 'the distinction between the Marxists and the anarchists on the question of the state.' (CW 35 pp. 230-1)

First half of September: Lenin and Krupskaya return to Zürich from Flums. The first letters from Zürich to Inessa Armand and Grigory Zinoviev are dated 15 September.

Between 15 September–5 October: Lenin writes from Zürich to Zinoviev in Hertenstein and advises him to 'reply more kindly to him [Bukharin]; for the present we have no reason to be angry' with him. (Briefe IV p. 293)

19 September: Lenin's sister Maria informs him of the arrest of his sister Anna in Russia.

20 September: Lenin writes to his brother-in-law, Mark Elizarov that he is horrified at the arrest of his sister Anna. 'Many thanks to Manyasha [Maria] for taking so much trouble over the publishers; I shall get down to writing something or other because prices have risen so hellishly that life has become devilishly difficult.' (CW 37 p. 530)

5 October: In a long letter to A G Shlyapnikov in Stockholm, Lenin writes: 'The main thing now, I think, is to publish popular leaflets and manifestos against tsarism . . . The most pressing question now is the weakness of the contacts between us and leading workers in Russia!! No correspondence!!' Lenin sees a split 'on an international scale' with the Second International as timely, and expresses support for the setting up of a 'a Third International *only* against the Kautskyites of all countries' based on the stand of the Zimmerwald Left. About his own situation Lenin says: 'As regards myself personally, I will say that I need to earn. Otherwise we shall simply die of hunger, really and truly!! The cost of living is devilishly high and there is nothing to live on.' (CW 35 pp. 232-6 Khr. III p. 554)

8 October: Lenin writes to Paul Levi but the letter has not yet come to light. (Khr. III p. 556)

22 October: Lenin writes to his sister Maria in Petrograd and asks if the new publisher has received his manuscript of the pamphlet on imperialism. 'I have not received the 500 roubles but shall receive them in a day or two, of course. I do not think it is an advance but payment for the manuscript received.' (CW 37 pp. 531-2)

25 October: Lenin writes to Franz Koritschoner in Vienna that Friedrich Adler's assassination of Karl Stürgkh, the Austrian Prime Minister, was 'the act of despair of a Kautskyite'. But 'we revolutionaries cannot fall into despair. We are not afraid of a split. On the contrary, we recognise the necessity of a split.' (CW 35 pp. 237-9)

October: During October Lenin completes the article which he had begun in August, 'A Caricature of Marxism and Imperialist Economism'. (CW 23 pp. 28-76) It is directed against Pyatakov's theses on imperialism. Lenin writes that for many the word 'imperialism' has become all the rage; they have 'memorised the word' and confused the workers. Lenin reproaches Pyatakov for having confused the economic substance of imperialism with its political tendencies. Lenin comes up with the remarkable view that 'socialism is impossible without democracy because 1) the proletariat cannot perform the socialist revolution unless it prepares for it by the struggle for democracy 2) victorious socialism cannot consolidate its victory and bring humanity to the withering away of the state without implementing full democracy.' On "the road to socialism", Lenin writes: 'All nations will arrive at socialism — this is inevitable, but all will not do so exactly the same way; each will contribute something of its own to some form of democracy, to some variety of the dictatorship of the proletariat, to the varying rate of socialist transformation of the different aspects of social life. There is nothing more primitive from the point of view of theory or more ridiculous from that of practice, than to paint, "in the name of historical materialism", *this* aspect of the future in a monotonous grey.'

October–November: Lenin's articles 'The Junius Pamphlet' and 'The Discussion on Self-Determination Summed up' appear in *Sbornik Sotsial-Demokrata* (Volume of Social Democrat) no 1. (CW 22 pp. 305-60) The article directed against Rosa Luxemburg under the pseudonym of Junius, and her pamphlet 'The Crisis of Social Democracy' was written in 1916. To Lenin opportunism and social chauvinism belong together, they are sociologically products of the labour aristocracy. This leads to his proposal to split the Party immediately. Lenin criticises Junius for not taking this view. 'A very great defeat in revolutionary Marxism in Germany as a whole is its lack of a compact illegal organisation.' Lenin criticises the Gruppe Internationale and maintains that Borchardt's International Socialists of Germany (ISD) 'clearly and definitely' remain at their post. However first and foremost Lenin makes clear the differences on the national question and defends the right of national self-determination against Rosa Luxemburg. This theme is also taken up in the latter article which is directed against Polish social democrats, especially Karl Radek. 'If we do not wish to abandon socialism then we *must* support *every* uprising against our main enemy, the bourgeoisie of the Great Powers, when it is not an uprising of a reactionary class.' Elsewhere he elucidates Engels and states: 'An economic revolution will be a stimulus to *all* peoples to *strive* for socialism: but at the same time revolutions – against the socialist state – and wars are possible . . . Engels mentions as "certain" only one, absolutely internationalist principle, and this he applies to *all* "foreign nations", i.e. not to colonial nations only; to force a blessing upon them would mean to undermine the victory of the proletariat.'

3 November: Lenin attends a meeting of left delegates to the Swiss Social Democratic Congress. He writes, on 9 November, to Inessa Armand: '. . . on Friday evening we arranged a meeting of the left (during which Radek and I were completely in agreement) and adopted (after we had nominated a commission) a resolution on Kienthal. Platten, Nobs, Münzenberg and a few others, i.e. *all* leaders of the left were present.' (Briefe IV p. 319)

4 November: Lenin, in the name of the CC, RSDLP, greets the Congress of the Social Democratic Party of Switzerland. (CW 23 pp. 121-4)

After 5 November: Lenin, in a letter to N D Kiknadze, writes: 'Marxism takes it stand on the facts and not the possibilities. A Marxist must, as the foundation of his policy, put *only* precisely and unquestionably demonstrated *facts*.' (CW 35 pp. 242-5)

6 November: Lenin's articles 'A Separate Peace' and 'Ten "Socialist" Ministers' appear in *Sotsial Demokrat* no 56. (CW 23 pp. 125–36) Lenin states in the former article that England is waging war to 'rob Germany of her colonies and to ruin her principal competitor'. Germany is fighting 'because her capitalists consider themselves – and rightly so – entitled to the "sacred" bourgeois right to world supremacy in looting and plundering colonies and dependent countries.' Russia is waging war 'for Galicia' and to conquer 'Armenia and specially Constantinople.' Tsarism has been striving to 'conquer Constantinople and a larger and larger part of Asia . . . Whatever the outcome of the present war, those who maintained that the only possible socialist way out of it is through civil war by the proletariat for socialism, will have been proved correct. The Russian social democrats who maintained that the defeat of Tsarism . . . is . . . the lesser evil, will have been proved correct.'

26 November: Lenin writes to his sister Maria: 'There have been no changes here. Prices are rising more than ever.' He has no Russian newspapers and asks her to send those she has already read. (CW 37 pp. 533–4)

30 November: Lenin sends a long letter to Inessa Armand at Clarens, Switzerland. He writes that the whole spirit of Marxism demands that each proposition should be considered only historically, only in connection with others, 'only in connection with the concrete experience of history'. He calls Radek who has squeezed him off the editorial board of *Vorbote*, 'impudent, insolent, stupid'. After further attacks on Radek, Lenin writes: 'Anyone who *forgives* such things in politics I consider a donkey or a scroundel. *I shall never forgive him*. For such things you punch a man's face or turn away.' The debate on self-determination is just beginning. 'To grant "equality" to little pigs and fools – never!' He will not allow his 'hands to be tied in politics'. Finally Lenin apologies for the length of the letter and for 'the abundance of sharp words: I can't write otherwise when I am speaking frankly. Well, after all, This is all *entre nous*, and perhaps the unnecessary bad language will pass.' (CW 35 pp. 250-5)

17 December: Lenin writes to Inessa Armand that 'something in the nature of a circle of left-wingers has been formed' in Zürich to which 'Nobs, Platten, Münzenberg and several others of the Young' group belong. (CW 43 pp. 587–8) Lenin devotes himself more intensively to work among Swiss social democrats at this time.

18 December: Lenin writes to Inessa Armand that his manuscript on imperialism has arrived in Petrograd but the publisher, 'and this is Gorky, oh the calf!', is dissatisfied with the attacks on Kautsky. 'Both laughable and disappointing. There it is, my fate. One fighting campaign after another – against political stupidities, philistinism, opportunism and so forth. It has been going on since 1893. And so has the hatred of the philistines on account of it. But still I would not exchange this fate for "peace" with the philistines.' (CW 35 pp. 259-61)

After 23 December: Lenin writes to Inessa Armand that he is happy
that she has had a talk with Paul Levi and Henri Guilbeaux and says
that it would be a good thing to do so more often. 'How stupid that
Levi is attacking parliamentarism!! Stupid!! And a "Left" too!! God,
how much muddle there is in people's heads.' (CW 35 pp. 264-5)
25 December: Lenin writes to Inessa Armand: 'One should know how
to *combine* the struggle for democracy and the struggle for the socialist
revolution, *subordinating* the first to the second.' He defends Engels:
'In my day I have seen an awful lot of hasty charges that Engels was an
opportunist and my attitude to them is supremely distrustful. Try, I
say, and prove first that Engels was wrong!! You won't prove it!'
Engels and Marx are '*not* infallible but if you want to point out their
"fallibility" you have to set about it differently, really, quite differently.' (CW 35 pp. 266-9)
28 December: Lenin applies for an extension, until 31 December 1917,
to his residence permit in Zürich; he deposits a 'savings book containing
100 francs' as surety. (Khr III p. 583)
December: Several articles by Lenin, including 'Imperialism and the
Split in Socialism' appear in *Sbornik Sotsial-Demokrata* no 2. (CW 23
pp. 105-20) In it Lenin bases himself, to a large extent, on the material
and conclusions of his pamphlet on imperialism; he lays greatest
emphasis on the elaboration of his thesis on the appearance of 'a labour
aristocracy' as a consequence of imperialism and the carrier of opportunism in the labour movement. Every imperialist Great Power can 'and
does bribe *smaller* strata . . . of the labour aristocracy.' To Lenin therefore the 'bourgeois labour party', representing this labour aristocracy,
is 'inevitable and typical for all imperialist countries.' In his article
'The Youth International: A Review' (CW 23 pp. 163-6), Lenin
analyses the journal of the same name which has been appearing since
September 1915. He regards it as the 'organ of seething, turbulent,
inquiring youth', an organ which '*still* lacks theoretical clarity and
consistency'. Adults often do not know how to go about approaching
youth 'for youth must, of necessity, advance to socialism *in a different
way, in other forms, in other circumstances* than their fathers.' He
is strongly in favour of the organisational independence of the Youth
League. This includes also 'complete freedom of comradely criticism
of their errors. We must not flatter youth.' In his article 'The "Disarmament" Slogan' (CW 23 pp. 94-104) Lenin calls disarmament 'the ideal
of socialism'. Only under socialism will wars cease and disarmament
be possible. 'But whoever expects that socialism will be achieved
without a social revolution and the dictatorship of the proletariat is not
a socialist. Dictatorship is state power based directly on *violence*. And
in the twentieth century . . . violence means neither a fist nor a club but
troops.' Lenin also states: 'We are by no means opposed to the fight for
reforms. And we do not wish to ignore the sad possibility – if the worst

comes to the worst — of mankind going through a second imperialist war, if revolution does not come out of the present war . . . We favour a programme of reforms directed *also* against the opportunists.'

End of 1916: 'In the autumn of 1916 and the beginning of 1917 Ilich steeped himself in theoretical work. He tried to utilise all the time the library was open. He got there at exactly 9 o'clock, stayed until 12 . . . after lunch he returned to the library and stayed there until 6 o'clock. It was not very convenient to work at home . . . the windows faced a yard from which came an intolerable stench, for a sausage factory adjoined it . . . On Thursdays, after lunch, when the library was closed, we went to the Zürichberg mountain. On his way home from the library Lenin usually bought two bars of nut chocolate, in blue wrappers, at 15 centimes a piece, and after lunch we took the chocolate and some books and went to the mountain. We had a favourite spot there in the very thick of the woods, where there was no crowd. Ilich would lie there on the grass and read diligently. At the same time we instituted a doubly rigid economy in our personal life. Ilich searched everywhere in an effort to earn something.' (Krupskaya p. 284)

1917

4 January: Lenin fills in a Zürich authorities' questionnaire and writes that he is engaged on 'literary and journalistic work for a Petrograd publisher', that he possesses no fortune and is not 'a deserter, not a refracteur but a political émigré since the revolution of 1905'. (Gautschi p. 180)

6 January: Lenin writes to Inessa Armand: 'We need 1) translators 2) more money. So far we have neither.' The question whether Lenin, through various channels, obtained money from German sources is still a matter for dispute and cannot be answered definitely. (Compare 30 March, 31 March–4 April, 25 April and 4 May 1917). Russian émigrés had manifold contacts and it is likely that German money, through various channels, also went to the Bolsheviks. As well, the German imperial government disbursed 40–80 million marks for subversive activity in Russia. However 'one cannot demonstrate that Lenin had direct contacts with the German authorities in Switzerland before mid March 1917 and even his indirect contacts are inconclusive'. (Gautschi p. 175)

14 January: Lenin writes to Inessa Armand: 'Believe me, absorbing work is most important and soothing for health and mind!' (CW 43 pp. 599–601)

15 January: Lenin informs Inessa Armand that a Conference on 'the anti-Grimm protest' has just ended; it was attended by a German from Gruppe Internationale [Paul Levi]. Lenin would like her to 'take a change of air . . . I would dearly love to say a lot of kind words to you to make things easier for you until you get into your stride with work that will engross you completely.' (CW 43 pp. 601-2)

16 January: Lenin, in a letter to Inessa Armand, develops the following plan: 'If Switzerland is drawn into the war, the French will occupy Geneva immediately. To be in Geneva then is to be in France, and from there, to be in touch with Russia. I am therefore thinking of turning over the *Party* funds to you (For you to keep *on your person*, sewed up in a special little bag).' (CW 43 p. 603)

19 January: Lenin writes to Inessa Armand: 'Engels was the father of "passive radicalism"?? Untrue! Nothing of the kind. You will never be able to prove this. (Bogdanov and Co tried but disgraced themselves).' (CW 35 pp. 272-4)

22 January: Lenin lectures on the revolution of 1905 in German at a youth rally in the Volkshaus in Zürich. (CW 23 pp. 236-53) He stresses that one should 'not be deceived by the present grave-like stillness in Europe'. Europe is 'pregnant with revolution'. On the date of the outbreak of the revolution Lenin is, however, less optimistic. 'We of the older generation may not to see the decisive battle of the coming revolution. But I can, I believe, express the confident hope that the youth which is working so splendidly in the socialist movement of Switzerland, and of the whole world, will be fortunate enough not only to fight, but also to win, in the coming proletarian revolution.'

30 January: Lenin, in a letter to Inessa Armand, writes: 'I am still "in love" with Marx and Engels and cannot calmly stand any abuse of them. No, these were real people! We must learn from them. We must not leave that basis.' (CW 35 pp. 279-81)

1 February: In Olten Lenin meets representatives of the Zimmerwald Union, including Radek, Levi and Münzenberg.

6 February: Lenin attends the General Meeting of Zürich social democrats.

14 February: Lenin writes to Inessa Armand that 'there is ground in the Swiss party for building up a *left trend*.' (CW 43 pp. 610-11)

15 February: Lenin writes to his sister Maria that he has received 808 francs and 500 francs and does not know 'what money this is'. He wants to keep an account of what the publisher has paid for and what he has not. 'Nadya [Krupskaya] says jokingly that I must have been "pensioned off". Ha, ha! The joke is a merry one, for the cost of living makes one despair and I have desperately little capacity for work because of my shattered nerves.' (CW 37 pp. 535-6)

17 February: Lenin writes to Inessa Armand that it is 'depressing' news that Trotsky has joined a bloc with the Zimmerwald Right. 'Trotsky is such a rascal, left phrases and a bloc with the Right against the Zimmerwald Left!!' (Briefe IV p. 385)

19 February: Lenin writes to Inessa Armand: 'I have been putting in a lot of study recently on the question of the attitude of Marxism to the *state*. I have collected a lot of material and arrived, it seems to me, at very interesting and important conclusions . . . I would terribly much like to write about this . . . Nadya is ill; she has caught bronchitis and has a temperature.' (CW 35 pp. 288-9)

22 February: Lenin, in a letter to Inessa Armand, writes: 'It is only worth working with youth.' Krupskaya is well again. (Briefe IV p. 391)

8 March: Lenin, in a letter to Inessa Armand, complains that things are going badly in Zürich for the German left. 'After Nobs and Platten crossed "back to Grimm" the leaders of the Young tagged along behind them. Münzenburg *turned down* Radek's article against Grimm; Bucher and the other friends of Münzenberg repeat the same phrases about the danger of a "split"!! It would be funny were it not so disgusting!' He envies Inessa and Zinoviev who 'have fresh people in front' of them when they lecture in public. To his 'theoretical understanding of the rottenness of the European parties has now been added a *practical* understanding of some use'. (CW 43 pp. 614-5)

12 March: The February Revolution begins in Russia — 27 February according to the Julian calendar. Tsarism is overthrown.

13 March: Lenin writes to Inessa Armand: 'From Russia — nothing, not even letters!! We are making arrangements via Scandanavia.' (CW 43 pp. 615-6)

15 March: The first news of the revolution in Russia reaches Lenin in Zürich. 'But once, after lunch, when Ilich was getting ready to leave for the library and I had finished the dishes, Bronski ran in with the announcement, "Haven't you heard the news? There is a revolution in Russia!" and told us what was written in the special editions of the newspapers that were issued . . . We read the telegrams over several times . . . Ilich's mind worked intensely . . . Ilich immediately took a clear, uncompromising line but he had not yet grasped the scope of the revolution.' (Krupskaya pp. 286-7) Lenin writes to Inessa Armand: 'We here in Zürich are in a state of agitation today . . . I am *beside* myself that I cannot go to Scandanavia!! I will not forgive myself for not risking the journey in 1915.' (CW 35 p. 294)

16 March: Lenin writes to A M Kollontai in Oslo that the revolution will not be confined to Russia. 'Of course we shall continue to be against defence of the fatherland, against the imperialist slaughter . . . All our slogans remain the same.' (CW 35 pp. 295-6)

17 March: Lenin develops, with Zinoviev, the 'Draft Theses, March 4 (17), 1917'. (CW 23 pp. 287-91) According to the theses the new government cannot give peace or freedom or bread to the masses; the 'ideological and organisational independence' of the Party, the formation of the Soviets, the arming of the workers are therefore necessary to ensure 'victory in the next stage of the revolution'. Lenin writes to Alexandra Kollontai that it is almost ironical that he should provide directions from Zürich when he has very little news. 'We are afraid that it will be some time before we succeed in leaving accursed Switzerland.' (CW 35 pp. 297-9)

18 March: Lenin lectures in La Chaux-de-Fonds on the Paris Commune and the outlook for the Russian revolution. He writes to Inessa Armand: 'We are all dreaming of leaving. If you are going home drop in to see us first. We'll have a talk. I would very much like you to find out for me in England discreetly whether I would be granted passage.' (CW 43 p. 616)

19 March: Lenin writes to V A Karpinsky in Geneva that the latter should procure papers for a journey to France and England and 'I will *use them* to travel through England (and *Holland*) to Russia.' Lenin wants a photograph to be taken of himself wearing a wig. (CW 35 p. 300) Lenin writes to Inessa Armand that he is convinced that he would be arrested in England if he travelled under his own name. 'My nerves naturally are overstrung. No wonder! To have to sit here on tenterhooks.' He develops for the first time a plan through 'Russian social patriots' to obtain permission from the German authorities to allow the passage of 'a railway coach to Copenhagen for various revolutionaries'. He continues: 'Why not? I cannot do it. I am a "defeatist".' He wagers that the Germans will provide a railway coach. 'Of course, if they get to know that this idea comes *from me* or from *you*, the thing will be ruined. Are there any fools in Geneva for this purpose?' (CW 43 pp. 616-8)

After 19 March: Lenin writes to V A Karpinsky that 'Martov's plan is a good one'; he actually means his own plan to travel through Germany. 'We cannot take part, either directly or indirectly, our participation will *spoil* it all. But the plan, in itself, is a very *good* one and is *very* right.' (CW 36 p. 420)

20 March: Lenin writes the first of his five 'Letters from Afar' (CW 23 pp. 295-342) which appears in *Pravda* in Petrograd on 3 and 4 April. The others are published for the first time in 1924. In the fifth letter he summarises his main theses: 'The revolutionary proletariat must 1) find the surest road to the next stage of the revolution, or to the second revolution, which 2) must transfer political power from the government of the landlords and capitalists . . . to a government of the workers and the poorest peasants. 3) This latter government must be organised on the model of the Soviets of Workers' and Peasants' Deputies, namely 4) it must smash, completely eliminate, the old state machine, the army, the police force and bureaucracy (officialdom) that is common to *all* bourgeois states. It must substitute for this machine 5) not only a mass organisation but a universal organisation of the entire armed people.'

23 March: Lenin writes to Inessa Armand: 'What if *no passage whatsoever* is allowed *either* by England *or* by Germany!!! And this is possible!'

(CW 43 pp. 620-1) All his thinking is concentrated on his return. 'Ilich did not sleep and at night all sorts of incredible plans were made. We could travel by airplane. But such things could be thought of only in the semi-delirium of the night . . . A Swedish passport could have been obtained through the aid of the Swedish comrades but there was the further obstacle of one not knowing the Swedish language. Perhaps only a little Swedish would do. But it would be so easy to give one's self away. "You will fall asleep and see Mensheviks in your dreams and you will start swearing, and shout, scoundrels, scoundrels! and give the whole conspiracy away", I said to him teasingly. Still, Ilich inquired of Hanecki as to whether there was some way in which he could be smuggled through Germany.' (Krupskaya p. 288)

25 March: Lenin, in a letter to Lunacharsky, writes: 'Independence, separateness of our *Party*, *no rapprochement with other parties*, are indispensable conditions for me. Without this one cannot help the proletariat to move through the *democratic* revolution to the *commune*, and I will not serve any other ends.' (CW 35 p. 302)

27 March: Lenin lectures in Zürich on the tasks of the Russian Social Democratic Labour Party in the Russian Revolution. (CW 23 pp. 355-61) He opposes any support of the new governement and criticises Gorky's social pacifism.

Before 30 March: Lenin writes to Hanecki in Stockholm and asks him to check whether the British government would permit Fritz Platten to pass through England with a Russian group in a 'locked railway coach'. (CW 43 pp. 622-3)

30 March: Lenin writes a long letter to Hanecki. First of all he agrees that he 'cannot, of course, make use of the services of people who are connected with the publication of *Die Glocke* (The Bell).' Hence Lenin refuses further contact with Parvus and this is of significance for the question of the 'German money'. He wants 'the pamphlet by Lenin and Zinoviev on the war and socialism' and other literature to be republished in Petrograd. On policy he declares: 'Not a shadow of confidence in or support for the government of Guchkov-Milyukov and Co.!!' (CW 35 pp. 308-13)

31 March: Lenin sends a telegram to the Swiss social democratic MP Robert Grimm: 'Our Party has decided to accept without reservations the proposal that the Russian émigrés should travel through Germany and to organise the journey at once.' He asks Grimm to keep him informed. (CW 36 p. 427)

Between 31 March–4 April: Lenin, in a letter to Inessa Armand, writes: 'We have more money for the journey than I thought . . . The comrades in Stockholm have been a *great* help.' (CW 43 pp. 623-4)

2 April: Lenin informs the police in Zürich that Krupskaya and he are leaving and demands the 'return of the 100 franc surety in cash'. (Gautschi p. 260)

3–4 April: 'Platten finally declared himself willing, in place of Grimm, to conduct the negotiations with Romberg, then the German ambassador in Berne. The same evening he travelled to Berne with Lenin to begin negotiations with the embassy. They were successful. The demands of those travelling that they should occupy a sealed carriage and have complete freedom from passport and personal checks were accepted by the German government. The conditions were: 1) I, Fritz Platten, will conduct the carriage carrying political émigrés wishing to travel to Russia, through Germany, bearing full responsibility and personal liability at all times 2) The carriage will be granted extraterritorial rights 3) No control of passports or persons may be carried out either on entering or on leaving Germany.' (Willi Münzenberg *Die Dritte Front* p. 238)

5 April: Lenin gives up their home in Zürich and travels to Berne. Lenin wants to pull up roots immediately he hears the journey to Russia is on. 'The train is due to leave without two hours. We had just these two hours to liquidate our "household", settle accounts with the landlady, return the books to the library, pack up and so on.' (Krupskaya p. 293)

7 April: Socialist Internationalists issue a declaration; they back Lenin's decision to travel through Germany, they 'not only have the right but the duty to grasp the opportunity offered them to return to Russia'. (SW XX/2 pp. 267–8) The declaration was signed by Levi, Guilbeaux, Loriot, Bronski, Platten, Nerman, Hansen and others.

8 April: In a 'Farewell Letter to Swiss Workers' (CW 23 pp. 367–73) Lenin writes that the 'great honour' of beginning the revolution has fallen to Russia. 'But the idea that the Russian proletariat is the chosen revolutionary proletariat among the workers of the world is absolutely alien to us . . . Russia is a peasant country . . . Socialism *cannot* triumph there *directly* and *immediately*.' However it 'may make our revolution the *prologue* to the world socialist revolution, a step towards it'.

9 April: Lenin leaves Switzerland. Besides Lenin and Krupskaya, the Zinovievs, Radek and Inessa Armand are also on the train; 32 émigrés in all, as well as Fritz Platten. The travellers enter the specially prepared German carriage at Gottmadingen, near Singen. Their names are not checked, they are only counted. Three doors of the carriage are locked (Platten wrote 'sealed' on them, hence the legend of the 'sealed carriage'), the rear door is left unlocked, hence only Platten and the accompanying Germans may leave the carriage.

11 April: During the evening the train arrives as Sassnitz, the last German station. The travellers spend the night in the train.

12 April: Lenin and the émigrés travel to Trelleborg in a Swedish freighter and from there to Stockholm via Malmö.

13 April: They arrive in Stockholm at 10 am. Lenin is greeted by left socialists and Carl Lindhagen, the mayor. Lenin stays in the Hotel Regina. (*Lenin v Svetsii* p. 156) Lenin buys trousers and shoes on the

insistence of his friends. He attends a meeting of Swedish social democrats and sets up a bureau of the RSDLP Abroad, headed by Radek
who is not permitted to enter Russia. Lenin leaves Stockholm at 6.37
pm for Russia.

14 April: Lenin sends a telegram to Karpinsky in Geneva: 'German
government faithfully guarded extraterritoriality of our coach. Continuing journey. Publish farewell letter.' (CW 43 p. 628)

15 April: Lenin arrives at Tornio on the Swedish–Finnish border. The
British officers who are in charge of the crossing body search Lenin.
Lenin remarks to one of the accompanying comrades, Zkhakaya: 'Our
investigations concerning Misha are over. We are on our own soil and
we shall show them . . . that we are the true masters of the future.'
(Biographie p. 408) Lenin sends a telegram to his sisters Maria and
Anna in Petrograd: 'Arriving Monday 11 pm. Inform *Pravda*.' (CW 37
p. 539)

16 April: Lenin is in Russia again. He arrives in Petrograd at 11 pm; he
delivers his first speech to enthusiastic crowds on the station forecourt,
standing on an armoured car, and concludes: 'Long live the world
socialist revolution!'

17 April: Lenin visits his mother's and his sister Olga's graves. At a
meeting of Bolshevik delegates to the All-Russian Conference of
Soviets, Lenin develops his 'April Theses'. They are published in *Pravda*
on 20 April under the heading 'The Tasks of the Proletariat in the
Present Revolution'. (CW 24 pp. 19–26) Lenin calls the Russian revolution the prologue of the world revolution and advocates the further
development of the revolution. The bourgeois February revolution
must be followed by a socialist revolution. 'The programme must be
altered. It is out of date. The Soviets of Workers' and Soldiers' Deputies
is a step towards socialism. Abolution of the police, the army and the
bureaucracy.'

19 April: *Pravda* no 25 announces that Lenin has commenced work on
the editorial board.

Between 21–26 April: Lenin writes the pamphlet 'Letters on Tactics'
and it appears at the end of the month. (CW 24 pp. 42–54) Lenin
declares that the 'bourgeois democratic revolution in Russia' is 'completed'. He opposes the 'old Bolsheviks', Kamenev, Kalinin, also Stalin,
who reiterate 'formulas senselessly learned by rote' instead of analysing
the new reality. He advocates again a state where there is '*no* police, *no*
army standing apart from the people, *no* officialdom standing all
powerful *above* the people'.

22 April: Lenin's article 'Dual Power' appears in *Pravda* no 28. (CW 24
pp. 38–41) He writes: 'The basic question of every revolution is that of
state power.' In Russia besides a provisional bourgeois government
there is already '*another government* . . . that . . . is growing', the
Soviets of Workers' and Soldiers' Deputies. He is for the overthrow

of the Provisional Government but that cannot happen 'immediately', the Soviets, councils, must be split from the bourgeoisie first.

23 April: Lenin finishes work on his pamphlet 'The Tasks of the Proletariat in Our Revolution' and it appears in September. (CW 24 pp. 55-8) Lenin further develops his 'April Theses'; he wants a workers' state without a bureaucracy, a militia instead of a police force. Lenin also pronounces on the role of women. 'Unless women are brought to take an independent part not only in political life generally but also in daily and universal public service, it is no use talking about full and stable democracy, let alone socialism.' Lenin proposes a change of name for the Party. 'We must call ourselves the *Communist Party* — just as Marx and Engels called themselves.'

25 April: Lenin writes to Hanecki and Radek that so far 'we have received nothing . . . no letters, no packets, no money.' They should be very 'careful' in their contacts (apparently also regarding money). Lenin writes that *Pravda* 'has wobbled towards "Kautskyism"', he hopes to correct that. (CW 36 pp. 444-5) Lenin writes to V A Karpinsky: 'Our journey was wonderful. Platten was not admitted by Milyukov. The atmosphere is a furious campaign of the bourgeoisie against us. Among the workers and *soldiers* — sympathy.' (CW 35 pp. 316-7)

27-28 April: Lenin writes and publishes a series of articles. He defends himself against attacks for travelling through Germany and against charges that his policies are playing into the hands of the Germans.

27 April-5 May: Lenin plays a leading role at the Petrograd City Conference of the RSDLP (Bolsheviks). He is elected honorary chairman and delivers the address and the concluding remarks on the political situation; his draft resolutions are adopted. (CW 24 pp. 139-66) Lenin gets the Party to accept his 'refurbishment'; he says: 'The trouble with us is that comrades have wished to remain "old" Bolsheviks' and '"old" Bolshevism needs revising.'

28 April: Lenin speaks against the Provisional Government at a meeting of soldiers of an armoured car unit.

3 and 4 May: Lenin attends a meeting of the CC, RSDLP (B); his draft resolution is adopted. (CW 24 pp. 184-5)

4 May: Lenin writes to Jacob Hanecki in Stockholm: The money from Kozlovsky (2 thous.) has been received. The packets have not arrived yet.' (CW 43 pp. 629-30)

7-12 May: The April Conference of the Bolsheviks takes place in Petrograd (24-29 April according to the Julian calendar), the first All-Russian Conference after the revolution. Lenin is elected to the presidium; he opens the Conference with a short speech and delivers the main report on the political situation. (CW 24 pp. 225-313) The Conference is a great success for Lenin; the Party (80,000 members) now officially adopts his radical line. On the new goal of the Bolsheviks

Lenin declares: 'We are all agreed that power must be wielded by the Soviets of Workers' and Soldiers' Deputies . . . This would be a state of the Paris Commune type. Such power is a dictatorship, i.e. it rests not in law, not on the formal will of the majority, but on direct, open force. Force is the instrument of power. How then will the Soviets apply this power? Will they return to the old way of governing by means of the police? Will they govern by means of the old organs of power? In my opinion they cannot do this. At any rate, they will be faced with the immediate task of creating a state that is not bourgeois. Among Bolsheviks, I have compared this state to the Paris Commune in the sense that the latter destroyed the old administrative organs and replaced them by absolutely new ones that were the direct organs of the workers.' On tactics Lenin states that it is 'impossible nonsense' to shout that force should be used. As long as the government does not begin war we shall engage in peaceful propaganda. There is no more dangerous mistake than to base tactics on subjective wishes. Lenin speaks also on the revision of the Party programme; his draft resolution is adopted, in which a correction of the theses on the state is advocated. The goal is a 'democratic proletarian-peasant republic (i.e. a type of state, functioning without police, without a standing army and without a privileged bureaucracy)' and no longer a 'bourgeois parliamentary republic'. Lenin is elected to the CC of the Party with the most votes, 104; he is the unchallenged leader of the Bolsheviks.

After 17 May: Lenin begins an autobiography after being asked by the Petrograd Soviet about his origins. He writes: 'I was born in Simbirsk on 10 April 1870. In the spring of 1887, my elder brother Aleksandr was executed by Alexander III for an attempt on his life (1 March 1887). In December 1887, I was arrested for the first time and expelled from Kazan University for students' disturbances. I was then banished from Kazan. In December 1895, I was arrested for the second time for social democratic propaganda among the workers in St Petersburg.' Here the manuscript breaks off. (CW 41 p. 430)

19 May: Lenin's article 'A Strong Revolutionary Government' appears in *Pravda* no 50 (CW 24 pp. 360-1) in which it was stated that the revolution against the capitalists is now the chief task. During these months articles by Lenin appear almost daily in *Pravda*.

21 May: Lenin speaks at the Petrograd city meeting of the RSDLP (B) on the results of the April Conference. (CW 41 pp. 431-3) He declares that the chief task is patiently to win over the workers and peasants. 'You cannot disregard the people. Only dreamers and plotters believe that a minority could impose their will on a majority . . . When the majority of the people refuse, because they do not yet understand, to take power into their own hands, the minority, however revolutionary and clever, cannot impose their desire on the majority of the people.'

23 May: Lenin speaks at a Conference of the *Mezhraiontsy*, the 'middle group' to which Trotsky, Lunacharsky, Uritsky and others belong. The middle group does not yet accept fusion with the Bolsheviks: Lenin's resolution at the Conference is rejected.

25 May: Lenin addresses workers at several meetings arranged by the Bolsheviks.

27 May: During a lecture on war and revolution Lenin declares: 'The most important thing . . . is the question of the class character of the war . . . The war which the capitalist governments have started can only be ended by a workers' revolution.' (CW 24 pp. 398–421)

31 May: Three articles by Lenin, including 'The Question of Uniting the Internationalists' appear in *Pravda* no 60. (CW 24 pp. 431–2) In it Lenin supports the fusion of the *Mezhraionsty*, the Inter-Borough Organisation, the 'middle group', of Trotsky and the Bolsheviks. (Compare 23 May.)

3 June: Lenin speaks to workers in several factories in Petrograd.

4 June: Lenin speaks on the agrarian programme at the 1st All-Russian Congress of Peasants' Deputies. (CW 24 pp. 486–505) He is in favour 'of the immediate organised seizure by the peasants of the landed estates.'

11 June: Lenin writes to Radek in Stockholm that Zimmerwald has become 'a hindrance' and the sooner they 'break with it the better'. He proposes a meeting of the left. 'We shall send the money (a sum of about 3–4 thous. roubles) soon.' (CW 43 p. 632)

12 June: At a meeting of the Petrograd Committee of the RSDLP (Bolsheviks) Lenin comments on the publication of a 'popular organ' and says that the CC wants 'Comrade Trotsky' to edit it. (CW 24 pp. 543–4)

13 June: Lenin speaks on workers' control in industry at the Petrograd Conference of Factory Committees.

16 June–7 July: The 1st All-Russian Congress of Soviets of Workers' and Soldiers' Deputies meets. The Bolsheviks have only 105 delegates out of more than a thousand at the Congress.

17 June: Lenin speaks at the 1st Congress of Soviets on the attitude to the Provisional Government. (CW 25 pp. 15–28) Amid applause and laughter he says in reply to the remark of I Tseretelli, the Menshevik leader, that there was no party in Russia prepared to assume full power: 'Yes, there is. No party can refuse this, and our Party certainly doesn't. It is ready to take over full power at any moment.'

22 June: At the 1st Congress of Soviets Lenin speaks on the war. (CW 25 pp. 29–42) According to Lenin the war is 'a continuation of bourgeois politics, nothing else'; he traces it back to imperialism. The only way to stop the war 'is the revolution'. During a night sitting the Bolshevik CC decides to accede to one of the demands of the Congress of Soviets, to abandon the 'peaceful demonstration' planned for 23

June. 'Ilich then insisted that the demonstration, called by the Petrograd Committee, be abandoned. He argued that since we recognised the power of the Soviets, we were obliged to submit to the decisions of the Congress, otherwise we would be playing into the hands of our enemies.' (Krupskaya p. 305)

24 June: Lenin explains why the demonstration was cancelled at a session of the Petrograd Committee (Bolsheviks). (CW 25 pp. 79–81) He states that the revolution has 'entered a new phase of its development' and calls for 'maximum calmness, caution, restraint and organisation . . . We must give them no pretext for attack'.

30 June: Lenin writes to Radek in Stockholm that a '*real* Third International' should be founded 'of the lefts *alone*'. (CW 43 pp. 634–5)

1 July: A demonstration organised by the Congress of Soviets is dominated to a considerable extent by the Bolsheviks and their slogans of 'Peace' and 'All Power to the Soviets' stand out. Lenin writes on 3 July about the demonstration in *Pravda*. (CW 25 pp. 109–11) 'The demonstration in a few hours scattered to the winds, like a handful of dust, the empty talk about Bolshevik conspirators', the 'overwhelming majority' of the industrial proletariat and the troops in Petrograd support the slogan that the 'Party has always advocated'.

11 July: Completely exhausted by overwork, and suffering from insomnia, Lenin travels to the village of Neivola, in Finland, to rest for a few days.

17 July: Lenin returns early in the morning to Petrograd where in his absence there have been mass demonstrations against the government and demands for power to pass to the Soviets. Lenin addresses the demonstrators. During the night of 17–18 July he attends a meeting of the CC and it decides to call off the demonstrations. On the same day G A Aleksinsky, a former Bolshevik and otsovist, accuses Lenin of being a German spy. A press campaign against Lenin begins.

18 July: Officer cadets smash the editorial offices of *Pravda*; arrests of Bolsheviks begin. Lenin moves into an illegal flat. He writes several articles, including 'Where is State Power and Where is Counter-Revolution?' (CW 25 pp. 155–9) to counter Aleksinsky's assertions. 'The Bolsheviks *never* received *any money* from either Hanecki or Kozlovsky. All that is a lie, a complete vulgar lie.' (Compare 25 April and 4 May.)

Between 18–20 July: Lenin considers the possibility of assassination after the 'July Days' and because of the campaign against him. He writes to Lev Kamenev: '*Entre nous*, if they do me in, I ask you to publish my notebook: "Marxism and the State".' (CW 36 p. 454)

20 July: The government issues a warrant for Lenin's arrest. He says to Krupskaya: 'Grigory [Zinoviev] and I have decided to appear, go and tell Kamenev.' Lenin declares to Krupskaya: 'Let us say good bye . . . we may not see each other again.' (Krupskaya p. 311) But the Party leadership decides that Lenin should not appear in court since no guarantee of safety is forthcoming. Lenin writes the article 'Three Crises' (CW 25 pp. 169–73) and states that the crisis of 3–4 July (16–17 July New Style) erupted 'despite the Bolshevik efforts' to check it and it led to a furious outburst of counter-revolution'.

21 July: In an article 'The Question of the Bolshevik Leaders Appearing in Court' (CW 25 pp. 174–5) Lenin states that one must not 'commit the folly of appearing in court of one's own free will'.

23 July: Lenin leaves Petrograd where he had been hiding in the house of Alliluev, a worker. He travels to Razliv station (near Sestroretsk, 35 km from Petrograd) and hides a few days in a barn belonging to N A Emelyanov, a worker. He had rented a piece of land for hay on the shores of lake Razliv; Lenin and Zinoviev hide in a hay-covered hut. Lenin writes the article 'The Political Situation' (CW 25 pp. 176–8) and states that counter-revolution has actually 'taken state power into its hands'. The slogan 'All Power to the Soviets' was correct during the peaceful development of the revolution but now a military dictatorship has taken over and the 'preparation of forces for the armed uprising' is now necessary.

End of July: Lenin writes the pamphlet 'On Slogans'. (CW 25 pp. 183–90) Sharp turns in history cause formally correct slogans to lose 'all meaning'. This applies to the slogan calling for the 'transfer of all state power to the Soviets', hence it is no longer valid. 'A peaceful course of development has become impossible. A non-peaceful and most painful course has begun.' New Soviets have to be established. 'The substitution of the abstract for the concrete is one of the greatest and most dangerous sins in a revolution.'

Beginning of August: Lenin writes the article 'Lessons of the Revolution'. (CW 25 pp. 223–39) 'Revolution enlightens all classes with a rapidity and thoroughness unknown in normal, peaceful times.'

3 August: The Petrograd Supreme Court indicts Lenin for treason and the organisation of an armed uprising.

Between 4–8 August: Lenin writes the article 'An Answer' (CW 25 pp. 208–18) to refute the charge and among other things says that it is an 'infamous lie' that he 'was in contact with Parvus'.

8 August: Lenin writes the article 'Constitutional Illusions'. (CW 25 pp. 194–207) 'For the majority in the state really do decide, definite conditions are required, one of which is the firm establishment of a political system, a form of state power, making it possible to decide matters by a majority and guaranteeing the translation of this possibility into reality.'

8–16 August: The 6th Congress of the RSDLP (Bolsheviks) meets in Petrograd; the Party has about 140,000 members. Although absent Lenin is elected to the CC with the largest number of votes, 133, next comes Zinoviev, also in hiding, with 132 and Trotsky, in prison, with 131 votes.

30 August: Lenin writes to the Bureau of the CC Abroad in Stockholm and asks Radek and Hanecki to undermine the 'shameful campaign of slander' directed against some Bolsheviks, 'not sparing toil, trouble or money'. He is opposed to any postponement of a 'Conference of the Left to found a Third International'. (CW 35 pp. 318–24)

August–September: Lenin writes his important pamphlet 'State and Revolution'. (CW 25 pp. 381–491) Lenin intends to *'re-establish'* the Marxist theory of the state. Marxist theory is for Lenin the application of the theory of development, in its most consistent, most complete, most pondered and most significant form to modern capitalism. The state is at any given time the instrument of oppression by which the economically dominant class effects its suppression of the exploited class. Lenin underlines first and foremost the revolutionary aspect of the theory of the state. He writes that after the proletarian revolution the transition from a capitalist to a communist society is impossible without a 'political transition period', a state of the 'dictatorship of the proletariat'. To Lenin dictatorship of the proletariat means: 'Democracy for the vast majority of the people and suppression by force, i.e. exclusion from democracy, of the exploiters and oppressors of the people.' The 'reduction of the remuneration of *all* servants of the state to the level of *workmen's wages*' is according to Lenin necessary in the transition society, in the 'worker's state'. Also 'all officials, without exception' should be 'elected and [be] subject to recall *at any time*'. The state loses its 'political' function and is reduced to accounting and control 'which any literate person can perform . . . The whole of society will have become a single office and a single factory with equality of labour and pay'. This is 'by no means our ideal or our ultimate goal', rather a 'necessary *step*' on the road to communism. Lenin declares that the state ceases to exist in the communist classless society since there is no exploitation and nothing exists which 'arouses indignation, evokes protest and revolt, and creates the need for *suppression*'.

End of August–Beginning of September: Lenin leaves Razliv and moves to Finland. According to *Biographie* p. 406 he moved on 8 August (Old Style) or 21 August (New Style), according to CW 25 p. 540 he moved on 21–22 August (Old Style) or 3–4 September (New Style). His papers are made out in the name of Konstantin Petrovich Ivanov, a worker. He has shaved off his beard and is wearing a wig. 'A Finnish comrade, Jaslava, an engine driver on the Finnish railway . . . undertook to get Ilich across, disguised as a fireman.' (Krupskaya p. 315) Lenin lives first in Lahti, then in Helsinki.

11 September: Lenin's article 'From a Publicist's Diary: Peasants and Workers' (CW 25 pp. 274–82) appears in *Rabochii* (The Worker) no 6. 'We are not doctrinaires. Our theory is a guide to action, not a dogma. We do not claim that Marx or Marxists know the road to socialism down to the last detail. It would be nonsense to claim anything of the kind. What we know is the direction of this road and the class forces to follow it; the specific, practical details will come to light only through the *experience of the millions* when they take things into their own hands.'

12 September: Lenin writes a letter to the CC, 'To the Central Committee of the RSDLP' (CW 25 pp. 285-9) and calls the Kornilov revolt a 'most unexpected' sharp turn in events which makes new tactics necessary, not support fo the Kerensky government, of course, but: 'We shall fight against Kornilov' and 'we shall not overthrow Kerensky right now.'

14-16 September: Lenin writes the article 'On Compromises' and it appears in *Rabochii Put* (The Way for the Workers) no 3 on 19 September. (CW 25 pp. 305-10) He states that a 'peaceful advance of the whole Russian revolution' is now possible and because of this the Bolsheviks are now ready to propose a compromise. 'Now, and only now, perhaps *during only a few days* . . . such a government could be set up and consolidated in a perfectly peaceful way. In all probability it could secure the peaceful *advance* of the whole Russian revolution.' He calls this an '*extremely* valuable' but '*extremely* rare opportunity'.

23-27 September: Lenin writes the pamphlet 'The Impending Catastrophe and How to Combat it'. (CW 25 pp. 319-65) He proposes the nationalisation of the banks and syndicates and demands 'an advance towards socialism'.

25-27 September: Lenin writes to the CC 'The Bolsheviks Must Assume Power'. (CW 26 pp. 19-22) Since the Bolsheviks are in a majority in the Soviets in Petrograd and Moscow 'the present task must be an *armed uprising* in Petrograd and Moscow . . . the seizing of power and the overthrow of the government . . . It would be naive to wait for a "formal" majority for the Bolsheviks. No revolution ever waits for *that*.' Lenin is convinced that the Bolsheviks will 'win *absolutely and unquestionably*'.

26-27 September: Lenin writes a letter to the CC 'Marxism and Insurrection'. (CW 26 pp. 22-7) He is against seeing preparation for insurrection as 'Blanquism'. Marx called insurrection 'an art' and it depends for success 'not upon a conspiracy and not upon a Party', but upon the advanced class. Insurrection must rely on a revolutionary upsurge of the people and its enemies must vacillate. This is now the case in Russia. '*Our victory is assured.*'

27 September: Lenin's article 'One of the Fundamental Questions of the Revolution' appears in *Rabochii Put* no 10. (CW 25 pp. 366-73) 'The key question of every revolution is undoubtedly the question of state power. Which class holds power decides everything.' The slogan 'Power to the Soviets' means 'radically reshaping the entire old state apparatus, that bureaucratic apparatus which hampers everything democratic. It means removing this apparatus and substituting for it a new, popular one, i.e. a truly democratic apparatus of Soviets.'

29 September: Lenin's article 'The Russian Revolution and the Civil War: They Are Trying to Frighten Us with Civil War' appears in *Rabochii Put* no 12. (CW 26 pp. 28–42) Lenin states that 'only an alliance of the Bolsheviks with the Socialist Revolutionaries and Mensheviks, only an immediate transfer of all power to the Soviets would make civil war in Russia impossible.' To the argument that there would be 'rivers of blood' during a civil war Lenin replies that this cannot be compared with the 'seas of blood' which Russian imperialism is shedding during the present war.

30 September: Lenin moves from Helsinki to Vyborg so as to be nearer to Petrograd.

Beginning–14 October: Lenin writes the pamphlet 'Can the Bolsheviks Retain State Power?' (CW 26 pp. 87–136) He again states that the Bolsheviks are ready to assume power. The proletariat must 'smash' the old state apparatus (standing army, police and bureaucracy). '*Without big banks socialism would be impossible*. The big banks *are* the "state apparatus" which we need to bring about socialism and which we *take ready made* from capitalism. A single State Bank, the biggest of the big, with branches in every rural district, in every factory, will constitute as much as nine-tenths of the *socialist* apparatus. There will be countrywide *book-keeping*, countrywide *accounting* of the production and distribution of goods; this will be, so to speak, something in the nature of the *skeleton* of socialist society.' The confiscation of the property of the capitalists will not be the decisive point but rather workers' control carried out by all the people. Russia since 1905 has been governed by 130,000 landowners. 'We are told that the 240,000 members of the Bolshevik Party will not be able to govern Russia . . . govern her in the interests of the poor and against the rich.' The Bolsheviks are not utopians. 'We know that an unskilled labourer or a cook cannot immediately get on with the job of state administration.' But a beginning must be made to train all the working people to administer the state.

9–10 October: Lenin's article 'The Tasks of the Revolution' appears in *Rabochii Put* nos 20 and 21. (CW 26 pp. 59–68) In it he argues that 'power to the Soviets', 'peace', 'land to those who till it' and 'struggle against famine and economic ruin' should be the chief elements in the Bolshevik programme. He sees 'possibly . . . the last chance' for a peaceful development of the revolution.

10 October: Lenin writes a letter to I T Smilga; the latter is to make full use of his 'high position' in Finland. (CW 26 pp. 69–73)

12 October: Lenin writes the article 'The Crisis Has Matured'. (CW 26 pp. 74–86) 'The whole future of the international workers' revolution for socialism is at stake.' In a postscript to the CC Lenin maintains that the victory of the insurrection is 'now *guaranteed*'. However as the CC does not respond to his instructions 'I am compelled to *tender my resignation from the Central Committee*, which I hereby do, reserving for myself freedom to campaign among the *rank and file* of the Party and at the Party Congress'.

Between 12–17 October: Lenin writes about Trotsky that the latter 'upon his arrival . . . took up an internationalist stand' and during the 'July Days' had proved himself 'equal to the task and a loyal supporter of the Party'. (CW 41 pp. 446–8)

14 October: In a 'Letter to the Central Committee, the Moscow and Petrograd Committees and the Bolshevik Members of the Petrograd and Moscow Soviets' (CW 26 pp. 140–1) Lenin demands insurrection. In Germany 'the beginning of a revolution is obvious, especially since the sailors were shot. The elections in Moscow — 47 per cent Bolsheviks — are a tremendous victory'. Delay is 'criminal' and a 'betrayal of the revolution'.

20 October: Lenin returns to Petrograd from Vyborg; he stays illegally in the flat of M V Fofanova, a Bolshevik.

21 October: Lenin writes 'Advice of an Onlooker'. (CW 26 pp. 179–81) He makes concrete proposals for the overthrow of the government (occupy the telephone exchange, telegraph offices, railway stations and bridges). 'The success of both the Russian and the world revolution depends on two or three days' fighting.'

23 October: Lenin attends a meeting of the CC. In his speech he supports armed insurrection. His resolution is adopted by 10 votes to 2 (Zinoviev and Kamenev). The armed uprising is stated to be 'inevitable' and the time to be 'fully ripe'. (CW 26 pp. 188–90)

29 October: Lenin attends a meeting of the expanded CC. After long debate it approves his position on insurrection. (CW 26 pp. 191–4)

31 October: Lenin writes a 'Letter to Bolshevik Party Members'. (CW 26 pp. 216–9) He attacks a declaration against an uprising which Zinoviev and Kamenev have published in the press. Lenin calls it 'noisy pessimism' and a 'grave betrayal' and condemns both of them regardless of his 'earlier close relations with them'.

1 November: Lenin writes in a 'Letter to Central Committee Members' (CW 26 pp. 234–5) that delay in launching the uprising would be fatal. 'We must not wait! We may lose everything!' The government is tottering and it must be given the coup de grâce. Lenin leaves his hiding place during the evening, he leaves behind a note for 'Margarita Fofanova: "I am going where you did not want me to go. Good-bye".' (CW 43 p. 638) Disguised, he turns up at Smolny, the Bolshevik headquarters, to join the leadership of the uprising.

7 November: The Bolshevik uprising, led by Trotsky and Lenin, is victorious; all important institutions, bridges, railway stations are occupied; the government takes refuge in the Winter Palace. Lenin remarks to Trotsky: 'The transition from illegality and being hounded from pillar to post to power is too abrupt. It makes one dizzy.' (Trotsky *Über Lenin* p. 84) Lenin writes at 10 am the appeal 'To the Citizens of Russia' (CW 26 p. 236) in which he proclaims the fall of the Provisional Government. 'The immediate offer of a democratic peace, the abolition of landed proprietorship, workers' control over production and the establishment of Soviet power' have been achieved. Lenin declares during the afternoon at a session of the Petrograd Soviet that the revolution has been 'accomplished'. He concludes his speech on the tasks of Soviet power with the cry 'Long Live the World Socialist Revolution'. (CW 26 pp. 239-40)

8 November: Lenin learns of the storming of the Winter Palace and the arrest of the government at 2 am. He goes to the home of V D Bonch-Bruevich, his secretary. Lenin attends a meeting of the CC in the afternoon. During the evening Lenin appears, amid great applause, at the 2nd All-Russian Congress of Soviets of Workers' and Solders' Deputies. 'In a battered suit, in trousers that were too long for him, to be the idol of a mob but loved nevertheless and honoured as seldom a leader in history.' (John Reed p. 132) The 2nd Congress elects Lenin head of the government, as 'Chairman of the Council of People's Commissars'. He speaks on peace (decree on peace) and on the agrarian question; his draft resolutions are adopted at the Congress. (CW 26 pp. 243-61)

9 November: Lenin attends a meeting of the All-Russian Central Executive Committee (CEC); he visits the headquarters of the Petrograd Military District.

12 November: Lenin speaks on the radio in the name of the Council of People's Commissars (Sovnarkom). (CW 26 p. 273) He states that the Soviet government is making every effort to avoid bloodshed. If 'Kerensky's units do begin to shoot', the Soviet government will not hesitate to suppress them 'ruthlessly'. Lenin wants no mercy to be shown, 'he feared his own soft-heartedness and those of the masses'. (Krupskaya 1959 p. 448)

14 November: Lenin opposes Kamenev and others at a meeting of the CC. (CW 26 pp. 275-6)

17 November: Lenin speaks several times during a meeting of the All-Russian Central Executive Committee (CEC). (CW 26 pp. 284-92) He declares: 'Socialism cannot be decreed from above. Its spirit rejects the mechanical bureaucratic approach; living creative socialism is the product of the masses themselves.' The Bolshevik opposition leaders – Kamenev, Rykov, Zinoviev, Milyutin and Nogin – leave the CC and the government; they are, unlike Lenin and Trotsky, for co-operation with other 'socialist parties'.

22 November: After a telephone conversation between Lenin and Dukhonin, the commander-in-chief, (CW 26 pp. 308-10) the latter is dismissed for refusing to begin negotiations for an armistice immediately. Lenin informs the CEC on 23 November of his talks with General Dukhonin.

27 November: Lenin addresses the Extraordinary All-Russian Congress of Soviets of Peasants' Deputies. (CW 26 pp. 321-32)

End of November-December: Lenin attends almost daily meetings of the Council of People's Commissars (Sovnarkom); he participates in discussions which include economic questions, trade, nationalisation, the courts, finance, libraries and the limiting of the salaries of people's commissars to 500 roubles per month.

10 December: Lenin drafts an outline programme for peace negotiations. (CW 26 pp. 349-50) The fundamental principle should be 'no annexations or indemnities'.

Before 12 December: Lenin, in a letter to the CC, supports Hanecki. It is 'unworthy of a workers' Party' to pass judgment on the basis of 'intellectualist scandal' (concerning his links with Parvus). (CW 44 pp. 46-8)

12 December: Lenin, at a meeting of the CC, opposes an editorial board for *Pravda* composed of Stalin, Sokolnikov and Bukharin. He proposes Sokolnikov, Stalin and Trotsky. (CW 36 pp. 456-7)

20 December: In a note to F E Dzerzhinsky, Lenin demands extraordinary measures to 'fight counter-revolutionaries and saboteurs', also the first steps towards 'universal labour conscription'. (CW 26 pp. 374-6)

21 December: Lenin receives Colonel Robins, representative of the US mission and discusses the possibility of American specialists providing military support for Soviet Russia.

31 December: In a draft resolution of Sovnarkom (CW 26 p. 397) Lenin demands 'intensified agitation against the annexationist policy of the Germans . . . Greater efforts to reorganise the army'.

December: Lenin drafts a decree on the socialisation of the national economy. (SW XXII pp. 139-42) Joint stock companies are to become state property, general labour service is to be introduced and trade unions are to exercise control functions.

1918

3 January: Lenin, in a letter to Charles Dumas, the French socialist, whom he knows from his émigré days in Paris, refuses a meeting. 'I regret very much that present relations between us have become impossible since very deep political differences of opinion separate us.' (Briefe V p. 20)

6-11 January: Lenin takes a holiday in Finland. 'We spent Christmas (24-29 December (Old Style), 6-11 January (New Style)) somewhere in Finland with Maria Ilinichna . . . The marked Finnish cleanliness, the white curtains on the windows, everything reminded Ilich of his illegal stay in Helsinki in 1907 and 1917, before the October Revolution, when he was working on 'State and Revolution'. The holiday did us little good, Ilich at times even spoke sotto voce, as during the days when he was in hiding. We went daily for walks but without really enjoying them. Ilich was too taken up with his thoughts and wrote practically the whole time.' (Krupskaya 1959 p. 477)

7-10 January: Lenin writes various articles during the holidays. In 'Fear of the Collapse of the Old and the Fight for the New' (CW 26 pp. 400-3) he repeats that 'socialism cannot be "introduced", that it takes shape in the course of the most intense, the most acute class struggle'. In 'How to Organise Competition?' (CW 26 pp. 404-15) Lenin states: 'Far from extinguishing competition, socialism, on the contrary, for the first time creates the opportunity for employing it on a really *wide* and on a really *mass* scale.' We must break the 'despicable prejudice' that 'only the so called "upper classes", only the rich, and those who have gone through the schools of the rich, are capable of administering the state'.

14 January: Lenin receives representatives of the diplomatic corps accredited to Petrograd for a discussion. The Romanian ambassador had been arrested the day before. Lenin speaks at the send-off of the 'first volunteers of the socialist army' (CW 26 p. 420) and demands that 'every obstacle on the way to world revolution' be overcome. During the return journey unknown assailants fire at Lenin's car. He is unhurt; only Fritz Platten, one of the passengers, is slightly injured.

15 January: Lenin speaks on the telephone to the Soviet delegation, led by Trotsky since 9 January, who are at Brest-Litovsk for peace negotiations with the Germans. He proposes an interruption in negotiations.

16 January: The All-Russian CEC adopts the 'Declaration of the Rights of the Working and Exploited People', drafted by Lenin. (CW 26 pp. 421-5) Private ownership of land 'is hereby abolished', workers' control is introduced as the first steps towards nationalisation, the banks become the property of the state, 'universal labour conscription' is brought in.

18 January: The Constituent Assembly convenes in Petrograd. The Bolsheviks are in the minority; they obtained 25 per cent of votes at the elections in November 1917. The majority refuses to debate Lenin's Declarations of the Rights of the Working and Exploited People. The Bolsheviks leave the assembly and it is dissolved.

19 January: The All-Russian CEC adopts Lenin's decree on the dissolution of the Constituent Assembly since it allegedly represented only the 'old relation of political forces'. (CW 26 pp. 434-6)

21 January: Lenin presents his theses on the 'immediate conclusion' of peace with Germany (CW 26 pp. 442-50) to a Conference of 63 leading Bolshevik functionaries. Lenin proposes the acceptance of the severe German terms — loss of the occupied areas, indemnity payments — the only alternative is to 'wage immediately a revolutionary war'. This latter tactic would only be correct 'if the German revolution were to break out and triumph in the coming three or four months'. This is improbable, hence it would be inexcusable to 'stake the fate of the socialist revolution which has already begun in Russia' on the mere chance of the German revolution breaking out in the near future. Lenin's demand for immediate peace receives 15 votes, 32 are for 'revolutionary war', 16 for Trotsky's slogan, 'neither war nor peace'.

24 January: Lenin delivers the Sovnarkom report at the 3rd All-Russian Congress of Soviets of Workers', Soldiers' and Peasants' Deputies. At a meeting of the RSDLP (Bolsheviks) Lenin makes two speeches on war and peace. (CW 36 pp. 467-70) He outlines the three views in the Party: 1) sign a separate annexationist peace 2) wage a revolutionary war 3) proclaim the war to be at an end, demobilise the army but do not sign a peace treaty. The last proposal, Trotsky's, he calls an 'international political demonstration'. Lenin is not completely in agreement with his 'supporters Stalin and Zinoviev . . . If we believe that the German movement can develop immediately, in the event of the interruption of the peace negotiations, then we must sacrifice ourselves, for the German revolution will have a force much greater than ours'. Since Lenin cannot obtain a majority for his policy of immediate peace he is in favour of delaying the signing of the peace; this is adopted by 12 votes to 1. 'Revolutionary war' is thrown out by 11 votes to 2. Trotsky's thesis not to wage war or sign a peace treaty is adopted by 9 votes to 7. Since Lenin's point of view is not adopted by the CC he does not publish his theses.

27 January: Lenin proposes severe measures in the struggle against famine during a meeting with representatives of food supply organisations. 'We can't expect to get anywhere unless we resort to terrorism: speculators must be shot on the spot. Moreover bandits must be dealt with just as resolutely: they must be shot on the spot.' (CW 26 pp. 501-2)

28 January: Lenin writes, in identical letters to V A Antonov-Ovseenko and Sergo Ordzhonikidze: 'Take the *most* decisive and *revolutionary* measures and send *grain*, *grain* and again *grain*!! Otherwise Petrograd will starve to death . . . For God's sake!' (Briefe V p. 30)

31 January: Sovnarkom adopts Lenin's draft decree on the nationalisation of the merchant marine and inland water transport. (CW 26 pp. 505-6) Lenin attends at least ten meetings of Sovnarkom in January.

4 February: Lenin receives J Sadoul, the French diplomatic representative and has a long conversation with him on the problems of a separate peace with Germany. Lenin speaks to agitators — propagandists — who are going to the provinces. (CW 26 pp. 512-6) He states that 'international capital' is not the only enemy of Soviet power. 'Chaos is our other enemy' and it has to be fought against. Lenin also says that an old Bolshevik was right when he told a Cossack what Bolshevism was. The 'Cossack asked him: "Is it true you Bolsheviks plunder?" "Yes, indeed", said the old man, "we plunder the plunderers".'

17 February: The CC rejects, by 6 votes to 5, Lenin's proposal to accept the German peace terms. Lenin does not regard a 'revolutionary war' as possible since the peasants would not fight in one. Radek states: 'Do you not understand that the peasant has voted against war?', Lenin asked me. "Excuse me, but how has he voted?" "He has voted with his feet, he is leaving the front". Hence the case for him was closed.' (Lenin *Leben und Werk* p. 49)

18 February: The CC dicusses, in two sessions, the situation after the new German offensive. Lenin maintains that 'an offer of peace must be made to the Germans'. (CW 26 pp. 522-4) In a radio message to the German government Lenin accepts the German peace conditions.

19 February: Lenin delivers a two-hour speech on war and peace at a meeting of Bolshevik and Left Socialist Revolutionary members of the All-Russian CEC. The separate peace is necessary 'since the Germans were advancing all along the front en masse'. After the conclusion of peace 'the deepening of the socialist revolution' is necessary. (CW 42 pp. 58-9)

19-20 February: Lenin writes the article 'The Revolutionary Phrase' (CW 27 pp. 19-29) and it appears on 21 February in *Pravda* no 21 (signed: Karpov). With it Lenin begins an open campaign for the signing of the peace. up till now he has only fought inside the Party for his point of view. 'The repetition of revolutionary slogans irrespective of objective circumstances . . . The slogans are superb, alluring, intoxicating, but there are no grounds for them; such is the nature of the revolutionary phrase.' Lenin is very critical of the 'left communists' of the time. 'You are worse than hens. A hen has not got the courage to step over a chalk line: but it can be said in her defence that the line was drawn by an unknown hand. You, however, have drawn your own chalk circle and are now staring at the chalk line instead of looking at reality.' (Fülöp-Miller *Lenin und Ghandi* p. 97)

21 February: Sovnarkom adopts, after a further German advance, the decree, drafted by Lenin 'The Socialist Fatherland is in Danger'. (CW 27 pp. 30-3) 'The country's entire manpower and resources are placed entirely at the service of revolutionary defence.'

23 February: During the morning Lenin writes the article 'Peace or War?' (CW 27 pp. 40-1) and it appears in the evening edition of *Pravda* no 34. Those who oppose an immediate, even an extremely onerous peace are endangering Soviet power. He has been fighting against 'revolutionary phrase-making' since January 'in the mildest and most

comradely fashion (I now profoundly condemn this mildness of mine)',
now he must act publicly against it. After receiving the latest, yet more
severe German peace conditions, Lenin declares at a meeting of the CC:
'If the policy of revolutionary phrase-making is continued I shall
leave the government and the CC.' (SW XXII pp. 297, 766) Seven
members of the CC now vote for Lenin's resolution to accept the
German terms, four left communists are against and four abstain. Lenin
speaks to the all-Russian CEC, at a session beginning at 3 am on 24
February, on the German peace conditions. (CW 27 pp. 43-7) Lenin's
proposal to sign an immediate peace treaty is adopted by 116 votes to
85 with 26 abstentions.

24 February: Lenin publishes the Sovnarkom decision to accept the
German peace conditions. (CW 42 p. 60) Lenin's article 'An Unfortunate Peace' appears in *Pravda* no 34. (CW 27 pp. 51-2) 'Trotsky was
right when he said: "the peace may be a triply unfortunate peace, but
the peace ending this hundred-fold obscene war cannot be an obscene,
disgraceful, dirty peace".' Despair is unnecessary, the humiliation
and the burdens can be sustained. 'We are not alone in the world.'

25-27 February: Lenin works on his article 'Strange and Monstrous'
(CW 27 pp. 68-75) which appears in *Pravda* nos 37 and 38 — 28
February and 1 March. Its starting point is a resolution of the Moscow
Regional Bureau of the Party, the stronghold of the left communists.
This expresses a lack of confidence in the CC and an unwillingness to
obey decisions connected with the implementation of the terms of
the peace treaty and 'considers a split in the Party in the very near
future hardly avoidable'. Lenin calls this criticism the 'legitimate
right of Party members'. However he opposes the view which holds
that it is expedient, in the interests of the international revolution, to
'accept the possibility of losing Soviet power, which is now becoming
purely formal'. This would not only be 'expedient' but a 'duty' if the
already existing German revolution could be saved by the defeat of
Soviet power. In reality the German revolution does not exist, hence it
is 'strange and monstrous' to propagate the defeat of supposedly
'formal' Soviet power.

5 March: Lenin writes the article 'A Serious Lesson and a Serious
Responsibility'. (CW 27 pp. 79-84) His comment on the peace signed
on 3 March is 'We have signed a *Tilsit peace*'.

6-8 March: The Extraordinary 7th Congress of the All-Russian Communist Party (Bolsheviks) (RCP) meets. Forty-six delegates attend. Lenin
delivers the report of the CC, speaks on the revision of the Party
programme and intervenes often during the discussion — he speaks
eighteen times in all. (CW 27 pp. 85-158) Lenin states, during his
report of the CC, 'it is the absolute truth that without a German revolution we are doomed'. Lenin's resolution, which endorses peace, is carried
by 30 votes to 12 votes of the left communists with 2 abstentions. The

Party is renamed the All-Russian Communist Party (Bolsheviks). With reference to the revision of the Party programme Lenin again maintains: 'Socialism cannot be implemented by a minority, by the Party. It can be implemented only by tens of millions when they have learnt to do it themselves. We regard it as a point in our favour that we are trying to help the masses themselves set about it immediately.'

10-11 March: Lenin and the other members of the government move from Petrograd to Moscow. He lives first of all in the Hotel National, then he obtains a flat next to his study in the Kremlin. He, his wife and his sister occupy four rooms; he lives a spartan existence. 'Ilich loved to go walking in the Kremlin. From there the view over the city was marvellous. His favourite walk was along the footpath opposite the Large Palace.' (Krupskaya 1959 p. 507)

11 March: Lenin writes the article 'The Chief Task of Our Day'. (CW 27 pp. 159-63) He stresses that it is 'our unbending determination to ensure that at any price Russia ceases to be wretched and impotent and becomes mighty and abundant in the full meaning of these words'.

14-16 March: Lenin attends the Extraordinary 4th All-Russian Congress of Soviets. He speaks on the ratification of the peace treaty. (CW 27 pp. 169-201) His resolution on the ratification of the Brest-Litovsk treaty is carried by 784 votes to 261 with 115 abstentions.

Between 23-28 March: Lenin dictates to a stenographer the 'original draft' of his 'The Immediate Tasks of the Soviet Government'. (CW 42 pp. 68-84) He outlines proposals for the development of the Russian economy since in future 'political tasks [will] occupy a subordinate position to economic tasks'. It is necessary to 'introduce the Taylor system and scientific American efficiency of labour' throughout Russia with a reduction in hours of work and without harming the labour force. Democratic centralism is necessary as a principle of administration but 'in no way excludes autonomy', rather it presupposes the necessity of it. 'There is nothing more mistaken than confusing democratic centralism with bureaucracy and routinism.' What is needed is to 'spread co-operative organisations throughout society'. (CW 27 pp. 203-18)

30 March: Lenin advocates, during a meeting of Sovnarkom, the setting up of a revolutionary court which will be 'mercilessly severe in dealing with counter-revolutionaries, hooligans, idlers and disorganisers'. (CW 27 pp. 219-20) Lenin attends at least twenty meetings of Sovnarkom during February and March.

5-6 April: Lenin approves the mobilisation measures of the CEC of Siberia in the face of the advance of Japanese troops. He promises money 'although our difficulties are extremely great'. (CW 44 p. 75)

23 April: Lenin addresses the newly elected Moscow Soviet. (CW 27 pp. 229-33) He states: 'Our revolution is entering its most dangerous and difficult phase.' We have advanced to the forefront 'not because the Russian proletariat is superior to the working class of other countries, but solely because we were one of the most backward countries in the world'. He is for the 'iron dictatorship of the working people. There is no doubt that in many cases the Soviet government has not displayed sufficient determination in the struggle against counter-revolution and in this respect it has had the appearance not of iron but of jelly, from which socialism cannot be built'.

26 April: The CC, RCP (B) approves Lenin's pamphlet 'The Immediate Tasks of the Soviet Government' and it is published on 28 April in *Pravda* no 83. (CW 27 pp. 235–77) Higher labour productivity, the organisation of competition and the strict administration of production and control by the people appear to him to be particularly important. (Compare also 23 and 28 March). He does not forget the goal of socialism: the 'old bourgeois method' of paying experts high wages has to be adopted. It is for him a necessary 'departure from the principles . . . of every proletarian power which calls for the reduction of all salaries to the level of the wages of the average worker, which urges that careerism be fought not merely in words but in deeds'. He wants this made clear to the masses.

1 May: Lenin speaks to May Day demonstrators in Red Square and at a meeting of Latvian riflemen. He also attends a parade of Red Army troops.

3–5 May: Lenin writes the article '"Left-Wing" Childishness and The Petty-Bourgeois Mentality'. (CW 27 pp. 323–54) Lenin turns on the left communists and takes issue with their organ *Kommunist*. Lenin declares that in the Soviet republic there are elements of socialism and capitalism present. 'State capitalism' would be a *'step forward'* compared with the present state of affairs. 'The most concrete example of state capitalism . . . is Germany. Here we have "the last word" in modern large scale capitalist engineering and planned organisation, subordinated to *Junker bourgeois imperialism*. Cross out the words in italics . . . and put . . . a Soviet state . . . and you will have the *sum total* of the conditions necessary for socialism. Socialism is inconceivable without large-scale capitalist engineering based on the latest discoveries of modern science. It is inconceivable without planned state organisation which keeps tens of millions of people to the strictest observation to a unified standard in production and distribution . . . Complete socialism' can only be created by the 'revolutionary co-operation of the proletarians of *all* countries'.

14 May: At a joint session of the All-Russian CEC and the Moscow Soviet Lenin delivers the 'Report on Foreign Policy'. (CW 27 pp. 365–81) Most important for Lenin is to 'preserve our socialist island in the middle of stormy seas'. We can finally only be victorious on a world scale and through the efforts of the workers of all countries. Lenin writes to S G Shaumyan: *'So far* we are being saved *only* by the contradictions and conflicts and struggles among the imperialists.' (CW 35 p. 332)

18 May: Lenin speaks on the critical financial situation to representatives of the financial departments of the Soviets. (CW 27 pp. 383–7) He states: 'You know that all socialists are against indirect taxation because the only direct tax from the socialist point of view is the progressive income and property tax.'

23 May: Lenin severely reprimands V D Bonch-Bruevich, the head of the Sovnarkom Bureau, for not giving a convincing reason as to why his 'salary as of 1 March 1918' is to be raised 'from 500 roubles to 800 roubles a month'. Lenin maintains that the increase is 'obviously illegal'. (CW 35 p. 333)

26 May: Lenin favours, in the 'Theses on the Current Situation' (CW 27 pp. 406–7) placing the struggle agaist famine in the forefront and waging a 'war for grain'. Martial law should be declared throughout the country and 'shooting for indiscipline' introduced.

28 May: Lenin writes to A G Shlyapnikov: 'The Central Committee has passed a decision *to direct the maximum number* of Party workers to the food front. For *obviously* we shall perish and ruin the *whole* revolution if we do not conquer famine in the next few months.' (CW 44 p. 95)

May: Lenin sends greetings, through Albert R Williams, to the 'American comrades'. He is 'absolutely convinced that the social revolution will finally prove victorious in all civilised countries. When it begins in America it will surpass the Russian revolution by far'. (Briefe V p. 83) During April and May Lenin attends over 40 meetings of Sovnarkom (and also many sessions of the CC and the All-Russian CEC) at which internal and foreign policy questions are discussed, as well as nationalisation, exchange of POWs and the granting of concessions. Complaints, the provision of funds for a Marx statue and other questions of secondary importance are also discussed.

2 June: Lenin sees the play *The Village of Stepanchikov* at the Moscow Art Theatre.

18 June: Lenin instructs A A Ioffe, the Soviet ambassador in Berlin, to collect and forward the publications and works of the left during the revolutionary period (the Junius pamphlet and others). He is 'really indignant' that this has not already been done. (Briefe V pp. 98–9)

27–28 June: Lenin attends the 4th Conference of Trade Unions and Factory Committees and delivers the 'Report on the Current Situation'. (CW 27 pp. 457–90) He comments on the famine and the uprising of the Czech legionaries in Siberia and declares in conclusion: 'Our policy was the right policy, our way was the right way.'

1 July: Lenin complains, in a letter to A A Ioffe, that the latter is always sneering at Chicherin. 'This is enough to drive one mad.' Chicherin is a splendid, cultured colleague. 'It is no misfortune that his weakness is that he lacks the ability to command. There are so many people with the opposite weakness around!' (Briefe V pp. 106–7)

5 July: At the 5th All-Russian Congress of Soviets, Lenin delivers the Sovnarkom report. (CW 27 pp. 505–32) Lenin's speech is interrupted for minutes on end by Left Socialist Revolutionary shouts and objections.

6 July: Left Socialist Revolutionary uprising in Moscow. The German ambassador, Count von Mirbach, is murdered. Lenin, Trotsky and Sverdlov pay a visit to the German embassy and express their condolences. 'He laughed a little, at half pitch, dressed and said firmly to Sverdlov: "We are going". His face changed and became ashen grey. It was not easy for Ilich to go to the Hohenzollern embassy after the death of Count von Mirbach. Deep inside this was probably one of the most difficult moments of his life.' (Trotsky *Über Lenin* p. 111)

7 July: Lenin states in a telegram to Stalin that the Left Socialist Revolutionaries who 'have launched an uprising against us' must be 'mercilessly suppressed'. (Briefe V p. 110)

8 July: The Left Socialist Revolutionaries in Moscow are disarmed and taken prisoner. On his way to visit their headquarters Lenin's car is fired upon by Red Guards. 'Ilich began to talk to them. "Comrades, this will not do, you cannot just start firing without seeing whom you are firing at." They were very embarrassed . . . As we approached the tunnel under the railway bridge we came upon a Komsomol patrol. "Stop." We stopped. "Identity cards." Ilich showed his identity card: V Ulyanov, Chairman of the Council of People's Commissars. "Pull the other one, it has bells on!" The young people arrested Ilich and took him to the nearest police station. He was immediately recognised there and everyone laughed heartily.' (Krupskaya 1959 p. 533)

20 July: Lenin demands, in a letter to Zinoviev, Lashevich and Stasova, a dozen leaders and a few thousand Petrograd workers for the struggle against the Czechs so as to 'make something solid out of the jellied mass.' The situation is 'extremely grave . . . If you are stingy with numbers . . . *you* will be responsible for our defeat.' (Briefe V pp. 120–1)

26 July: Lenin makes a speech at a joint session of the All-Russian CEC, the Moscow Soviet, Factory Committees and Trade Unions of Moscow. (CW 28 pp. 17–34) The Bolsheviks have been harbouring the illusion that the 'forces of the proletariat and the revolutionary people of any one country . . . could overthrow international imperialism. This can only be done by the joint efforts of the workers of the world . . . We knew that our efforts were inevitably leading to a world wide revolution.'

2 August: Lenin speaks at five meetings to workers and Red Guards on the theme 'The Soviet Republic Is in Danger'.

9 August: Lenin writes to G F Fedorov, the chairman of the Nizhny Novgorod (now Gorky) Soviet that 'it is obvious that a White Guard insurrection is being prepared' there. He demands that energetic action be taken. 'Mass searches. Executions for concealing arms. Mass deportation of the Mensheviks and unreliables.' (CW 35 p. 349)

16 August: Lenin speaks at a meeting of the Moscow Party Committee on organising groups of sympathisers. (CW 28 pp. 60-1) Young people must be won over. But 'we must not accept people who try to join for careerist motives; people like this should be driven out of the Party.'

20 August: Lenin writes a 'Letter to Armenian Workers'. (CW 28 pp. 62-75) 'We are now, as it were, in a besieged fortress, waiting for the other detachments of the world socialist revolution to come to our relief.'

23 August: Lenin addresses a meeting in the Polytechnic Museum in Moscow. (CW 28 pp. 79-84) He states that the world revolution will certainly come, it 'is inevitable. But only a fool can answer when revolution will break out in the West. Revolution can never be forecast; it cannot be foretold; it comes of itself. Revolution is brewing and is bound to flare up.'

29 August: Lenin proposes, at a meeting of Sovnarkom, that all members should report in writing on their activities since November 1917. During the three months from June to August Lenin attends over 40 meetings of Sovnarkom at which all aspects of social life are touched upon.

30 August: Lenin speaks at three meetings in Moscow. Leaving the former Michelson Works Lenin is hit by two bullets from a revolver fired by Fanya Kaplan, a Socialist Revolutionary. One bullet penetrates the top of the lung and the other the shoulder. He is taken to the Kremlin. 'Ilich's bed was in the middle of the room and he lay there quite pale, no blood visible in his face. He looked at me, a minute passed, and then he said in a soft voice: "You have come, you are tired. Go and lie down". The words had no meaning but the eyes said something quite different: "It is almost over." I left the room so as not to upset him.' (Krupskaya 1959 p. 538)

7 September: Lenin sends a telegram to Trotsky: 'Recovery proceeding excellently.' (CW 35 p. 359)

12 September: Lenin sends a telegram to Trotsky: 'Congratulations on taking Simbirsk.' Simbirsk is Lenin's home town. (Briefe V p. 173)

16 September: Lenin has recovered and attends a meeting of the CC.

17 September: Lenin chairs once more a meeting of the Sovnarkom.

24 or 25 September: Lenin moves to Gorki, until mid-October, to rest after his health deteriorates. He goes to 'the former estate of von Reinbot, a former city head of Moscow. It was a beautiful, comfortably-furnished house with balconies, a bathroom, electric light and a wonderful park. The guards were housed on the ground floor. Before the attack on Ilich the question of a guard was never solved. Ilich was never accustomed to it . . . [he] was received by the guards with a speech of welcome and a large bouquet of flowers. Ilich was quite embarrassed and the guards were as well. Everything was somehow strange here. We had always been used to small, simple flats . . . We chose the smallest rooms as our living room, the same room in which Ilich, six years later, closed his eyes for the last time.' (Krupskaya 1959 p. 542)

1 October: Lenin writes to Sverdlov and Trotsky that the international revolution has 'come so close in *one week* that it has to be reckoned with as an event of the *next few years* . . . We are all ready to die to help the German workers to advance the revolution which has begun in Germany'. (CW 35 pp. 364-5)

9 October: Lenin writes the article 'The Proletarian Revolution and the Renegade Kautsky'. (CW 28 pp. 105-13) He begins: 'This is the title of a pamphlet I have begun to write.' Kautsky 'has renounced Marxism', the renegade must be unmasked. 'Europe's greatest misfortune and danger is that it has *no* revolutionary party.' But 'world Bolshevism will conquer the world bourgeoisie.'

18 October: Lenin asks A A Ioffe, in Berlin, to forward him all newspaper cuttings on socialist questions. 'We must play the role of an international bureau for ideological questions but we are doing nothing!! Publications must be increased one hundredfold.' (Briefe V p. 189) Lenin writes to the members of the Spartacus Group that their work has 'saved the honour of German socialism and the German proletariat.' They have an important role to play in the 'rapidly maturing German revolution'. (CW 35 p. 369)

22 October: Lenin speaks for the first time in public after his recovery at a joint session of the All-Russian CEC, the Moscow Soviety, Factory Committees and Trade Unions. (CW 28 pp. 114-27) He touches on the German revolution. 'Three months ago people used to laugh when we said there might a revolution in Germany.' The situation is, however, dangerous and this should not be hidden from the masses. 'The workers are mature enough to be told the truth.'

23 October: Lenin tells A A Ioffe during the course of a telephone conversation. 'Immediately transmit our very warm greetings to Karl Liebknecht. The liberation from prison of the representative of the revolutionary workers of Germany is the portent of a new era, the era of victorious socialism.' (CW 35 p. 371)

3 November: Lenin says during a speech at a rally in honour of the Austro–Hungarian revolution: 'The time is near when the first day of the world revolution will be celebrated everywhere. Our labour and sufferings have not been in vain!' (CW 28 p. 131)

6 November: On the first anniversary of the revolution Lenin addresses a celebration meeting of the All-Russian Central and Moscow Trade Union Councils. (CW 28 pp. 132-4) He declares that the working class has demonstrated that 'it is capable of organising industry without intellectuals or capitalists.' Lenin speaks on the anniversary of the revolution and on the international situation at the Extraordinary 6th All-Russian Congress of Soviets. (CW 28 pp. 135-64) 'We did not decree socialism immediately throughout industry, because socialism can only take shape and be consolidated when the working class has learnt how to run the economy and when the authority of the working people has been firmly established.' The complete victory of the socialist revolution 'in our country alone is inconceivable and demands the most active co-operation of at least several advanced countries, which do not include Russia'. Lenin further adds: 'We have never been so near to world proletarian revolution as we are now' but 'the situation is more dangerous than ever before.'

10 November: In a telegram to 'All Soviets of Deputies, to Everyone' Lenin proclaims the victory of the German revolution. (CW 28 p. 179)

19 November: During a speech at the 1st All-Russian Congress of Working Women Lenin states that the task is to 'abolish all restrictions on women's rights.' He is opposed to 'offending religious feelings . . . in fighting religious prejudices.' He describes the previous position of women as that 'of a slave; women have been tied to the home and only socialism can save them from this.' (CW 28 pp. 180-2)

27 November: Lenin speaks at a meeting of Moscow Party workers on petty bourgeois parties. (CW 28 pp. 201-24)

November: Lenin completes the pamphlet 'The Proletarian Revolution and the Renegade Kautsky' (CW 28 pp. 227-325) which *Kommunist*, the Moscow publishing house, still manages to bring out in 1918. It is a reply to Kautsky's *Die Diktatur des Proletariats* (Vienna 1918). Lenin repeats his theses on the state, revolution and the dictatorship of the proletariat. 'The revolutionary dictatorship of the proletariat is rule won and maintained by the use of violence by the proletariat against the bourgeoisie, rule that is unrestricted by any laws.' However 'proletarian democracy is a *million times* more democratic than any bourgeois democracy; Soviet power is a million times more democratic than the most democratic bourgeois republic'. Lenin defines his attitude to war, defensive war, and to the form of government. His hatred of Kautsky finds expression in many terms of abuse – twaddle, stuff and nonsense, lackey of the bourgeoisie, monstrously absurd and untrue statement, fraud and so on.

1 December: Lenin attends the first meeting of the newly-formed Council of Defence.

4 December: Lenin writes to G M Serrati: 'We all hope that a proletarian revolution will soon begin in Italy and other Entente countries.' (CW 36 p. 496)

12 December: Lenin writes to A G Shlyapnikov in Astrakhan that speculators have penetrated Soviet organs there and this is sabotaging the provisioning of the troops. 'Spare no effort to catch the speculators and the bribe takers in Astrakhan and execute them. One must deal

153

with this riff-raff in such a way that everyone will remember it *for years to come*.' (Briefe V p. 213) Lenin telegraphs Trotsky that Perm is in danger. 'I think it is absolutely essential to send reinforcements.' (Briefe V p. 214)

15 December: Lenin instructs E M Sklyansky, Trotsky's deputy, to strengthen, above all, the Southern Front where the Bolsheviks are also gaining ground after the successes in the east.

23 December: Lenin writes the article '"Democracy" and Dictatorship'. (CW 28 pp. 368–72) For Lenin the democratic republic is 'in practice, the dictatorship of the bourgeoisie.'

27 or 28 December: Lenin writes to G V Chicherin: 'We must *urgently* prepare an international socialist conference for founding the Third International, in Berlin (openly) or in Holland (secretly), say, by 1 February 1919.' This should be confirmed by the CC 'before the departure of the Spartacist.' The Spartacist is Eduard Fuchs who had arrived from Berlin and who had also had discussions with Lenin. Lenin proposes to take 'the theory and practice of Bolshevism' which Bukharin is to formulate, and *Was will der Spartakusbund?*, the programme drawn up by Rosa Luxemburg, as the guide lines of the new International. (CW 42 pp. 119–21) Lenin is more precise on 31 December. A platform 'based on the programme of the Spartacus League and the All-Russian Communist Party (Bolsheviks) in Russia' should be the 'basis of the new International.' (Briefe V p. 456)

1919

Beginning of the year: Kruspskaya, who is resting in a school tucked away in the woods, has invited Lenin to spend a Russian Christmas with her. 'On their way to us their car was stopped by bandits. They were quite nonplussed when they recognised Ilich; everyone had to leave the car; Vladimir Ilich, Maria Ilinichna, even the chauffeur, comrade Gil and the comrade who was Ilich's personal body guard; and he never let the jug of milk he was holding out of his hands. Then the bandits got in and drove off. We waited in the school and wondered why Ilich and Maria Ilinichna were so long in coming. When they finally arrived they looked rather bedraggled.' (Krupskaya 1959 p. 553)

6 January: Lenin demands in a telegram to the Kursk Cheka: 'Immediately arrest Kogan, a member of the Kursk Central Purchasing Board, for refusing to help 120 starving workers from Moscow and sending them away empty-handed.' This is to be published so that 'all employees of the central purchasing boards and food organisations should know that formal bureaucratic attitudes to work and incapacity to help starving workers will earn severe reprisals, up to and including shooting.' (CW 36 p. 499)

17 January: Lenin speaks at a joint session of the All-Russian CEC, the Moscow Societ and the All-Russian Trade Union Congress. (CW 28 pp. 391–404) The socialist revolution will last when 'Russia is governed by the proletariat', when there is 'universal training of the working people in the art of governing the state.'

18 January: Lenin addresses the Moscow City Conference of the RCP (B). 'Our enemy today is bureaucracy and profiteering.' (CW 28 pp. 405–6)

19 January: Lenin delivers a speech at a protest rally following the murder of Karl Liebknecht and Rosa Luxemburg in Berlin.

20 January: Lenin delivers a report to the 2nd All-Russian Trade Union Congress. (CW 28 pp. 412–28) The revolution has provided the trade unions with new tasks. 'The trade unions should know that there is higher and more important work than those tasks . . . registration, establishing work standards, the amalgamation of organisations. This task is to teach the people the art of administration . . . the tasks of the trade unions are to build a new life and train millions and tens of millions who will learn by experience not to make mistakes and will discard the old prejudices, who will learn by their own experiences how to run the state and industry.'

21 January: Lenin writes the 'Letter to the Workers of Europe and America' which appears on 24 January in *Pravda* no 16. (CW 28 pp. 429–36) He refers to his letter of 20 August 1918 and states that since then 'the maturing of the world proletarian revolution' and the turning of the workers towards communism 'has proceeded very rapidly.' The foundation of the Communist International became a fact when the Spartacus League with such 'world famous' leaders as 'Liebknecht, Rosa Luxemburg, Clara Zetkin and Franz Mehring' set up the Communist Party of Germany (KPD).

14 February: Lenin writes a 'Reply to a Peasant's Question'. (CW 36 pp. 500–3) He comments on rumours of differences of opinion between himself and Trotsky. 'There are no differences between us', also none where the middle peasants are concerned. He confirms that Trotsky has said that no communist 'has ever entertained the idea of violence against the middle peasants'.

18 February: Lenin telegraphs Zinoviev in Petrograd that he has heard that the Soviet has expelled 'Vera Zasulich and other well known [Menshevik] revolutionaries from the House of Writers. This is scandalous! This is surely not true!' It was, in fact, only a rumour. (Briefe V p. 250)

22 February: Lenin demands that the Menshevik newspaper *Vsegda Vperyod* (Always Ahead) should be shut down because it has launched the slogan 'Stop the Civil War'. This has happened at a time when Kolchak's troops 'are not only occupying Siberia but also Perm' and this is equivalent to 'support of Kolchak.'

1 March: Lenin has a preparatory meeting with a group of delegates attending the founding Congress of the Communist International.

2 March: Lenin declares the 1st Congress of the Communist International open. (CW 28 pp. 453-6) Fifty-two delegates from 30 countries represent for the most part small communist groups. First Lenin asks all present to 'rise in tribute to the finest representatives of the Third International: Karl Liebknecht and Rosa Luxemburg.'

4 March: Lenin speaks on 'Bourgeois Democracy and the Dictatorship of the Proletariat' at the 1st Congress of the Communist International. (CW 28 pp. 457-74) He delivers all his speeches in German at the Congress. He is opposed to the use of the concepts 'democracy in general' and 'dictatorship in general' without posing the 'question of the class concerned'. In his theses he declares that the chief task is to 'explain to the broad mass of the workers the historic significance . . . of the new, proletarian democracy which must replace bourgeois democracy and the parliamentary system.'

6 March: Lenin makes the concluding speech at the 1st Congress of the Communist International which has set up (with the German representative, Eberlein, abstaining) the Third International with headquarters in Moscow. Lenin states: 'The victory of the proletarian revolution on a world scale is assured. The founding of the international Soviet republic is on the way.' (CW 28 pp. 476-7)

8 March: Lenin telegraphs to Tsaritsyn where an employee has been arrested for defacing a portrait of Lenin: 'Nobody should be arrested for defacing a picture. Free Valentina Pershikova immediately.' (Briefe V p. 259)

12 March: Lenin is in Petrograd and delivers a report on the foreign and home policy of Sovnarkom at a session of the Petrograd. (CW 29 pp. 19-37) The Soviet government has won great military victories and has expanded its influence. On the subject of administration Lenin remarks: 'We threw out the old bureaucrats but they have come back, they call themselves "commonists" when they can't bear to say the word "Communist" and they wear a red ribbon in their button-holes and creep into warm corners. What to do about it? We must fight this scum again and again.'

13 March: Lenin attends the funeral of his brother-in-law, Mark Elizarov, in Petrograd. Lenin speaks on the organisation of a farm labourers' union at the 1st Congress of Farm Labourers of Petrograd Gubernia. (CW 29 pp. 38-46) He also speaks at a meeting in the People's House in Petrograd.

14 March: Lenin returns to Moscow.

18 March: Lenin delivers a speech in memory of J M Sverdlov, the former chairman of the All-Russian CEC at a special session of the All-Russian CEC. (CW 29 pp. 89-94) Lenin calls Sverdlov the 'most perfect type of professional revolutionary', a man who possessed an 'exceptional organising talent'. After the session Lenin accompanies the funeral procession to Red Square where he delivers a funeral oration at Sverdlov's grave. Lenin opens the 8th Congress of the RCP (B) which remains in session in Moscow until 23 March. Four hundred and three delegates represent 313,000 members. Lenin delivers the report of the CC. (CW 29 pp. 146-64) The Russian revolution was 'largely a *bourgeois* revolution until the Committee of Poor Peasants (Kombedy) were set up, i.e. until the summer and even the autumn of 1918.' When future historians try to discover who administered Russia during the last 17 months 'nobody will believe that it was done by so few people. The number was so small because there were so few, intelligent, educated and capable political leaders in Russia'.

19 March: Lenin delivers the report on the Party programme at the Congress. (CW 29 pp. 165-96) Already in February he had prepared a rough draft of the Party programme and written detailed notes on some sections. (CW 29 pp. 97-140) According to Lenin the programme should be based on the premise that the 'era of the world proletarian, communist revolution has begun'. He passes from the analysis of world capitalism to the 'chief tasks of the dictatorship of the proletariat in Russia' and underlines the necessity of continuing the 'struggle against bureaucratism'. He adheres, as before, to the right of national self-determination. In Lenin's view Bukharin has missed the main point. 'How is it that comrade Bukharin has forgotten a small trifle, the Bashkirs? There are no Bushmen in Russia, nor have I heard that the Hottentots have held claim to an autonomous republic, but we have Bashkirs, Kirghiz and a number of other peoples and to these we cannot deny recognition.' Each nation is travelling 'in the same historical direction' but 'by very different zigzags and bypaths'; the 'more cultured nations are obviously proceeding in a way that differs from that of the less cultured nations. Finland advanced in a different way. Germany is advancing in a different way.'

22 March: Lenin sends 'ardent greetings', on behalf of the Party Congress, to the government of the Hungarian Soviet Republic. 'Our Congress is convinced that the time is not far distant when communism will triumph all over the world . . . Long live the world communist republic!' (CW 29 p. 197) In a radio message he says: 'This is Lenin. Sincere greetings to the proletarian government of the Hungarian Soviet Republic and especially to Comrade Béla Kun.' (CW 29 p. 226)

23 March: Lenin delivers the 'Report on Work in the Countryside' at the Congress and makes the final speech. (CW 29 pp. 198-225) He concentrates on the middle peasants who 'must be helped'. He is convinced that it will 'be the last difficult half-year' and this has been strengthened by the 'news of the success of the proletarian revolution in Hungary'. Lenin is re-elected to the CC, RCP (B). In a radio message to Béla Kun, Lenin asks if the communists have a majority in the government. It would be a mistake 'given the specific conditions' in Hungary to 'imitate our Russian tactics in all details . . . I must warn you against this mistake'. (CW 29 p. 227)

25 March: The CC plenum re-elects Lenin to the Politburo.

End of March: Eight speeches by Lenin are recorded on gramophone records (CW 29 pp. 237-53) including one against anti-Semitism. 'Shame on accursed tsarism which tortured and persecuted the Jews. Shame on those who foment hatred towards the Jews, who foment hatred towards other nations.'

2 April: In reply to a request by artisans in Cherepovits Gubernia for permission to complete the building, begun in 1915, of their church, Lenin writes: 'Of course the building of the church may be completed.' (Briefe V p. 265)

3 April: Lenin speaks at a session of the Moscow Soviet. (CW 29 pp. 255-71) He underlines the 'extremely grave situation' of Soviet power. 'We shall allow no opposition. The imperialists of the whole world have got us by the throat, they are trying to defeat us by all the force of an armed attack and we must fight a life and death struggle.' He adds: 'We shall live to see the day when the world Soviet republic will be added to the Russian and Hungarian Soviet Republics.' Lenin writes to E M Sklyansky: 'The twelve French prisoners are suffering from the cold. Provide them with clothing and food.' (Briefe V p. 265)

5 April: Lenin asks for the Council for the Protection of the Child to be helped as much as possible.

7 April: Lenin requests Béla Kun, by radio, to 'greet the Bavarian Soviet Republic'. (CW 44 p. 208)

10 April: In a letter Lenin appeals to Petrograd workers to 'help the Eastern Front'. Kolchak's victories in the east are endangering Soviet power. (CW 29 p. 275)

11 April: Lenin speaks at a meeting of the All-Russian Central Council of Trade Unions (CW 29 pp. 281-301) and describes the military situation. It was correct to concentrate almost all forces in the south, the capture of Odessa proved that. However Kolchak is now threatening the Volga in the east. Lenin makes concrete proposals for the mobilisation and arming of trade unionists.

13 April: Lenin informs the publishing house of the Petrograd Soviet that he has received 'The 20,000' fee and '15,000 of it should be paid into the publisher's account in the name of P Petrov.' (Briefe V p. 272)

15 April: Lenin writes 'The Third International and its Place in History'. (CW 29 pp. 305-13) The Third International has 'gathered the fruits of the work of the Second International', has discarded its 'petty-bourgeois dross' and has begun to 'give effect to Marx's cardinal slogan', the dictatorship of the proletariat. This is creating 'democracy for the masses' for the first time. However history is moving along paths that 'are anything but smooth, simple and straight.'

17 April: Lenin speaks at the 1st All-Russian Congress of Communist Students. (CW 29 p. 324) It is important to 'learn'. The future society 'in which all must work, the society in which there will be no class distinctions' will be built later by the youth of the country; at present the task is to work under the guidance 'of your seniors'.

27 April: Lenin sends a message of greetings to the Bavarian Socialist Republic. (CW 29 pp. 325-6) He has many questions: Have councils of workers and servants been formed in the different parts of the city; have the workers been armed; have the bourgeoisie been disarmed ... ; have the capitalist factories ... been confiscated; have mortgage and rent payments by small peasants been cancelled; have the wages of farm labourers and unskilled workers been doubled and trebled; Further he asks if workers have been given the houses and the flats of the rich. 'Have you taken hostages from the ranks of the bourgeoisie' and have higher rations for workers than for the bourgeoisie been introduced? An improvement in the living standards of workers, farm labourers and small farmers has to be achieved irrespective of the cost.

1 May: Lenin delivers three speeches in Red Square.

2 May: Lenin proposes more 'aid in kind be rendered to workers' children'. (CW 42 p. 136)

13 May: Lenin sends a telegram to Béla Kun. He is 'sure that in spite of the vast difficulties the proletarians of Hungary will retain power and consolidate it.' (CW 36 p. 509)

15 May: Lenin proposes to the All-Russian CEC that the salary of A D Tsyurupa, his assistant, be raised since his family is always hungry. 'The children are adolescents, they need *more* than an adult.' (CW 44 p. 230)

19 May: Lenin delivers a speech 'Deception of the People with Slogans of Freedom and Equality' at the 1st All-Russian Congress on Adult Education. (CW 29 pp. 339-76) Class struggle in its most extreme form occurs after the overthrow of the bourgeoisie. 'We want to abolish classes and in this sense we are for equality. But the claim that we want all men to be alike is just nonsense, the silly invention of an intellectual.' The dictatorship of the proletariat is inevitable but it 'does not mean only force, although it is impossible without force, but also a form of the organisation of labour superior to the preceding form'.

20 May: Lenin sends a telegram to the town of Gomel: 'If Rabkin's bicycle was acquisitioned for the duration of the uprising why was it not returned afterwards?' (Briefe V p. 309)

22 May: Lenin telegraphs Trotsky that the situation in Astrakhan gives cause for alarm; Trotsky is to 'go there a second time' and solve the problem. 'Evidently Sokolnikov is not up to it.' (Briefe V p. 312)

27 May: Lenin sends 'Greetings to the Hungarian Workers' (CW 29 pp. 387-91) and states that Hungary is revealing the international significance of Soviet power but the transition is altogether different from that in Russia. The essence of the dictatorship of the proletariat is 'not in force alone' but in organisation and discipline so as to achieve socialism 'and remove the basis for all exploitation of man by man'. This goal cannot be achieved 'at one stroke'. Lenin sends a message to King Aman Ullah of Afghanistan: 'We greet the intention of Your Majesty to establish close relations with the Russian people.' (Briefe V p. 380)

28 May: Lenin writes the article 'The Heroes of the Berne International' (CW 29 pp. 392–401) directed against the Independent SPD.

29 May: Lenin telegraphs S I Gusev, M M Lashevich and K K Yurenev in Simbirsk: 'If we don't win the Urals before the winter, I consider that the revolution will inevitably perish.' (CW 35 p. 393)

30 May: Lenin writes to the Orgluro of the CC: 'I am in favour of expelling members who engage in religious observances.' (Briefe V p. 321)

31 May: Lenin's appeal, also signed by Dzerzhinsky: 'Beware of Spies!' appears in *Pravda* no 116. (CW 29 p. 403) The advance of the 'White Guards' on Petrograd reveals that they have spies everywhere. 'Death to Spies!'

8 June: Lenin writes to Sklyansky: 'More hostages from the ranks of the bourgeoisie and the families of officers must be seized because of the increasing incidence of treason.' (Briefe V p. 334)

18 June: Lenin writes to Béla Kun that it is quite in order for Hungary to enter into negotiations with the Entente but the Entente should not be trusted 'for a moment'. (CW 36 p. 512)

28 June: Lenin completes his pamphlet 'A Great Beginning' (CW 29 pp. 409–34) and it is published in July. He touches on fundamental questions following the organisation of the communist subbotniks, voluntary unpaid work carried out on free Saturdays. The success of the dictatorship of the proletariat depends on 'a higher type of social organisation of labour'. Leadership must be exercised by industrial workers. Lenin defines classes thus: 'Classes are large groups of people differing from each other by the place they occupy in an historically determined system of social production, by their relation (in most cases fixed and formulated in law) to the means of production, by the role in the social organisation of labour and consequently by the dimensions of the share of social wealth of which they dispose and the mode of acquiring it.' Labour productivity, for Lenin, is 'in the last analysis the most important, the principal thing for the victory of the new social system.' Capitalism can only be defeated by 'socialism creating a new and much higher productivity of labour.' Despite the laws emancipating every woman she still remains a house slave 'because *petty housework* crushes, strangles, stultifies and degrades her, chains her to the kitchen and the nursery and she wastes her labour on barbarously unproductive, petty, nerve-racking, stultifying and crushing drudgery.' The liberation

of women and 'real communism' begin only with the wholesale transformation of petty housekeeping into 'a large-scale socialist economy'.
1 July: Lenin congratulates the 'liberators of the Urals' who have taken
Perm and Kungur. (Briefe VI p. 1)
Before 3 July: Lenin writes the CC letter 'All Out for the Fight Against
Denikin!' (CW 29 pp. 436–55) and it is carried at a CC plenum on 3–4
July. 'The Soviet Republic is besieged by the enemy. It must become a
single military camp, not in word but in deed.'
4 July: Lenin reports on the current situation at a joint session of the
All-Russian CEC, the Moscow Soviet, the Council of Trade Unions and
representatives of Moscow factory committees. (CW 29 pp. 456–69)
Compared with July 1918 the situation has improved, especially on the
industrial front.
8 July: Lenin writes to Maxim Gorky in Petrograd and asks him to
come. 'We must speak about various things urgently.' Lenin writes to
Kamenev and asks for 'firewood to be delivered' to Gorky. (Briefe VI
p. 8)
9 July: Lenin writes to his wife Nadezhda Krupskaya, who is sailing on
the Volga in the *Krasnaya Zvezda* (Red Star), a steamer engaged on
propaganda work. 'I read the letters asking for help that sometimes
come for you and try to do what I can ... on Sundays we take a holiday at "our" country house. Trotsky is better; he has left for the south
and I hope he will manage all right . . . I embrace you fondly and ask
you to write and to telegraph more often.' (CW 37 pp. 543–4)
11 July: Lenin lectures on 'The State' at the Sverdlov University in
Moscow. (CW 29 pp. 470–88) He reiterates his concept of the role of
the state and says that to approach the 'question scientifically' means
'not to forget the underlying historical connections, to examine every
question from the standpoint of how the given phenomenon arose in
history and what were the principal stages in its development; and from
the standpoint of its development to examine what it has become today'.
12 July: Lenin predicts, in a report delivered at the Moscow Conference
of the RCP (B) (CW 29 pp. 489–93) that 'this July will be the last
difficult one and next July we shall welcome the victory of the world
Soviet republic.'
14 July: Lenin writes the article 'The Tasks of the Third International'
(CW 29 pp. 494–512) directed against Ramsay MacDonald.
15 July: Lenin writes to Krupskaya: 'Yesterday and the day before I
was in Gorki with Mitya [his brother Dmitri] (he has been here for
four days) and Anya [his sister Anna]. The limes are in bloom. We had
a good rest. I embrace you fondly and kiss you. Please rest more and
work less.' (CW 37 p. 546)
18 July: Lenin writes to Gorky: 'Come here for a rest — I often go
away for two days to the country where I can put you up splendidly.'
(CW 35 p. 409)

31 July: Lenin writes to Maxim Gorky that Petrograd has been 'one of the sickest places in recent times' since the workers there have suffered most. These impressions led Gorky to 'sick conclusions', such as when Gorky writes that the 'divergence' from communism 'is deepening'. This is a mood which demands that you 'change your circumstances radically, your environment.' (CW 25 pp. 410–4)

End of July: Lenin replies to the request of Béla Kun for immediate aid; he is not to despair, but 'immediate aid at present is physically impossible.' Béla Kun should try to 'hold on as long as possible. Every week is precious. Supply Budapest with provisions, fortify the city.' (Briefe VI p. 26)

10 August: Lenin writes to Sklyansky: 'I am not well. I have had to go to bed.' He wants an offensive in the direction of Voronezh. (CW 35 p. 417)

20 August: Lenin telegraphs the War Councils of the 10th and 4th Armies: 'Issue the strictest order: the peasants are to be protected in every way during the bringing-in of the harvest, and robbery, violence and illegal procurement of grain by soldiers are to be ruthlessly punished by execution by a firing squad.' (Briefe VI p. 35)

23 August: Lenin asks the agricultural section of the Moscow Soviet food department 'kindly' not to send him any fruit from state farms in future but to inform him if it 'is given to hospitals, sanatoria, children.' (CW 44 p. 277)

24 August: In a 'Letter to the Workers and Peasants Apropos of the Victory over Kolchak' (CW 29 pp. 552–60) Lenin writes: 'Red troops have liberated the entire Urals area from Kolchak and have begun the liberation of Siberia.'

28 August: Lenin replies (CW 29 pp. 561–6) to a letter from Sylvia Pankhurst. He is convinced that to 'renounce participation in the parliamentary elections is a mistake on the part of the revolutionary workers in Britain' but it would be preferable to 'make that mistake than to delay the formation of a big workers' Communist Party in Britain'.

15 September: Lenin, in a letter to Maxim Gorky, defends the arrest of 'bourgeois intellectuals of the near-Cadet type . . . No. There is no harm in such "talents" being made to spend some weeks or so in prison, if this *has* to be done to *prevent* plots . . . and the death of tens of thousands'. (CW 44 pp. 283–5)

21 September: An article by Zinoviev, 'On the Numerical Composition of Our Party' appears in *Pravda*. Lenin writes, in a foreword, that everyone is to take note of the article; 'purge' the Party of 'hangers-on' and recruit all the best elements among the mass of workers and peasants. (CW 36 p. 514)

23 September: Lenin speaks at the Conference of Non-Party Women Workers. (CW 30 pp. 40–6) He repeats that the 'complete equality of women' will be achieved when housework has been overcome. The task now is to 'make politics available to every working woman.'

5 October: Lenin replies to questions put by the correspondent of the *Chicago Daily News*. (CW 30 pp. 50-1) The Soviet government is prepared to guarantee absolute non-intervention in the internal affairs of foreign states; it is 'the most democratic government . . . of the world' and it is in favour of 'an economic understanding with America — with all countries, but *especially* with America'.

10 October: Lenin expresses 'Greetings to Italian, French and German Communists'. (CW 30 pp. 52-62) In Germany 'the Kautskyite (or Independent) party is dying' whereas the Communist Party 'will grow stronger and become as hard as steel'. The 'victory of commumism' is 'inevitable'.

14 October: Lenin writes, in a letter to Dutch communists: 'Our position is very difficult owing to the offensive of 14 states.' (CW 44 p. 291)

17 October: Lenin writes to Trotsky that Petrograd will be defended to the last. 'As you see, your plan has been adopted.' (CW 44 pp. 294-5)

19 October: Lenin writes the appeal 'To the Red Army Men'. (CW 30 p. 70) 'The tsarist generals — Yudenich in the north and Denikin in the south — are once again bending every effort in an attempt to vanquish Soviet power.' The defeat of Kolchak in the Urals and in Siberia has demonstrated the possibilities of the Red Army; forward 'against the landowners and the tsarist generals!'

24 October: Lenin criticises, in a letter to V V Vorovsky of the state publishing house, the published report on the founding Congress of the Communist International (Comintern). 'A slovenly mess. No table of contents. Some idiot or sloven, evidently an illiterate, has lumped together, as though he were drunk, all the "material", little articles, speeches, and printed them *out of sequence* . . . An unheard-of disgrace!' (CW 35 pp. 427-8)

28 October: Lenin writes to Paul Levi, Clara Zetkin, Eberlein and other members of the CC, KPD, that he has learnt of the split among German communists; it should not be deepened. The left opposition obviously has 'very gifted propagandists, inexperienced and young, like our own Left Communist of 1918.' The unity of the KPD is necessary. (CW 30 pp. 87-8) Lenin also writes to the 'communist comrades' who have now 'formed a new party'. (CW 30 pp. 89-90) He thinks an exchange of views could assist in 'advancing the cause of German communism and in mustering its forces. I shall be very glad if we manage to exchange opinions on these questions.' Lenin writes to V A Kugushev in Ufa that his secretary L A Fotieva is ill. 'It is our business to *repair* this "state property".' He asks that she be 'fixed up, have medical treatment and be fed to *bursting point*'. (CW 44 p. 305)

30 October: Lenin writes 'Economics and Politics in the Era of the

Dictatorship of the Proletariat'. (CW 30 pp. 107–17) 'Socialism means the abolition of classes.' At present the 'essence' of socialism consists in demarcating the 'working peasant from the peasant owner'.

21 November: Lenin asks A S Enukidze to provide additional food for 'Keeley, an American engineer, who has come to help the Soviet government' and for Ursin, the founder of Finnish Social Democracy; 'in particular, *butter*'. The 'Finns helped us very considerably before 1905. It is now our duty to help them.' (CW 44 pp. 311–2)

22 November: Lenin addresses the 2nd All-Russian Congress of Communist Organisations of the Peoples of the East. (CW 30 pp. 151–62) 'It is self-evident that final victory can be won only by the proletariat of all the advanced countries of the world, and we, the Russians, are beginning the work which the British, French or German proletariat will consolidate. But we see that they will not be victorious without the aid of the working people of the oppressed colonial nations; first and foremost, of Eastern nations.'

2 December: Lenin opens the 8th All-Russian Conference of the RCP (B) and delivers the report of the CC. (CW 30 pp. 167–94) Lenin states that one may say 'without any exaggeration . . . that our main difficulty is now behind us.' Terror was forced on Soviet power. A draft resolution states that the Russian Socialist Federative Soviet Republic 'wishes to live in peace with all peoples and devote all its efforts to internal development.'

5 December: Lenin delivers the All-Russian CEC and Sovnarkom report at the 7th All-Russian Congress of Soviets. (CW 30 pp. 205–42) 'Our banking on the world revolution . . . has on the whole been fully justified.' However 'we have seen for ourselves that the revolution's development in more advanced countries has proved to be considerably slower, considerably more difficult, considerably more complicated.' A new 'scourge' is threatening the country; lice and typhus. *'Either the lice will defeat socialism or socialism will defeat the lice!'*

16 December: Lenin completes the article 'The Constituent Assembly Elections and the Dictatorship of the Proletariat' (CW 30 pp. 253–75) and it is published in *Communist International*. Lenin analyses the election results of November 1917 in order to explain the victory of the Bolsheviks. The Bolsheviks had polled over 25 per cent of all votes cast, they had achieved a majority in the capital cities and had received half the votes cast by the armed forces; without this they 'could not have been victorious'. The thesis of the 'opportunists', that a majority at the polls had first to be achieved is false. 'The proletariat must first overthrow the bourgeoisie and win *for itself* state power and then use that state power, that is, the dictatorship of the proletariat, as an instrument of its class for the purpose of winning the sympathy of the majority of the working people.'

21 December: Lenin requests, in a telegram to Ryazan, that the promised potatoes for Moscow be delivered more quickly. 'The working class of Moscow is in the throes of starvation. Saving it means saving the revolution.' (CW 44 pp. 319-20)

23 December: At a meeting of Sovnarkom Lenin goes into the problem of improving conditions for scientists. During 1919 he attended numerous meetings of Sovnarkom, the All-Russian CEC, the CC and Politburo of the RCP (B) and the Council of Defence and worked intensively on many internal, foreign and military problems; he also concerned himself with innumerable petty matters.

28 December: Lenin writes, in a 'Letter to the Workers and Peasants of the Ukraine Apropos of the Victories over Denikin' (CW 30 pp. 291-7) that 'Red troops have taken Kiev, Poltava and Kharkov and are advancing victoriously on Rostov'. The Ukraine will be liberated. A '*voluntary* union' of nations is necessary. Mutual mistrust should be fought and Russian communists 'must repress with the utmost severity the slightest manifestation in our midst of Great Russian nationalism.'

End of 1919: Lenin writes an introduction to John Reed's book *Ten Days that Shook the World*. He recommends the book unreservedly to 'the workers of the world' since it 'gives a truthful and most vivid exposition' of the October Revolution. (CW 36 p. 519)

1920

4 January: Lenin writes to G V Chicherin that Bolshevik organisations should collect '4-5 copies of *every* socialist and anarchist and communist pamphlet and book, *every* resolution, *all reports* and minutes of congresses, etc., etc., in all languages'. Foreigners are to be employed. 'Russians are slovenly and will *never* do this meticulously.' (CW 44 pp. 325-6) Lenin writes to V D Bonch-Bruevich: 'I am paying *personally* for my library.' (CW 44 p. 327)

17 or 18 January: Lenin pushes through a resolution in the Politburo against V M Frunze who had protested against an order by Trotsky. 'The order by Lenin and Trotsky given by telephone is found to be correct.' (CW 42 pp. 159-60)

20 January: Lenin drafts a reply to a letter from the Independent SPD (USPD). (CW 30 pp. 337-44) Lenin regards the 'recognition' of the dictatorship of the proletariat by the USPD as being 'purely verbal' and he is opposed to their joining the Comintern.

23 January: Lenin writes to G M Krzhizhanovsky that there are too few 'specialists with a wide horizon and an eye for the future'; Lenin develops a plan for electrification. 'Let's set to work and in 10-20 years we shall make all Russia, both industrial and agricultural, *electrical*.' A programme for the next 10-20 years must sweep along 'the mass of workers and politically conscious peasants'. (CW 35 pp. 435-6)

24 January: Lenin speaks at a Non-Party Conference of Workers and Red Army Men of Presnya District, Moscow. (CW 30 pp. 302-6) According to Lenin the victories of the Red Army and the raising of the blockade have made the situation easier. The workers in Western Europe do not want to fight against Russia. 'We were . . . victorious not because we were the stronger but because the working folk of the Entente countries proved to be closer to us than to their own governments.'

27 January: Lenin addresses the 3rd All-Russian Congress of Economic Councils. (CW 30 pp. 309-13) He favours moving from corporate (collegiate) to 'one man management'.

2 February: Lenin delivers the Sovnarkom report at a meeting of the All-Russian CEC. (CW 30 pp. 315-36) After the defeat of Kolchak's army in the Far East, the annihilation of Yudenich's troops before Petrograd and the victories in the south it is now clear to the West that the 'hopes of crushing the military forces of the Soviet Republic' have vanished. As a consequence the blockade has also been lifted. The 'lie' that the Bolsheviks stayed in power only by force has been refuted. Terror was forced on the Bolsheviks by the Entente. Even before the end of the Civil War we 'renounced capital punishment and have therefore proved that we intend to carry out our own programme as we had promised.' It is important to make use 'of the technical knowledge, culture and the apparatus created by bourgeois capitalist civilisation.' The new technical base is to be electricity.

14 February: Lenin writes 'A Publicist's Notes'. (CW 30 pp. 352-62) He takes umbrage at a letter from Jean Longuet, Marx's grandson and a French socialist. Lenin attacks the 'Centrists' and also goes into some of Otto Bauer's arguments. 'Speaking abstractly', Lenin regards a 'regular' (peaceful) transition to socialism as possible and advantageous, but this is only possible if beforehand the proletariat has been victorious in nine or ten countries, 'including all the Great Powers'.

18 February: Lenin answers the questions of the correspondent of the *New York Evening Journal*. (CW 30 pp. 365-7) Soviet power desires 'peaceful co-existence with all peoples'. The victory of Soviet power throughout the world cannot be prevented. 'I, for one, do not know of any means of preventing it.'

19 February: Lenin writes to the members of the Politburo: 'I am against summoning Stalin. He is cavilling.' (CW 44 pp. 342-3)

1 March: Lenin speaks at the 1st All-Russian Congress of Working Cossacks. (CW 30 pp. 380-400) He states that Soviet Russia has emerged stronger from the war. Some people have tried to 'slander Comrade Trotsky' by declaring that the victories were due to the 'iron discipline' of the Red Army. 'We have never denied this. War is war and it demands iron discipline.' The dictatorship of the proletariat is, however, vital. There is the threat of a new capitalist war 'not because the capitalists, taken individually, are vicious — individually they are just like other people' — but because 'private property has led and always will lead to war'. He points out the danger of a war with Poland. 'We know that it was a heinous crime to divide Poland up among the German, Austrian and Russian capitalists . . . We therefore understand the hatred the Poles feel.' Lenin rejects a war 'on account of frontiers' but 'we shall defend' the Russia of the Soviet revolution 'to the last drop of blood'.

4 March: Lenin demands that 'activities in the organisation of medical and educational institutions for defective juveniles' be stepped up. (CW 42 pp. 182-3)

6 March: Lenin delivers a speech, at a special session of the Moscow Soviet, on the occasion of the first anniversary of the founding of the Third International. (CW 30 pp. 417-25) 'Europe is not moving towards revolution the way we did, although essentially Europe is going through the same experience . . . And it is because they are experiencing this independently that we can be sure the victory of the communist revolution in all countries is inevitable.'

19 March: In a telegram to Maxim Gorky in Petrograd Lenin informs him that his request for better provisions for scientists will be granted. A V Sapozhnikov, a chemist, whom Gorky had asked to be released from prison, is now free. (CW 44 p. 359)

29 March: Lenin opens the 8th Congress of the RCP (B) and delivers the CC report before more than 700 delegates representing 611,000 members. He also speaks on economic construction and the co-operatives. (CW 30 pp. 439-90) 'And after these victories we may now proceed with calm and firm assurance to the immediate tasks of peaceful economic development.' Lenin fills in the questionnaire for Congress delegates. (CW 42 pp. 443-4) He answers, among others the following questions: Former profession: Barrister's assistant, publicist; Nationality: Russian; Party work done: member of the CC and editor of the Central Organ; Doing illegal work: 1893-1917; Present Party work: member of the CC, chairman of Sovnarkom and the Council of Defence; Arrested: 1887, 1894 and 1900; In prison: 14 months plus several days; In exile: 3 years, in emigration 1900-5 and 1908-17.

30 March: Lenin replies to the discussion on the report of the CC. He takes issue with his critics, the Democratic Centralists, Sapronov and others, who accuse the leadership of bureaucraticism.

31 March: Lenin speaks at the Congress on economic development. He against proposes one-man management in the economy, and on the trade unions he says: 'It is essential for the CC to be constituted in such a way as to have a transmission belt to the broad masses of the trade unions . . . to connect the CC simultaneously with the united will of 600,000 Party members and the 3,000,000 trade union members. We cannot govern without such a transmission belt.'

March: Lenin writes to A V Lunacharsky: 'A number of monasteries outside Petrograd should be taken over to accommodate defective and *homeless* children and adolescents.' (CW 44 p. 366)

1 April: Lenin addresses the 1st All-Russian Congress of Mineworkers. (CW 30 pp. 495-501) 'We continue to be a besieged fortress towards which the world's workers are turned, for they know that their freedom will come from here; and in this besieged fortress we must act with military ruthlessness, with military discipline and self-sacrifice.'

2 April: Lenin telegraphs G K Ordzhonikidze on the Caucasian Front: 'Display caution and maximum good will towards the Moslems . . . Do everything to demonstrate, and in the most emphatic manner, our sympathy for the Moslems, their autonomy, independence, etc.' (CW 30 p. 494) He writes about this to Trotsky: 'Comrade Trotsky, if you are in agreement, send it in code by direct line. I have drawn it up toether with Stalin.' (Briefe VI p. 180)

3 April: Lenin speaks on co-operatives at the 9th Congress of the RCP (B).

5 April: Lenin is reelected to the CC, RCP (B) at the 9th Congress. His forthcoming birthday leads to him being specially honoured by the delegates and it is decided to publish a complete edition of his works. Whem Kamenev informs Lenin that he intends to prepare a complete edition of his works and to make a corresponding proposal, 'Ilich began to protest. "Why? Completely superfluous. Everything possible was written thirty years ago. It is not worth it." Only my remark that youth must learn and that it was better when they learned from his works, instead of from the writings of Martov and Tugan-Baranovsky, caused him to hesitate.' (Kamenev *Lenins literarische Erbe* pp. 19-20) Radek writes later: 'When I remarked on one occasion to Vladimir Ilich that I had been thumbing through the volume of his works for 1903, which had just been published, a crafty smile spread over his face and he said mockingly: "It's interesting now to read how stupid were were then".' (Lenin *Leben und Werk* p. 44) Lenin makes the closing speech at the Congress. The rapid growth of the Party causes him a 'certain apprehension'. The chief task is the education of Party members. The condition for the maintenance of 'discipline is loyalty to the cause'.

7 April: Lenin speaks at the 3rd All-Russian Trade Union Congress. (CW 30 pp. 502-15) 'We are surrounded by the petty bourgeoisie who are reviving freedom of trade and capitalism.' The chief slogan is: 'let us get closer to one-man management, let us have more labour discipline, let us pull ourselves together and work with military determination, staunchness and loyalty, brushing aside all groups and craft interests, sacrificing all private interests.'

8 April: Lenin writes the article 'From the Destruction of the Old Social System to the Creation of the New'. (CW 30 pp. 516-8) 'It will take many years, decades, to create . . . new forms of social ties between people and new forms and methods of drawing people into labour.'

19 April: Lenin speaks at the 3rd All-Russian Congress of Textile Workers. (CW 30 pp. 519–25) The 'unparalleled privations of the last two years' are not yet over for the proletariat. It must achieve 'unparalleled miracles' on the labour front, comparable to those achieved by the Red Army on 'the war front'.

22 April: Lenin asks the Petrograd Soviet to afford Gorky *'every* assistance'. (CW 44 p. 370) Lenin receives many telegrams, letters and so on on the occasion of his fiftieth birthday.

23 April: Lenin addresses a meeting held in honour of his fiftieth birthday. (CW 30 pp. 526–8) He thanks everyone for the congratulations and 'even more for having spared me congratulatory speeches'. He hopes that the Party will not get a big head. Lenin opposes the personality cult which was then developing around him. He forbade the collection of material for a future Lenin museum. On this he remarked to M S Olminsky: 'You have no idea how unpleasant I find the constant promotion of my person.' (Biographie p. 660)

27 April: Lenin completes the pamphlet '"Left Wing Communism" – An Infantile Disorder'. (CW 31 pp. 17–118) He adds an appendix on 12 May. This work, which is published in June, is an attempt at a popular exposition of Marxist strategy and tactics and is directed against ultra-left currents. Lenin, basing himself on Bolshevik history, sets out to demonstrate that the struggle against pernicious 'petty-bourgeois radicalism' is also necessary. Refusing compromises 'on principle' is 'childish' as far as Lenin is concerned, for politics is a 'science and an art'. Lenin advises his followers to use every dodge and trick, to engage in compromises and to work in 'reactionary' trade unions and parliaments; however, never to lose sight of the goal of communism. A basic law of revolution for Lenin is: Only when the 'lower strata' no longer want the old order and the 'upper strata' can no longer live in the *old way*, only then can the revolution be victorious. A revolution is impossible without a crisis within the whole nation. Development is 'different' in each country and under no circumstances may tactical rules be applied in a stereotyped manner.

1 May: During the morning Lenin helps move timber in the Kremlin during a subbotnik. He speaks at two meetings and at the ceremonial laying of the foundation stone of a monument to Karl Marx in Moscow.

5 May: Lenin addresses troops who are leaving for the Polish front. Soviet Russia and Poland have been at war since 26 April.

7 May: Lenin thanks the 30th Regiment in Turkestan 'for the macaroni and flour' which he has 'handed over to the children of Moscow.' (CW 44 p. 374)

20 May: In a message to the Indian Revolutionary Association (CW 31

p. 138) Lenin writes that only when the 'Indian, Chinese, Korean, Japanese, Persian and Turkish workers and peasants' get on with the 'cause of liberation' will the 'victory over the exploiters be ensured'.

26 May: Lenin has discussions with a British labour delegation.

30 May: Lenin writes a 'Letter to British Workers' on the nature of reformist politics. (CW 31 pp. 139-43) He writes to G V Chicherin that he is not satisfied with the letter. 'I am exhausted and the words would just not come to me.' (Briefe VI p. 207)

3 June: Lenin writes to Trotsky about Stalin's plan to launch an offensive in the Crimea. 'Won't it cost too many lives? We will be sacrificing most of our soldiers. We must think this over and weigh it up ten times.' He proposes as an answer to Stalin: 'Wait for our reply. Lenin, Trotsky.' (CW 44 p. 381)

4 June: Lenin states, in an interview with K Fusse, correspondent of the Japanese newspapers *Osaka Mainichi* and *Tokyo Nichi-Nichi*, that 'real communism' can succeed only in the West, 'but it must be remembered that the West lives at the expense of the East'; there imperialism is digging 'its own grave'. According to Lenin the chief tasks of Soviet power are: 'First, to beat the Polish landlords, second, to secure a lasting peace and then, third, to develop our economic life.' (CW 42 pp. 195-6)

5 June: Lenin writes the 'preliminary draft' of his theses on the national and colonial question for the 2nd Congress of the Communist International (Comintern). (CW 31 pp. 144-51) The interests of the 'proletarian struggle in any one country' must 'be subordinated to the interests of the struggle on a world-wide scale.' The victorious revolution in one country must 'make the greatest national sacrifices for the overthrow of international capital.'

Beginning of June: Lenin writes the 'preliminary draft theses on the agrarian question' for the 2nd Comintern Congress. (CW 31 pp. 152-64) According to Lenin, only the urban and industrial proletariat 'led by the Communist Party' can lead and liberate the peasantry.

12 June: Lenin reviews the journal *Kommunismus* which is published in Vienna. (CW 31 pp. 165-7) He criticises articles by György Lukács, a 'very left-wing and very poor' article, and by Béla Kun. Lenin speaks at the 2nd All-Russian Conference of Organisers Responsible for Rural Work. (CW 31 pp. 168-80) He discusses the war with Poland and refers to it as another 'instance of God (if he exists, of course) first depriving of reason those whom he would punish. The Entente is undoubtedly headed by very shrewd men, excellent politicians, yet these people commit folly after folly'. The slogan 'all for the war' must now be proclaimed in Russia to ensure victory.

19 June: Lenin attends a meeting of the Executive Committee of the Comintern (ECCI); he criticises the French and Italian socialists.

25 June: Lenin, in a letter to Zinoviev, writes that Pavlov, the famous psychologist, has requested, in view of his difficult material circumstances, to be permitted to travel abroad. This is hardly advisable since he will only oppose communism when there. This scholar is 'such a great cultural asset' that his 'forcible detention in Russia in conditions of material insecurity is unthinkable.' Lenin proposes that Pavlov be allowed 'a special ration' and 'more or less comfortable circumstances'. (CW 44 p. 392)

4 July: Lenin writes the 'Theses on the Fundamental Tasks of the 2nd Congress of the Communist International'. (CW 31 pp. 184–201) Lenin declares that it is the duty of communists 'not to gloss over short-comings in their movement but to criticise them openly.' The concepts 'dictatorship of the proletariat' and 'Soviet power' are to 'be defined as concretely as possible'. Since influential parties of the Second International (The Socialist Party of France, the Socialist Party of America, the Independent SPD and the Independent Labour Party in Great Britain) wish to affiliate to the Third International, although their 'activities' are 'not yet communist', conditions of entry must be drawn up. Lenin lists five.

7 July: Lenin receives Frossard and Cachin, representing French socialists, and Murphy, the delegate of the British Shop Stewards' Committee.

18 July: Lenin and Krupskaya travel together to Petrogard for the opening of the 2nd Congress of the Comintern.

19 July–7 August: Lenin takes part in the debates of the 2nd World Congress of the Third International. (CW 31 pp. 213–63) 217 delegates representing 67 organisations from 37 countries attend. Lenin is elected to the presidium on 19 July; he delivers a speech on the international situation and the fundamental tasks of the Comintern. He receives ovation after ovation. Lenin turns on the socialists who have been 'bribed' by 'the mention of thousands of cushy jobs'. 'Opportunism in the upper ranks of the working class movement is bourgeois socialism, not proletarian socialism.' Communists can proudly say: 'at the 1st Congress we were in fact merely propagandists . . . Today the advanced proletariat is everywhere with us.' Lenin makes a speech at the laying of the foundation stone of a memorial to Karl Liebknecht and Rosa Luxemburg in Petrograd. He lays a wreath in memory of the revolutionary dead on Mars Field in Petrograd.

20 July: Lenin returns to Moscow. Lenin publishes his 'Terms of Admission to the Communist International'. (CW 31 pp. 206–11) He lists nineteen conditions, including the removal of all 'centrists' from all important posts; the linking of legal and illegal work; work in the army; in the countryside; in the colonies; in the trade unions. Parties must be organised on the basis of 'democratic centralism'; Party purges are to be carried out; support is to be given to Soviet republics; parties are to change their names to Communist Party. These proposals form the basis of the 'twenty-one conditions' adopted at the Congress.

23 July: Lenin speaks on the role of the Communist Party (CW 31 pp. 235-9) at a session of the Congress which has moved to Moscow. 'A political party can comprise only a minority of a class . . . we are therefore obliged to recognise that it is only this class-conscious minority that can direct and lead the broad masses of the workers.'

26 July: Lenin delivers the report of the commission on the national and colonial questions at the 2nd Comintern Congress. He states that the 'cardinal idea' of the theses is the 'distinction between oppressed and oppressor nations. Unlike the Second International and bourgeois democracy, we emphasise this distinction.'

30 July: Lenin speaks at the session of the Comintern Congress devoted to the conditions for admission to the Communist International. He takes issue with Crispien of the Independent SPD and Serrati of the Socialist Party of Italy. It is no accident that there is nothing about the dictatorship of the proletariat in the Erfurt Programme of 1891; Russian social democrats have included this in their programme since 1903. When Crispien describes terror and coercion as two different things, such a distinction could be made perhaps in a 'manual of sociology' but not in political practice. The 'reformist tendency' has also 'nothing in common with communism'.

31 July: Lenin drafts a decision for the Politburo of the RCP (B) stating that Maxim Gorky's leading article on Lenin in *Communist International* no 12 is 'inappropriate' since it also contains a good deal that is 'anti-communist'. (CW 42 p. 205) Gorky glorifies Lenin in the article and calls him a 'saint'. Gorky states that he is convinced that 'the terror is for him [Lenin] unbearable and is very painful even though this is very skilfully concealed'. (*Communist International* no 12, 1920 pp. 7-8)

2 August: Lenin speaks on parliamentarism at the 2nd Comintern Congress. He opposes the anti-parliamentary theses of Bordiga: 'How will you reveal the true character of parliament . . . if you are not in parliament?'

3 August: Lenin states in a telegram to I T Smilga and M N Tukhachevsky: 'All measures should be taken to promulgate in Poland on the widest possible scale the Manifesto of the Polish Revolutionary Committee. Use our aircraft for this.' (CW 44 p. 409)

6 August: Lenin speaks on affiliation to the British Labour Party at the 2nd Comintern Congress. He is of the opinion that British communists should act 'in a revolutionary manner' in the British Labour Party.

7 August: At the end of the 2nd Comintern Congress the ECCI meets; Lenin is one of its members.

15 August: Lenin writes the 'Letter to the Austrian Communists'. (CW 31 pp. 267-9) He opposes the boycott of the parliamentary elections decided upon by the Communist Party of Austria.

17 August: Lenin writes to the administration of the health resorts and sanatoria of the Caucasus to 'do everything to help' Inessa Armand, (who has been head of the women's section of the RCP (B) since 1918) and her sick son and to 'provide the best accommodation and treatment'. (CW 44 p. 417)

18 August: Lenin asks G K Ordzhonikidze to ensure that Inessa Armand and her son 'are given proper accommodation', to inspect everything and to execute them in case of danger. 'Please reply by letter and, if possible, also by telegram.' (Briefe VI p. 268)

19 August: In a telegram to I T Smilga Lenin demands 'Belorussian workers and peasants, even if in bast shoes and unclothed, immediately, with revolutionary speed' to stand by as reserves for the army. (CW 44 p. 418)

5 September: Lenin stops in the village of Bogdanovo, en route for some hunting. The peasants complain to him that all their grain, including their seed, has been taken from them.

6 September: Lenin writes to the Podolsk uezd food committee. 'I can testify that Bogdanovo village . . . is very badly off for food.' He asks for the situation to be checked, and a lower level to be set for grain deliveries. (CW 44 p. 427)

17 September: Lenin fills in a form for the registration of members of the RCP (B) in Moscow (compare also 29 March). He replies to the question about relatives, their age and 'number of dependents' as follows: 'Wife 51, brother 45, sister 44.' Do you own immovable property? 'No'. To the question about knowledge of foreign languages, he replies: 'French, German, English: all 3 poorly.' Which part of Russia do you know well? 'I have lived only on the Volga and in the capital cities'. What is your salary and do you have any supplementary income '13½ thousand (13,500); supplementary income from literary work.' (His income has been raised because of inflation.) Has he ever been called before a Party court to explain his behaviour? 'By the Mensheviks in the RSDLP during splits.' What documents or certificates do you have to testify that you were in our illegal Party organisation? He simply replies: 'The history of the Party is such a document.' Lenin states that he does not belong to a trade union; he has read 'almost all' the writings of Marx, Engels, Kautsky and Plekhanov. Does he write newspaper articles and on what? 'Seldom, on political subjects.' Has he written any pamphlets? 'Yes. Rather too numerous to list.' On what subjects is he able to give instruction? 'Mostly political.' (CW 42 pp. 445–8)

20 September: Lenin proposes peace negotiations with Poland at a session of the CC, RCP (B).

22–25 September: The 9th All-Russian Conference of the RCP (B) meets. Lenin says in a speech (CW 31 pp. 275–9) that 'our presence at the walls of Warsaw' has had 'a powerful effect on the revolutionary movement in Europe'.

23 September: Lenin declares in a telegram to A A Ioffe that it is important to conclude 'an armistice in a short time' with the Poles. (CW 44 p. 434)

24 September: Lenin speaks on the immediate tasks of Party development at the 9th Conference of the RCP (B). (CW 42 pp. 207-13) He also submits a draft resolution recommending that 'literary organs be set up; discussion leaflets' which are the organs of 'criticism within the Party' are to be promoted. He also proposes that a 'control commission' be set up to receive and examine complaints. Lenin writes a 'Letter to German and French Workers'. (CW 31 pp. 280-2) He touches on the discussion in the Independent SPD and takes umbrage at 'the clamour about Moscow's dictates' in the Comintern; it is merely a Centrist 'red herring'.

2 October: Lenin speaks at the 3rd All-Russian Congress of the Russian Young Communist League. (CW 31 pp. 283-99) The tasks of youth can be summed up in a single word; 'learn'. This does not merely mean to assimilate 'communist slogans', but the 'store of knowledge which mankind has accumulated'. The purpose of training is to 'imbue' youth 'with communist morality' and 'this morality is entirely subordinated to the interests of the proletariat's class struggle.' He is convinced that those who are now 15 years old 'will see a communist society and will itself build this society'.

6 October: Lenin receives H G Wells, the English novelist.

8 October: Lenin drafts a resolution 'On Proletarian Culture'. (CW 31 pp. 316-7) The 'most valuable achievements of the bourgeois epoch' are not to be rejected; 'all attempts to invent one's own particular (proletarian) brand of culture' are 'theoretically unsound and practically harmful'.

9 October: Lenin addresses Party activists from the Moscow organisation of the RCP (B) (CW 42 pp. 214-7) and discusses the split in the Independent SPD. 'Zinoviev's arrival' in Germany 'will speed up and deepen the split' that has already started among the 'independents'. Part of the 'breakaway "independents"' and up to a million members' of the Communist Party of Germany [in reality the KPD has only 78,000 members!] will constitute 'an imposing revolutionary force'.

12 October: Lenin attends the funeral in Moscow of his friend, Inessa Armand. On her way to the Caucasus she had fallen ill (compare 17-18 August), had contracted cholera and had died on 24 September. Angelica Balabanoff reports on Lenin's appearance: 'His whole being, not only his face, expressed such grief that I did not even dare to nod to him once. It was clear that he wanted to be left alone in his sorrow . . . his eyes seemed to drown in tears which he held back with difficulty. And every time our circle moved he allowed himself to be carried along without any resistance, as though he was thankful to be brought nearer the dead one.' (A Balabanoff *Lenin* p. 49)

20 October: Lenin writes a 'Contribution to the History of the Question of Dictatorship: A Note'. (CW 31 pp. 340-61) 'Major questions in the life of nations are settled only by force. The reactionary classes themselves are usually the first to resort to violence, to civil war.' He points out the 'difference between dictatorship *over* the people and the dictatorship *of* the revolutionary people.'

Beginning of November: Clara Zetkin visits Lenin. He says to her: '"The revolution in Poland which we expected has not materialised. Radek had predicted to us the way it could come about . . . I was violently attacked for wanting to accept the (Polish) peace conditions . . . No, the thought of the agony of another winter at war was unbearable. We had to conclude peace". As Lenin spoke, his face before me was all shrivelled up. Countless wrinkles, great and small, furrowed deep into it. And every wrinkle spoke of a heavy sorrow or a gnawing pain. A picture of implicit and inexpressible suffering was visible on Lenin's face.' Lenin also discusses with Clara Zetkin the women's question, among others. He calls it a 'literary fashion' that a woman communist, Kety Guttmann, in Hamburg, published a newspaper for prostitutes. 'Freudian theory is also fashionable folly . . . I am distrustful of those who always concentrate on the sexual aspect . . . and I am in this regard, as far as some people are concerned, a Philistine to some extent, although I find philistinism repugnant. But I also hold the famous glass-water theory to be completely unmarxist and moreover unsocial. Sexual life is more than the purely physical, there is also the impact of culture.' (Zetkin *Erinnerungen an Lenin* pp. 20-2, 56-63)

4 November: Lenin writes an article on the struggle within the Socialist Party of Italy. He adds a postscript on 11 November 'False Talk on Freedom'. (CW 31 pp. 377-96) Again he attacks the Centrists and defends the 'twenty-one conditions'.

9 November: Lenin gets his views on trade unions, in opposition to Trotksy, adopted by the CC, RCP(B) by 10 votes to 4.

14 November: Lenin and Krupskaya travel to the village of Kashinov to attend the opening ceremony of a power station. He has discussions with peasants – he also receives many peasant delegations in Moscow.

21 November: Lenin makes a speech on the foreign and domestic situation at the Moscow Gubernia Conference of the RCP(B). (CW 31 pp. 408-26) After the victories of the Red Army during the summer, the defeat at Warsaw, the armistice with Poland in October and the annihilation of Wrangel, the chances of 'conclusive peace' have improved. However 'for victory to be lasting, we must achieve the victory of the proletarian revolution in all, or at least in several, of the main capitalist countries.' Lenin calls the demand of the opposition for the promotion of young people, a 'sound programme'.

26 November: Lenin addresses a meeting of secretaries of Party cells of the Moscow organisation of the RCP(B). (CW 31 pp. 430-3) He touches on the question of concessions for foreign capitalists. It is not opportunistic to make use of the contradictions among capitalists. Opportunism sacrifices real interests so as to secure a few, temporary advantages.

29 November: Lenin speaks at a meeting of communists of Zamos-
kvorechie District of Moscow. (CW 31 pp. 434–6) He is critical of the
left opposition and of bureaucratism. He refers to the 200,000 Soviet
functionaries in Moscow: 'It was only to be expected that red tape in
the Soviet apparatus would penetrate into the Party apparatus.'

5 December: Lenin congratulates M N Pokrovsky on his book *A Brief
Outline of Russian History*; it is 'original' in 'presentation and
approach'. He recommends that a chronological index be added so that
students when studying it 'will know the facts'. (CW 36 p. 530)

7 December: Lenin and his supporters find themselves in the minority,
by 7 votes to 8, against Bukharin and Trotsky, at a session of the CC,
RCP (B) devoted to trade union problems.

15 December: Lenin speaks at a meeting of peasants from the village
of Modenovo on the situation in Soviet Russia.

19–20 December: Lenin is in Gorki, outside Moscow; he works on his
report to the 8th All-Russian Congress of Soviets.

21 December: Lenin delivers a report on concessions to the RCP(B)
group of delegates to the 8th Congress of Soviets. (CW 31 pp. 463–86)
The experience of history teaches that 'a series of wars is inevitable',
therefore 'we must exert every effort' to 'conclude trade agreements'.
The existence of the Soviet republic depends on utilising disagreements;
to 'vanquish all the imperial powers would, of course, be a most
pleasant thing, but for a fairly long time we shall not be in a position to
do so.'

22 December: Lenin delivers the Sovnarkom report at the 8th Congress
of Soviets. (CW 31 pp. 487–518) 'We have, no doubt, learnt politics.
But things are bad as far as economic matters are concerned.' The
electrification plan must become 'the second programme of our Party'
aimed at 'restoring our entire economy and raising it to the level of
up-to-date technical equipment'. In this connection he coins the slogan:
*'Communism is Soviet power plus the electrification of the whole
country'*.

28 December: Lenin informs N P Gorbunov that a letter about electric
ploughs 'interests me very much. I feel quite ill because of insomnia and
therefore ask you to follow up this matter'. (Briefe VII p. 36) This
attitude is typical of the numerous letters and notes which he wrote on
all conceivable problems from 1918 onwards.

30 December: Lenin speaks on 'The Trade Unions, the Present Situation and Trotsky's Mistakes' at a joint meeting of communist delegates
to the 8th Congress of Soviets and Trade Union Functionaries. (CW 32
pp. 19–42) Lenin opposes Trotsky's thesis that the trade unions should
be 'nationalised'. Lenin calls the trade unions 'a school of economic
management, a school of communism'. He states: 'Ours is a workers'
state with a *bureaucratic twist to it*.' It is the business 'of the massively-
organised proletariat to protect itself, while we, for our part, must use

these workers' organisations to protect the workers from their state and to get them to protect our state.'

End of year: Lenin drafts a proposal on 'Polytechnical Education'. (CW 36 pp. 532–4) Polytechnical instruction is to be put into practice 'as far as possible'. General 'educational subjects' are to be expanded in all technical schools. He also proposes 'communism' as a subject.

1921

1–21 January: Lenin holidays in Gorki, near Moscow.

7 January: Lenin sends Mustafa Kemal a telegram: 'Warmest greetings to the Turkish people and their government.' (Briefe VII p. 306)

9 January: Lenin speaks on the position of Soviet Russia at a meeting of peasants in Gorki.

19 January: Lenin writes the article 'The Party Crisis' (CW 32 pp. 43–53) and it appears in *Pravda* no 13 on 21 January. He writes: 'The Party is sick. The Party is down with the fever.' There are deviations towards syndicalism. Party members must study both sides of the question. 'Only a hopeless idiot will believe oral statements.' He describes the various stages of the discussion on the trade unions. Bukharin has now made a mistake which is 'much more serious than all of Trotsky's put together' because he wants to transfer important management functions to the trade unions, functions which only the Party can carry out. Formerly he (Lenin) had fought the defenders of 'bureaucratic excesses', now the worst 'syndicalist deviation' must be combated, since 'in the last analysis' it means 'repudiating the Party's leading role in relation to the non-Party masses'.

23 January: At the 2nd All-Russian Congress of Miners Lenin repeats his thoughts on the discussion about the trade unions. (CW 32 pp. 54–63)

25 January: Lenin writes the article 'Once Again on the Trade Unions, the Current Situation and the Mistakes of Trotsky and Bukharin'. (CW 32 pp. 70–107) Lenin calls 'factional activity', a 'danger for the Party'. He outlines again the discussion, and states: 'Politics is a concentrated expression of economics . . . Politics must take precedence over economics. To argue otherwise is to forget the ABC of Marxism.' Lenin goes into 'dialectical logic', which demands that if 'we are to have a true knowledge of an object we must look at it and examine all its facets, its connections and "mediacies"', regard its 'development, its change' and see human experience as a 'criterion of truth'. Finally there is no abstract truth; 'truth is always concrete'. He refers to Plekhanov and remarks to the young Party member that he '*cannot* hope to become a *real* Communist' without having studied his philosophical writings.

27 January: Lenin receives Maxim Gorky and delegates of the United Council of Scientific Institutes of Petrograd. He discusses with them the possibilities of scientific research work.

2 February: Lenin writes to D B Ryazanov: 'Could we *buy* the letters of Marx and Engels, or photographs of them, from Scheidemann & Co. (you know, that dirty lot will sell anything)? Is there any hope of our collecting in Moscow everything published by Marx and Engels?'(CW 45 pp. 80-1) Lenin writes to the Central Committee of the Swedish Red Cross that the 'humanitarian help in the form of a consignment of various medicaments' is 'accepted with grateful thanks' by the Soviet government. (Briefe VII pp. 306-7)

7 February: Lenin writes the article 'The Work of the People's Commissariat of Education' (CW 32 pp. 123-32) and it appears in *Pravda* no 28 on 9 February. Lenin sees from the statistics that 'only the first steps in the transition from capitalism to communism are being taken . . . at the present time'.

8 February: Lenin submits a rough draft of his 'Theses Concerning the Peasants' (CW 32 p. 133) to the Politburo. It contemplates the transition to a new policy, replacing the forced deliveries of grain by a 'tax in kind'.

12 February: Lenin writes to the members of the Politburo (CW 32 pp. 134-6) that the output of oil in Baku is dropping; the situation is threatening and foreign concessionaries must be found. The head of the oil administration is 'extremely stupid' and 'stupidity in such high quarters is a menace'.

21 February: Lenin writes the article 'The Integrated Economic Plan' (CW 32 pp. 137-45) and it is published the following day in *Pravda*. He criticises planning and the authorities; one 'must learn how to run' Russia. What is needed is 'less intellectualist and bureaucratic complacency' and a 'deeper scrutiny' of practical experience and 'of the available achievements of science'.

24-25 February: Lenin chairs a CC session which discusses the replacement of compulsory grain deliveries by a tax in kind, demobilisation of the army, oil concessions and other matters.

1 March: Lenin writes to N Osinsky that he has spoken to the peasant I A Chekunov. 'He says the peasants have lost confidence in Soviet power. I asked him whether we could right things with a tax? He thinks we could . . . This is the kind of people we must *do our utmost* to hold on to, in order to restore the confidence of the peasant *mass*. This is the *main* political task.' (CW 45 pp. 90-2)

2 March: Beginning of the Kronstadt revolt.

4 March: Lenin writes an article on International Women's Day. (CW 32 pp. 161-3) The Bolshevik revolution has struck deeper 'at the roots of oppression and the inequality of women' than any party or revolution the world has ever dreamed of. Soviet power has eliminated the 'especially disgusting, base and hypocritical inequality in the laws on marriage and the family and inequality in respect of children'.

8-16 March: The 10th Congress of the RCP(B) meets. Almost 1,000 delegates representing 732,000 members attend. The Congress effects the transition from War Communism to the New Economic Policy (NEP). Lenin opens the Congress on 8 March; he intervenes several times, delivers speeches and moves resolutions. (CW 32 pp. 165-271) In his speech of welcome Lenin states that the Party has permitted itself the amazing 'luxury' of engaging in serious disputes when surrounded by mighty and powerful enemies. In his CC report he says that the 'transition from war to peace began when the last enemy soldier was finally driven from the territory of the RSFSR.' Demobilisation has produced unexpected difficulties. The problem of fuel is now the basic question of economic development. On discussion within the Party he states: 'We cannot have arguments about deviations and we must put a stop to that.' What is needed is 'unity, discipline and restraint'. The Kronstadt uprising is quickly suppressed.

9 March: At the 10th Congress Lenin delivers the summing-up speech on the debate on the CC report. He is most critical of the Workers' Opposition — Kollontai, Shlyapnikov — who have declared that an 'All-Russian Congress of Producers' should administer production. This to Lenin is an 'anarcho-syndicalist deviation' and a 'nonsense'. 'Quite a lot of time' has been spent in discussion. 'Comrades, this is no time to have an opposition.' The Party Congress must draw the conclusion that 'the opposition's time has run out and that the lid's on it. We want no more oppositions.' Reproached for having passed over Kronstadt, Lenin retorts: 'My report tied in everything — from beginning to end — with the lessons of Kronstadt.'

14 March: Lenin speaks on the trade unions at the 10th Party Congress. He repeats: 'Our state is one with bureaucratic distortions.' Engels spoke of producers in a communist society where there will be no more classes, but when Shlyapnikov comes 'in the midst of this furious class struggle' and talks 'about an All-Russian Congress of Producers — isn't that a syndicalist deviation which must be emphatically and irrevocably condemned?'

15 March: Lenin delivers the report and sums up the debate on the introduction of a tax in kind. Since workers form a minority in Russia the revolution, according to Lenin, 'can triumph only on two conditions': firstly, 'if it is given timely support by a socialist revolution in one or several advanced countries', secondly, through a workers' agreement with 'the majority of the peasant population'. The substitution of a tax in kind for compulsory deliveries is an 'incentive' for the peasants. 'We must adapt our state economy to the economy of the middle peasant which we have not managed to remake in three years, and will not be able to remake in another ten.' It is important to come to an agreement with the peasants but 'this must be done in practice, skilfully, efficiently and flexibly'.

16 March: Lenin speaks on Party unity and on the anarcho-syndicalist deviation and makes the closing Congress speech. He submits draft resolutions: 'On Party Unity' and 'On the Syndicalist and Anarchist Deviation in our Party'. Lenin attacks the 'anarcho-syndicalist deviation'; its propagation is said to be 'incompatible with membership of the RCP(B)'. The danger of a split in the Party exists, hence no factions may be formed; factionalism is to be 'completely eliminated'.

After 16 March: Lenin requests N A Semashko, the People's Commissar of Health, to 'appoint a special person' to arrange trips abroad; to Germany for Tsyurupa, Krestinsky, Osinsky, Kuraev, Gorky, Korolenko and others for medical treatment. Also 'the *best* physician to *give* N I Bukharin *a medical examination* (the *heart*, among other things) and let me know the result.' (CW 45 pp. 97-8)

17 March: Lenin writes to the American, Washington B Vanderlip, that he is pleased to hear 'of President Harding's favourable views on our trade with America'. He asks Vanderlip to excuse the fact that he cannot meet him; the Party Congress 'has taken so much of my time and forces that I am very tired and ill'. (CW 45 pp. 98-9) Lenin writes to A A Ioffe that he understands the latter's dissatisfaction, but he cannot understand why Ioffe can write 'such an *absolutely, impossible, absolutely impossible* thing: that I am the CC.' This 'could have been written only in a state of great nervous irritation and overwork. The old CC (1919-1920) defeated me on one of the vastly important questions, as you must know from the discussion [compare 7 December 1920]. I cannot say how many times I have been in a minority on organisational and personal matters.' (CW 45 pp. 99-100)

27 March: Lenin speaks at the All-Russian Congress of Transport Workers. (CW 32 pp. 272-84) He states: 'Socialism . . . implies the abolition of classes; and as long as there are workers and peasants, there will be different classes and, therefore, no full socialism.'

Between 9-21 April: Lenin writes to V M Molotov that something has been published somewhere which said '*expose the falsehood of religion*, or something to that effect. This is not right. It is tactless'. It is '*absolutely*' necessary to '*avoid any affront to religion*'. (CW 45 pp. 119-20)

11 April: Lenin reports on concessions at a meeting of trade unionists. (CW 32 pp. 300-15)

14 April: Lenin writes to the communists of Azerbaidzhan, Georgia, Armenia, Daghestan and the Gorny republic. (CW 32 pp. 316-8) It is necessary to 'refrain from copying our tactics but thoroughly to vary them and adapt them to the differing concrete conditions'.

16 April: Lenin writes to Clara Zetkin and Paul Levi that he has been 'so busy and so overworked in the last few weeks' that he has had 'practically no opportunity to read the German press'. He regards the 'Open Letter' of the KPD (of January, with the offer of a united front with the SPD) as *'perfectly correct* tactics'. Lenin has read nothing on the 'strike movement and the action in Germany' (of March 1921). He thinks that a representative of the (Comintern) executive defended the silly tactics, 'which were too much to the left — to take immediate action "to help the Russians"'. The representative, Béla Kun, 'is very often too Left'; one should 'not give in'. Lenin regards Paul Levi's plan to write a pamphlet to be wrong. 'Why not wait?' He proposes a private talk before the Comintern Congress 'without public polemics, without withdrawals, without pamphlets on differences'. (CW 45 pp. 124-5)

21 April: Lenin completes his pamphlet 'The Tax in Kind' (CW 32 pp. 329-65) and it is published in May. Under 'peculiar War Communism we actually took from the peasant all his surpluses', states Lenin. The 'tax in kind . . . is one of the forms of transition from . . . War Communism . . . to regular socialist exchange of products'. It is also possible to 'combine . . . the Soviet state . . . with state capitalism' since capitalism is a 'bane compared with socialism' but a 'boon compared with medievalism' and the small production which predominates in Soviet Russia. This gives rise to the 'evils of bureaucracy' which Lenin points out once again. The task is immense. 'We, the vanguard, the advanced contingent of the proletariat are passing directly to socialism, but the advanced contingent is only a small part of the whole of the proletariat; the latter, in its turn, is only a small part of the population.'

24 April: Lenin writes to L B Kamenev: 'Could you not arrange for flowers to be planted on the grave of Inessa Armand? 2) Moreover, that a small stone slab or gravestone be placed on it?' (Briefe VII p. 167)

5 May: Lenin writes to Grigory Zinoviev in Petrograd that Gintsburg, the sculptor working on Plekhanov's bust, 'is in need of *materials*, clay, etc. The graves of Plekhanov and Zasulich are neglected'. One must look after such things. (CW 45 p. 138)

6 May: Lenin, in a letter to A V Lunacharsky, opposes the printing of 5,000 copies of Mayakovsky's peom '150,000,000'. 'It is nonsense, stupidity, double-dyed stupidity and affectation.' (CW 45 p. 138) Lenin, in a letter to M N Pokrovsky, asks for his help to 'fight futurism'. (CW 45 p. 139)

26-28 May: Lenin attends the 10th All-Russian Conference of the RCP(B). He opens and closes the Conference and delivers a speech. (CW 32 pp. 399-437) He goes again into the significance of the tax in kind in his speech. In a closing address (28 May) he states that the 'disintegration of the capitalist world' is steadily progressing; the oppressed colonial peoples are becoming stronger all the time. 'We are now exercising our main influence on the international revolution through our economic policy . . . The Struggle in this field has now become global.'

28 May: Lenin informs Karl Radek and Grigory Zinoviev that Clara Zetkin has sent him a telegram, to the effect that she will not come to the Comintern Congress if her 'associates' among the opposition, Brass and Anna Geyer, are not permitted to attend. Lenin wants to know if he should intervene or 'say absolutely nothing'. (CW 45 p. 158)

30 May: Lenin speaks in the All-Russian CEC on local economic bodies. (CW 32 pp. 438–40) Lenin writes a long letter to Y K Lutovinov, a leader of the Workers' Opposition, who is working in Berlin. Lenin accuses him of playing 'opposition at all costs'. He tells Lutovinov, a former worker, that 'professional proletarians have repeatedly yielded up, in actual life, demagnetised petty-bourgeois intellectuals, according to their real class role'. He advises him, because of their past friendship, to 'do something about' his 'nerves'. (CW 45 pp. 160–5)

7 June: Lenin writes to I I Radchenko: 'The inventors are not our men but we must use them. It is better to let them have more, let them have money, make a killing — so long as *we, too*, can advance an undertaking which is of exceptional importance for the RSFSR.' (CW 45 pp. 181–2)

10 June: Lenin forwards his remarks on the theses on Comintern tactics to Zinoviev. The 'crux of the matter' is that Paul Levi 'is in very many things *right politically*'. August Thalheimer's and Béla Kun's theses are politically utterly fallacious; mere phrases and playing at Leftism. It was a mistake for him (Lenin) to vote for the admission of the ultra-Left Communist Workers' Party of Germany (KAPD) to the Comintern. He is critical and sceptical of the 'March action' (1921) and supports the expulsion of Paul Levi but only 'say, for six months'. (CW 42 pp. 319–23)

16 June: Lenin, in a letter to the KPD leaders Wilhelm Koenen, August Thalheimer and Paul Frölich, who are in Moscow, states: 'I take this opportunity to emphasise that I do most resolutely withdraw the rude and impolite expressions I used, and hereby repeat my oral apology in writing.' (CW 45 p. 187)

22 June–12 July: The 3rd Congress of the Communist International meets in Moscow. 605 delegates attend, representing 103 organisations from 52 countries. Lenin submits theses and delivers several speeches. (CW 32 pp. 451–96) In his theses he examines the international situation and that of Soviet Russia. 'A large-scale machine industry . . . is the only material base that is possible for socialism.' The dictatorship of the proletariat is necessary as long as 'classes exist' and the bourgeoisie has only been overthrown in one country.

28 June: Lenin speaks on the Italian question at the 3rd Comintern Congress. He states that 'the great misfortune of the working-class movement in Germany' is that the 'break was not brought about before the war'. The 'mark of true communism is a break with opportunism'. He takes umbrage at Serrati's 'tales' that the Russians want everyone to imitate them. 'We want the very opposite.' Principles 'must be adapted to the specific conditions in the various countries. The revolution in Italy will run a different course from that in Russia. It will start in a different way. How? Neither you nor we know.' The Comintern will never demand that 'you slavishly imitate the Russians'.

1 July: Lenin speaks at the Comintern Congress 'in defence of the tactics of the Comintern'. He opposes 'left stupidities' which are endangering the movement. 'We Russians are already sick and tired of these Leftist phrases.'

5 July: Lenin speaks at the Comintern Congress on the tactics of the RCP(B). It was clear to the Bolsheviks that 'without the support of the international world revolution the victory of the proletarian revolution was impossible'. On the colonial revolution he says: 'In spite of the fact that the masses of toilers – the peasants in the colonial countries – are still backward, they will play a very important revolutionary part in the coming phrase of the world revolution.' He points out the economic problems of the Soviet Russia: 'We are not alone in the world. We exist as a link of the world economy in a chain of capitalist states.' (In CW 32 p. 491 this last sentence is incorrectly reproduced)

6 July: Lenin speaks during a session of the commision on tactics of the Comintern Congress with reference to the Czechoslovak question.

7 July: Lenin writes to the members of the commission on tactics that his words of the day before, against the Hungarian communists, have produced dissatisfaction. 'I hasten therefore to inform you in writing: when I was an émigré myself (for more than 15 years), I took "too Leftist" a stand several times (as I now realise). In August 1917, I was also an émigré and moved, in our Party Central Committee, a much too "Leftist" proposal which, happily, was flatly rejected. [It is not known which proposal this was.] It is quite natural for émigrés frequently to adopt attitudes which are "too Leftist".' (CW 45 pp. 203–4)

8 July: Lenin asks the Orgburo to grant him 'a month's holiday, in accordance with Dr Getier's orders'. (CW 45 p. 204) The Politburo grants this request on 9 July. Lenin may only attend meetings of the Politburo.

11 July: Lenin addresses the German, Polish, Czechoslovak, Hungarian and Italian delegations to the 3rd Comintern Congress. (CW 42 pp. 324–8) 'We are not Blanquists, we do not want to rule with a minority of the working class against the majority.'

13 July: Lenin begins his holiday; he travels to Gorki, near Moscow, to spend a month there.

15 July: Lenin receives the US Senator Joseph I France from Maryland.

17 July: Lenin asks G K Ordzhonikidze about Stalin's state of health. (CW 35 p. 510)

19 July: Lenin inquires about Béla Kun's state of health.

20 July: Lenin writes to L B Krasin that private citizens in Great Britain want to send food parcels to Soviet Russia. 'Naturally we must simplify and accelerate the receipt of such packets.' (Briefe VIII p. 49)

27 July: Lenin has a talk with Clara Zetkin. He informs Zinoviev of it on 28 July (compare CW 45 pp. 231-2). Clara Zetkin intends to try to persuade Paul Levi to give up his parliamentary seat and to make a declaration of loyalty to the 3rd Comintern Congress. She is afraid that 'it could occur to some friend of Levi's to publish Rosa Luxemburg's manuscript against the Bolsheviks'. Then she would oppose it as erroneous, just as Rosa Luxemburg herself admitted later that it was 'wrong'.

2 August: Lenin writes an 'Appeal to the International Proletariat'. (CW 32 p. 502) Some areas of Russia are suffering from famine 'whose proportions are apparently only slightly less than those of the 1891 calamity . . . We need help'. After the 3rd Comintern Congress Lenin receives Willi Münzenberg. Lenin informs him of 'the threatening famine, to a certain extent already reality, on the Volga and in the Ukraine. Lenin analysed it for me . . . help could only be expected from the international proletariat. His plan consisted of . . . immediately setting in motion an international aid programme and entrusting me with the organisation of the programme. He asked me if I was prepared to take on the task. Naturally I accepted with pleasure and enthusiasm.' (Willi Münzenberg *Die Dritte Front* p. 348)

5 August: Lenin writes to G I Myasnikov. He opposes the latter's demand that there should be 'freedom of the press, from the monarchists to the anarchists, inclusively'. Lenin states: 'We do not believe in "absolutes". We laugh at "pure democracy" . . . We do not wish to commit suicide and, therefore, we will not do this.' (CW 32 pp. 504-9)

9 August: Lenin writes to Maxim Gorky: 'I am so tired that I am unable to do a thing.' Gorky should recover his health in a sanitorium in Europe. 'Over here we have neither treatment, or work — nothing but hustle. *Plain empty* hustle.' (CW 45 p. 249)

11 August: Lenin writes to V M Molotov that something has to be done to oppose Hoover. 'I can't work. There is absolute need of help from Trotsky, who has a capacity for these things (both diplomatic experience and a military and political instinct).' (CW 45 pp. 250-1)

13 August: Lenin proposes to Zinoviev that a 'Bureau be set up in Germany . . . an information-gathering institute' which would collect information on the international labour movement. 'We must and can cover the expenses. Without this institute we have neither eyes, nor ears, nor hands to play a part in the international movement.' (Briefe VIII pp. 120-2)

14 August: Lenin writes a 'Letter to the German Communists' on the occasion of the 7th Congress of the KPD. (CW 32 pp. 512-23) He states that 'essentially, much of Paul Levi's criticism of the March action in Germany in 1921 was correct', but Levi 'had to be expelled for breach of discipline'. The KPD must, 'at all costs, end the internal dissension', forget about Paul Levi and the 'Communist Workers' Party of Germany [KAPD] people'. The most important task is to 'win over the majority of the proletariat to our side.'

20 August: Lenin writes the article 'New Times and Old Mistakes in a New Guise' (CW 33 pp. 21-9) and it is published on 28 August in *Pravda* no 190. The enemy is no longer 'the hordes of White Guards' but 'everyday economics in a small peasant country with a ruined large-scale industry'. The proletariat is *déclassé* 'i.e. dislodged from its class groove'.

26 August: Lenin states, during a telephone conversation with A V Lunacharsky: 'I can't see you, since I'm ill.' The People's Commissar for Enlightenment should not concern himself with the theatre but with 'teaching people to read and write'. (Briefe VIII p. 147)

1 September: Lenin writes to Eugene Varga about the planned information-collecting institute (compare 13 August): 'We need *full* and *truthful* information. And the truth should not depend on whom it has to serve.' (CW 42 p. 339)

3 September: Lenin requests 'exact and regular information about the collection of donations by foreign workers in aid of the starving in Russia' in a letter to the secretary of the Comintern Executive Committee. (CW 45 p. 284)

20 September: Lenin writes the article 'Purging the Party' (CW 33 pp. 39-41) and it appears the following day in *Pravda* no 210. The Party must be purged of 'rascals, of bureaucratic, dishonest and wavering communists and of Mensheviks'.

27 September: Lenin writes the 'Tasks of the Workers' and Peasants' Inspection'. (CW 33 pp. 42-8, published for the first time in 1927) He is critical of the work of the commission.

September: Lenin writes to Trotsky: 'The wail about the lack of money is general and universal. We could very well blow up . . . We are late. The commercial tide is stronger than we are.' (CW 45 p. 321)

14 October: Lenin writes the article 'The Fourth Anniversary of the October Revolution' (CW 33 pp. 51-9) and it is published in 18 October in *Pravda* no 234. 'Experience has proved that we were wrong. It appears that a number of transitional stages were necessary — state capitalism and socialism — in order to *prepare* . . . for the transition to communism.'

16 October: Lenin replies to a suggestion by G V Chicherin on the subject of improving the international standing of Soviet Russia: 'There can be no question at all of Trotsky and myself withdrawing from the Executive Committee of the Communist International.' (CW 45 pp. 339-40)

17 October: Lenin delivers a speech on the New Economic Policy (NEP) at the 2nd All-Russian Congress of Political Education Departments. (CW 33 pp. 60-79) He calls NEP a necessary 'retreat' during which the 'principle of personal incentive' is to apply. He sees three enemies: 'communist conceit, illiteracy and bribery'.

19 October: Lenin writes a 'Letter to Polish Communists'. (CW 42 pp. 354-5) He warns against a *'premature* uprising'; if 10,000-30,000 workers 'are massacred', this *'may* delay the revolution *even for* several years . . . Do not yield to provocations. The revolution must be allowed to *grow to full* ripening of the fruit.'

22 October: Lenin and Krupskaya go to the Butyrsky Khutor, the training and experimental farm of the Moscow Zootechnical Institute where trials of the first Soviet electrical plough are being carried out.

28 October: Lenin writes to the committee of a Moscow borough of the RCP(B) that he cannot comply with their request to forward them his reminiscences of the October Revolution. 'A mass of current work, and I simply do not have the strength to start writing. I am becoming tired. And when I am tired I cannot write.' (Briefe VIII p. 325)

29 October: Lenin delivers a report and makes the closing speech at the 7th Moscow Gubernia Conference of the RCP(B). (CW 33 pp. 81-108) He develops his views on NEP. The 'development of small commercial enterprises, the leasing of state enterprises, etc.' means the 'development of capitalist relations' and this is dangerous; but there is just no other way.

5 November: Lenin writes the article 'The Importance of Gold Now and After the Complete Victory of Socialism'. (CW 33 pp. 109-16) It appears in *Pravda* no 251 on 6-7 November. The greatest danger for the revolutionary is exaggerated revolutionism, to write 'revolution' with a capital R, to elevate 'revolution to something almost divine'. However, our revolution 'has completed only its bourgeois-democratic work'. On the subject of gold Lenin writes: 'When we are victorious on a world scale I think we shall use gold for the purpose of building public lavatories in the streets for some of the largest cities in the world.' This would be an educational use of it, since 'for the sake of gold, ten million men were killed' in the war. However, in the meanwhile, 'we must save gold in the RSFSR'.

7 November: Lenin delivers two speeches on the fourth anniversary of the October Revolution.

28 November: Lenin meets the American economic specialist, P P Christensen, in his office in the Kremlin.

1 December: Lenin prepares notes on the history of the RCP(B) for N I Bukharin who is to write an article on the united front. Lenin refers to the 'subjects' of differences and splits as well as the 'alternation of periods of split and periods of unity' in the Party, and draws up a corresponding chronology. (CW 36 pp. 552-4)

6 December: Lenin is granted a period of sick leave; he goes again to Gorki, outside Moscow.

11 December: Lenin writes the article 'The Theses on the Agrarian Question Adopted by the Communist Party of France'. (CW 33 pp. 131-7)

14 December: Lenin fills in a questionnaire for delegates of the 11th All-Russian Conference of the RCP(B). He has a consultative vote. His reply to the question, Profession before 1917? is Publicist, from 1884 to 1917, i.e. 23 years. Principal sources of income before 1914? Literary earnings and salary from the Party; after 1917, salary from the Soviet government. (CW 42 pp. 455-6)

19 December: Lenin writes a letter to the members of the Politburo on the Party purge, which he regards as a success. He advises the adoption of 'stricter conditions for admission to the Party'. (CW 33 p. 138)

23 December: Lenin speaks at the 9th All-Russian Congress of Soviets on home and foreign policy. (CW 33 pp. 143-77) He states that a 'certain equilibrium . . . has been created in international relations'. For the first time he is able to report that a year has passed without any attack on Soviet power. He repeats his theses on NEP and discusses the economic situation of Soviet Russia.

30 December: Lenin drafts a resolution, adopted by the CC on 12 January 1922, on the role and functions of trade unions under NEP. (CW 33 pp. 184-96) The transfer of enterprises to profit and loss means that 'as regards the socialised enterprises, it is undoubtedly the duty of the trade unions to protect the interests of the working people, to facilitate as far as possible the improvement of their standard of living, and constantly to correct the blunders and excesses of business organisations resulting from bureaucratic distortions of the state apparatus.'

31 December: Lenin is present at a meeting of the Politburo at which he is granted a six weeks' leave of absence, from 1 January 1922.

1922

January: Lenin goes several times to the village of Kostino, near Moscow, for rest and relaxation.

Between 9-12 January: Lenin drafts a Politburo directive on NEP. (CW 33 pp. 197-8) NEP is to be tested 'in practice, as quickly and as widely as possible' and to become reality.

17 January: Lenin dictates 'Directive on the Film Business'. (CW 42 pp. 388-9) He is for a balance between films with a 'propaganda message' and films 'specially for advertisement or income (of course, without obscenity and counter-revolution)'.

23 January: Lenin, in a letter to members of the Politburo, is in favour of granting the firm of Krupp of Essen a concession of 50,000 desyatinas of land (about 55,000 hectares). It is important to 'conclude concession agreements with German firms'. (*Wissenschaftliche Zeitschrift der Universität Rostock* 1, 1970 p. 7)

2 February: The Politburo decides to extend Lenin's leave to the opening of the 11th Party Congress, 27 March.

6 February: Lenin draws up draft CC directives for the forthcoming (April-May) Genoa international conference. (CW 42 pp. 396-8) The Soviet delegation is to develop a plan; it should 'be a bourgeois pacifist programme', which contains the 'annulment of all debts' and 'radical revision of the Versailles Treaty' as well as proposals to combat inflation, the energy crisis and so on.

13 February: Lenin completes a census form handed to all members of the RCP(B). His Party card is no 224,332. His language is Russian. What other languages can he speak fluently? 'I can speak fluently in none.' Lenin states that he has been an atheist 'since the age of 16'; to a question about his grandfather's occupation, he replies: 'I don't know'; about that of his father: 'Headmaster of elementary schools'; he began earning his own living at 27 (approximately); his status in the organisation? '"Professional" revolutionary and CC member' (CW 42 pp. 457-61)

21 February: Lenin writes to A D Tsyurupa that one must shift the 'centre of gravity from writing decrees and orders (our stupidities in this respect verge on idiocy) to *selection of people* and *checking fulfilment* . . . The departments are shit; decrees are shit. To find men and check up on their work — that is the whole point.' (CW 36 p. 566)

23 February: Lenin dictates remarks on the Conference of the Three Internationals in Berlin and refers to the 'unity of action' as the most pressing task of the working class. (CW 42 pp. 400-1)

28 February: Lenin writes to D I Kursky: 'I shall try to see you personally, but I cannot promise it because I am not feeling well.' His state of health also does not permit him to go into the wording of individual articles of the Civil Code — something he has busied himself with on several previous occasions.

End of February: Lenin writes 'Notes of a Publicist'. (CW 33 pp. 204-11 and first published in 1924) Nowhere else in the world has the bourgeois-democratic revolution been completed so 'thoroughly' as in Russia; a new epoch has been ushered in with the Soviet type of state. 'But we have not finished building even the foundations of the socialist economy . . . we have always urged and reiterated the elementary truth — that the joint efforts of the workers of several advanced countries are needed for the victory of socialism.' At the 3rd Comintern Congress he found himself on the 'extreme Right flank'; that was the 'only correct stand to take'. But he was wrong 'about Levi'; he is republishing those works by Rosa Luxemburg 'in which she was wrong'. However 'in spite of her mistakes she was — and remains for us — an eagle'. And not only will 'communists all over the world cherish her memory' but 'her *complete* works (the publication of which the German communists are inordinately delaying)' are needed.

6 March: Lenin speaks on the current situation at a meeting of communists at the All-Russian Congress of Metalworkers. (CW 33 pp. 212-26) He discusses the impending Conference in Genoa. He states that he hopes to 'discuss these subjects with Lloyd George personally in Genoa and to tell him that *it is no use trying to frighten us with such trivialities* . . . I hope that I shall not be prevented from doing this by ill health, which during the past few months has prevented me from taking a direct part in political affairs.' He hopes in a few weeks' time to 'return' to his 'duties' but doubts that the 'victorious powers which rule the whole world' will agree among themselves.

12 March: Lenin writes the article 'On the Significance of Militant Atheism' (CW 33 pp. 227-36) for the journal *Pod Znamenem Marksizma* (Under the Banner of Marxism). According to Lenin this journal must be a 'militant atheist organ'. He asks for the 'study of Hegelian dialectics, materialistically interpreted'.

19 March: Lenin writes to I I Skvortsov-Stepanov that he is delighted by his book on the electrification of the RSFSR and tells him to 'write another such little book on the history of religion and *against all* religion'. (CW 36 p. 570)

23 March: Lenin writes to V M Molotov that 'on account of ill health' he will not be able to attend CC meetings or deliver a report at the Congress. He submits a plan for the report. (CW 33 pp. 251-3)

24 March: Lenin asks for more stringent measures to be adopted in selecting new Party members. 'If we have 30,000 to 40,000 members in the Party, even that number is excessive.' The level of training of members is inadequate. (CW 33 pp. 254-5)

27 March-2 April: The 11th Congress of the RCP(B) meets. Almost 800 delegates represent 532,000 members. Lenin opens and closes the Congress and delivers the CC report. (CW 33 pp. 259-326) Lenin states that Soviet Russia is going to Genoa to 'expand trade'; hence it is important to distinguish between those in the bourgeois camp who are inclined to settle the problem 'by war' and those who incline towards 'pacifism'. NEP is the 'basis of our entire policy' but 'we cannot run the economy'. He speaks of a 'drop in the ocean, called the Communist Party' and states: 'take Moscow with its 4,700 communists in responsible positions; and if we take the huge bureaucratic machine, that gigantic heap, we must ask: who is directing whom? I doubt it very much if it can be truthfully be said that the communists are directing that heap.' Something comparable to that of the vanquished nations who impose their 'higher culture' on the conqueror is taking place.

28 March: Lenin sums up the debate on the CC report at the Party Congress and attacks once again the Workers' Opposition which is only a 'wreck of the former Workers' Opposition'.

2 April: Lenin is re-elected to the CC; he delivers the closing speech at the Congress.

9 April: Lenin writes a letter when the Conference of the First and Second Internationals and the Vienna 'Centrist' International is over in Berlin. (CW 33 pp. 330-4) Radek and Bukharin made a mistake when they conceded that the Soviet government should not apply the death penalty to the 47 Socialist Revolutionaries and that representatives of the Three Internationals should be present at the trial.

11 April: Lenin drafts a decree on the functions of deputy chairmen of Sovnarkom and of the Council of Labour and Defence. (CW 33 pp. 335-43)

23 April: Lenin undergoes an operation at the Soldatenkovo (now Botkin) Hospital in Moscow for the removal of a bullet — from the assassination attempt of 30 August 1918.

2 May: Lenin writes an article on the tenth anniversary of *Pravda*. (CW 33 pp. 349-52)

5 May: In a letter to the Politburo, Lenin criticises various proposals, including some by Trotsky. (CW 33 pp. 353-5)

15 May: Lenin demands, in a note to Stalin, confirmation of the foreign trade monopoly. He adds a preamble to the Criminal Code of the RSFSR and directs that the death penalty under certain circumstances be commuted to deportation and the death penalty or deportation should be introduced for 'all forms of activity by the Mensheviks, *SRs and so on*'. (CW 42 pp. 418-9)

15 or 16 May: Lenin drafts a decision of the All-Russian CEC on the Genoa Conference; the delegation has 'carried out its task correctly' in defending the sovereignty of the RSFSR and 'in concluding a treaty with Germany'. (CW 33 pp. 356-7)

19 May: Lenin supports a plan to develop radio engineering, pointing out its political significance and the need to 'complete the organisation of wireless communication'. (CW 33 pp. 360-1)

23 May: Lenin writes to 'Comrade Stalin, for the *Politburo*' (CW 42 p. 420) He proposes that 'no less than 60 per cent' of the All-Russian CEC members should be 'workers and peasants not occupying any official posts in government bodies'.

26 May: Lenin suffers his first stroke, due to arteriosclerosis of the brain, at Gorki, near Moscow. N A Semashko writes later: 'Vladimir Ilich's final illness began with insigificant symptoms. He felt dizzy as he got out of bed and he had to grab hold of a cupboard which was nearby. The doctors, who were called immediately, at first attached no significance to these symptoms . . . But Vladimir Ilich was sad and pensive; he felt the impending disaster and answered all attempts to reassure him: "No, that is the first alarm signal".' (*Genosse Lenin* p. 170) Lenin is partially paralysed for a short time.

Mid June: Lenin is slightly better.

12 July: Lenin informs Sovnarkom that he has recovered and asks for books to be sent.

13 July: Stalin visits Lenin in Gorki. He reports on his visit during the autumn; he found Lenin 'fresh and recovered', but with traces of over-tiredness and overstrain. '"I may not read a newspaper", remarked comrade Lenin ironically. "I may not speak about politics. I go round every piece of paper lying on my desk, fearing it could be a newspaper and that it could lead to a breach of discipline".' (Stalin *Werke* Bd 5 p. 118)

5 August: Stalin visits Lenin again. 'This time I found comrade Lenin surrounded by a mountain of books and newspapers (he was permitted to read as much as he liked and to talk about politics). There was no trace of overtiredness and overstrain . . . It is our old Lenin who looks craftily, one eye half closed, at his interlocutor.' (Stalin *Werke* Bd 5 p. 119)

End of August–Beginning of September: Lenin writes his unfinished article 'A Fly in the Ointment'. (CW 33 pp. 368–9)

1 September: Lenin writes to V A Avanesov that the *'most necessary* thing for us now is to learn from Europe and America.' (CW 36 pp. 581–2)

17 September: Lenin writes, in a letter to the 6th All-Russian Congress of Trade Unions: 'This is the first time since my long illness that I am able to address a Congress, even though in writing.' Means to restore heavy industry, the 'main basis of socialism', are lacking. (CW 33 pp. 370–1)

26 September: Lenin writes to Lev Kamenev in connection with the founding of the USSR. 'Stalin tends to be somewhat hasty.' (CW 42 pp. 421–3)

2 October: Lenin returns to Moscow from Gorki. His working day is reduced at the request of his doctors. 'He was permitted to work between 11 am and 2 pm and from 6 pm to 8 pm on the condition that he (in addition to Sundays) added another rest day in the middle of the week.' But he often went 'to his office at 9.30 am, and if a secretary looked in he would reply with a smile "I'm not working, I'm just reading".' (Biographie p. 797)

6 October: Lenin writes in a note for the Politburo on the subject of the founding of the USSR: 'I declare war to the death on dominant nation chauvinism. I shall eat it with all my healthy teeth as soon as I have got rid of this accursed bad tooth.' He absolutely insists that the All-Russian CEC should be chaired in turn by a 'Russian, a Ukrainian, a Georgian, etc.' (CW 33 p. 372)

10 October: Lenin apologises that he cannot speak at the Congress of Textile Workers: 'I had a toothache which not only kept me from my work just when I had started it, but kept me fretting for a whole week'. (CW 42 p. 423)

13 October: Lenin writes the letter 'Re the Foreign Trade Monopoly'. (CW 36 pp. 375–8) He is opposed to any breach in the foreign trade monopoly.

27 October: Lenin grants Michael Farbman, correspondent of the *Observer* and the *Manchester Guardian*, an interview. (CW 33 pp. 383–9)

He is in favour of an Anglo–Soviet agreement. He declares: 'We are, of course, opposed to the League of Nations', which is 'so intimately bound up with the Versailles Treaty'.

31 October: Lenin speaks at the 4th session of the All-Russian CEC to stormy, prolonged applause. (CW 33 pp. 390–5) He states that the machinery of state, with 243,000 employees in Moscow, is 'inflated to far more than twice the size we need'. Louis Fischer, who was at the session, wrote later: 'The little man . . . with a bald head, parched yellow-brown skin and a small, sparse reddish beard walked, but walked so fast it seemed to me he was running on tiptoe, to the stage . . . What is remarkable is its [his speech's] quality – in no way inferior to that of his speeches in the heyday of his intellectual power.' (Fischer *The Life of Lenin* p. 616)

5 November: The 4th Congress of the Communist International opens in Petrograd; 408 delegates representing 66 communist organisations in 58 countries attend. The Congress moves to Moscow on 9 November and remains in session until 5 December.

7 November: Lenin writes to the workers of the former Michelson Works: 'I regret very much that precisely today a slight indisposition has forced me to stay indoors.' He sends greetings on the occasion of the fifth anniversary of the October Revolution. (CW 33 p. 411)

13 November: Lenin addresses the 4th Comintern Congress, in German, on 'Five Years of the Russian Revolution and the Prospects of the World Revolution'. (CW 33 pp. 418–32) He is met with tumultous applause and speaks first about state capitalism, which he again refers to as a step forward for Soviet Russia. He blames the state apparatus for mistakes and 'foolish things'. 'We took over the old machinery of state and that was our misfortune. Very often this machinery operates against us.' He asks foreign communists 'not to hang Russian experience in a corner like an icon and pray to it', but to assimilate part of it. 'The fascists in Italy may, for example, render us a great service by showing the Italians that they are not yet sufficiently enlightened and that their country is not yet ensured against the Black Hundreds.' The most important thing in the period just starting is to 'study'. Louis Fischer, who was present, has this to say about Lenin's speech: 'At Lenin's feet sat Karl Radek . . . and whenever Lenin could not find the German word he needed, he gave the Russian equivalent to Radek, who raised his impish face and offered the translation' Lenin 'spoke with machine-gun rapidity in a rather high-pitched voice'. (Fischer *The Life of Lenin* p. 619)

20 November: Lenin address the Moscow Soviet (CW 33 pp. 435–43); it is his last official speech. Lenin states: 'We still have the old machinery.' Communists should control the apparatus they 'have been assigned to, and not, as so often happens with us' allow the apparatus to control them. Socialism 'is no longer a matter of the distant future or an abstract picture, or an icon' but it 'has been brought into everyday life'.

21 November: Lenin receives visitors, as can be seen from the diary of his secretaries; he attends meetings of Sovnarkom.

25 November: In the morning Lenin does not feel well. 'He stayed only five minutes, dictated three letters over the phone.' He comes again at 6 pm to his office. (CW 42 pp. 467-8)

2 December: The doctor instructs Lenin to go away for a rest once or even twice for several days every two months. (CW 42 p. 471) He writes a letter to Willi Münzenberg (CW 35 pp. 559-60) that the organisation of aid by the international working class has 'helped Soviet Russia in considerable measure'.

4 December: Lenin makes 'Notes on the Tasks of Our Delegation at the Hague'. (CW 33 pp. 447-51) He gives instructions on the peace conference (10-15 December in the Hague) and thinks that it must be stated that war 'is hatched in the greatest secrecy and that the ordinary workers' organisations, even if they call themselves revolutionary organisations, are utterly helpless in face of a really impending war.' His remarks are sent to a commission 'consisting of Zinoviev, Trotsky and Bukharin'. (CW 42 p. 474)

7 December: Lenin arrives 'at 10.55 am in his office; at 11 am a Politburo meeting started with Kamenev in the chair. Vladimir Ilich attended. Vladimir Ilich left the meeting at 2.20 pm . . . Left for Gorki at 6.15 pm, taking with him current papers'. (CW 42 p. 476) Lenin remains at Gorki until 12 December.

8 December: Lenin dictates by telephone a proposal for a Politburo standing order; the Politburo should meet 'on Thursdays from 11 to 2 (not later)'. (CW 42 pp. 429-30)

12 December: Lenin arrives in Moscow at 11 am. 'Rykov, Kamenev and Tsyurupa sat with him until 2 pm.' Lenin is in his office again at 5.30 pm and works there for the last time. He 'left at 8.15 pm'. (CW 42 p. 478)

13 December: Lenin suffers two attacks of illness, thrombosis of the brain, during the morning. The doctors order complete rest for Lenin. He writes to Kamenev, Rykov and Tsyurupa, his Sovnarkom deputies: 'Owing to a recurrence of my illness I must wind up all political work and take a holiday again.' However he insists on 'complete freedom' to receive visitors and even to extend visiting hours. (CW 42 pp. 432-3)

15 December: Lenin gives his secretary L A Fotieva 'a letter he had written to Trotsky, telling Fotieva to type it herself and send it off, keeping a copy in a sealed envelope in the secret files. He found it very difficult to write'. (CW 42 p. 480)

16 December: During the night of 15-16 December Lenin suffers a attack lasting over an hour, his second stroke. Lenin does not want to go to Gorki since that would tire him. A dog, called Aida, is to be brought 'every day at 9.30 am, to him; he plays with it and is very fond of it'. (CW 42 p. 481) Lenin's workload is again enormous; between 2 October and 16 December he 'wrote 224 official letters and notes, saw 171 persons (125 visits) and chaired 32 meetings and discussions of Sovnarkom, the Council for Labour and Defence, the Politburo and its commissions'. (Biographie pp. 797-8)

23 December: Despite his illness Lenin begins to dictate his thoughts. M A Volodicheva, one of his secretaries, states: 'A little after 8 pm Vladimir Ilich called me to his flat and dictated for four minutes. He fet bad. Doctors were called. Before starting to dictate he said: "I want to dictate to you a letter to the Congress. Take it down." He dictated quickly but it was obvious that he was ill.' (CW 42 p. 481)

24 December: After a discussion between Stalin, Kamenev and Bukharin and the doctors it is decided, at Lenin's insistence, that he be permitted to dictate '5-10 minutes daily'. Visitors are forbidden; he is not to receive any political news so as not to 'give him any reason to brood or become excited'. (Tagebuch pp. 10-11) Lenin continues dictating his 'Letter to the Congress' known as his 'Testament'. (CW 36 pp. 591-611) He emphasises again and again the confidentiality of the material and it is to be 'kept in a special place under special responsibility'. (CW 42 p. 482) In his 'Testament' Lenin concentrates first and foremost on the Party leadership. 'I think that . . . the prime factors in the question of stability are such members of the CC as Stalin and Trotsky.' Relations between them present the greatest danger of a split which Lenin hopes to avoid mainly by increasing the size of the CC, from 27 to 50-100 members. 'Comrade Stalin, having become Secretary General, has unlimited authority concentrated in his hands and I am not sure that he will always be capable of using that authority with sufficient caution. Comrade Trotsky is distinguished not only by outstanding ability. He is personally perhaps the most capable man in the present CC but he has displayed excessive self-assurance and shown excessive preoccupation with the purely administrative side of things. These two qualities of the two outstanding leaders of the present can inadvertently lead to a split.' In assessing the other leaders Lenin recalls 'the October episode with Zinoviev and Kamenev was, of course, no accident; but neither can the blame for it be laid upon them personally any more than now Bolshevism can upon Trotsky.' Lenin also mentions Bukharin, 'the favourite of the Party'; but there is something 'scholastic' about him. 'He has never made a study of dialectics and, I think, never fully understood it.' Pyatakov is 'a man of outstanding will and outstanding ability' but he reveals 'too much zeal for . . . the administrative side of the work'.

26 December: Lenin continues dictating his remarks; he returns to the subject of increasing the number of CC members and suggests how the apparatus 'which, in effect, we took over . . . from the tsar' can be improved.

27 December: Lenin dictates notes on the granting of legislative functions to the State Planning Commission; he continues dictating on 28 and 29 December.

30 December: Lenin goes into the nationality problem in his notes. He repeats that the apparatus was taken 'over from tsarism and slightly annointed with Soviet oil'. He attacks Great Russian chauvinism. The right of secession from the Union will be a 'mere scrap of paper' and quite incapable to 'defend the non-Russians from the onslaught of that really Russian man, the Great Russian chauvinist, in substance a rascal and a tyrant, such as the typical Russian bureaucrat is.' Lenin again criticises Stalin. 'I think that Stalin's haste and his infatuation with pure administration, together with his spite against the notorious "nationalist-socialism", played a fatal role here.' Lenin calls the 'Georgian' on 31 December a 'real and true nationalist-socialist'.

End of the year: As Krupskaya reports, Lenin went to the theatre for the last time, in 1922, (probably in November or December) 'where he saw Dickens' *A Christmas Carol*. Ilich felt bored after the first act. Dickens' petty-bourgeois sentimentality got on his nerves . . . and he left in the middle of the performance'. (Krupskaya *Das ist Lenin* p. 117)

1923

2 January: Lenin dictates the article 'Pages from a Diary' (CW 33 pp. 462–6) which appears in *Pravda* no 2 on 4 January. He examines the problem of illiteracy and writes: 'At a time when we hold forth on proletarian culture . . . facts and figures reveal that we are in a very bad way even as far as bourgeois culture is concerned.'

4 January: Lenin dictates to L A Fotieva, his secretary, an addendum to his 'Letter to the Congress' of 24 December 1922. 'Stalin is too rude and this defect, although quite tolerable in our midst and in dealings amongst us communists, becomes intolerable in a Secretary General. This is why I suggest that the comrades think about a way of removing Stalin from that post and appointing another man in his stead who in all other respects differs from comrade Stalin in having only one advantage, that of being more tolerant, more loyal, more polite and more considerate to the comrades, less capricious, etc.' From the point of view of avoiding a split 'it is not a detail, it is a detail which can assume decisive importance.'

4–6 January: Lenin dictates 'On Co-operation'. (CW 33 pp. 467–75) Co-operatives mean the 'social ownership of the means of production' and they produce the 'system of socialism'. It is important to 're-organise our machinery of state, which is utterly uesless, and which we took over in its entirety from the preceding epoch'.

16–17 January: Lenin writes 'Our Revolution (Apropos of N Sukhanov's Notes)'. (CW 33 pp. 476-9) Lenin accuses the Mensheviks of being 'impossibly pedantic' in their Marxism and being incapable of grasping its 'revolutionary dialectics'. If a 'definite level of culture is required for the building of socialism . . . why cannot we begin by first achieving the prerequisites for that definite level of culture in a revolutionary way and *then*, with the aid of the workers' and peasants' government and the Soviet system, proceed to overtake the other nations?'

22 January: Lenin calls his secretary to him for 25 minutes. He makes 'corrections in the second variant of the article on the Workers' and Peasants' Inspection. He finally choses his variant. As his time is limited he is in a great hurry.' Krupskaya, who had let the secretary in, 'said he had stolen several minutes to look through the article'. (CW 42 p. 483)

23 January: Lenin completes the article 'How We Should Reorganise the Workers' and Peasants' Inspection' (CW 33 pp. 481-6) and it appears in *Pravda* no 15 on 25 January. Lenin proposes that members of the Central Control Commission should be present at 'meetings of the Politburo'.

1 February: 'Vladimir Ilich said: "If I were at large (at first he made a slip, then repeated, laughing, if I were at large) I could easily do all this myself".' (CW 42 p. 485) This was to his secretary in connection with the instructions he had given her on how to deal with Politburo papers.

2 February: Entry by M A Volodicheva in the journal. (CW 42 p. 486) 'I had not seen him [Lenin] since 23 January. Outwardly, a considerable change for the better; fresh, cheerful-looking. Dictates, as always, excellently.'

5 February: Entry by M I Glyasser, another secretary, in the journal. (CW 42 p. 489) 'I saw him [Lenin] for the first time since his illness. I thought he looked well and cheerful, only slightly paler than before. He speaks slowly, gesticulating with his left hand and moving the fingers of his right. There was no compress on his head.'

14 February: L A Fotieva writes in the journal (CW 42 p. 493) 'Vladimir Ilich sent for me a little after 12. He had no headache. He said that he was quite well, that his was a nervous illness, that sometimes he felt quite well, i.e. his head was quite clear, but sometimes he felt worse. Therefore we had to hurry with his requests as he wanted to put some things through without fail in time for the Congress.' He finds speaking difficult during the evening; the Georgian question, in which he opposes the Russian nationalism of Stalin and Ordzhonikidze, occupies him most. He wants to make it clear that 'he is on the side . . . of the injured party', i.e. the Georgians. (CW 42 p. 621)

2 March: Lenin completes the article 'Better Fewer But Better' (CW 33 pp. 487-502) and it appears in *Pravda* no 49 on 4 March. It is Lenin's last public utterance. 'Our state apparatus is so deplorable, not to say wretched' that fundamental changes are necessary. Bureaucratism occurs not only in 'Soviet offices' but also in 'our Party offices'. Lenin emphasises the need to 'learn' and to be thrifty.

5 March: Lenin arranges for his secretary, M A Volodicheva, to come about 12 noon and dictates a letter to Trotsky and one to Stalin. (CW 42 p. 493) In his letter to Trotsky he asks him, Trotsky, to 'uphold the "Georgian case" at the plenum of the CC. The matter is now being "looked into" by Stalin and Dzerzhinsky and I cannot trust their impartiality.' Lenin writes to Stalin 'after he has learned of Stalin's rude attack on N K Krupskaya'. He asks Stalin to decide whether he wishes to apologise or whether he prefers to 'break off relations between us'.

6 March: Lenin 'dictates a letter to the Mdivani group. He feels ill'. (CW 42 p. 493) The letter to the Georgian communists is probably Lenin's last written work. He is 'very annoyed by the coarseness of Ordzhonikidze and the indulgence of Stalin and Dzerzhinsky. I am preparing a memorandum and a speech for you. Greetings. Lenin'.

9 March: Lenin's third stroke (according to Biographie p. 850 it takes place on 10 March) confines Lenin to bed. The doctors discover paralysis of the right leg and arm, loss of speech and a cloudy consciousness.

15 May: Lenin, ill, is moved from Moscow to Gorki.

19 June: Nadezhda Krupskaya writes to Clara Zetkin: 'Lenin did not sleep the night before last and was extremely nervous and excited . . . The most important thing now is not a diagnosis but careful, attentive nursing. Everything depends on the general state of his strength. In this regard a visible improvement has been noticeable during the past month and there are days when I begin to hope that recovery is not impossible.' (L Dornemann *Clara Zetkin* pp. 395–6)

Summer: G E Lozgachev-Elizarov, the adopted son of Lenin's sister Anna, describes a visit to Gorki: 'Vladimir Ilich was sitting in his wheelchair in a white summer shirt with an open collar . . . A rather old cap covered his head and the right arm lay somewhat unnaturally on his lap. Vladimir Ilich hardly noticed me even though I stood quite plainly in the middle of the clearing.' (G E Lozgachev-Elizarov *Gora und sein bester Freund* pp. 291–2)

End of July: Lenin's state of health slowly improves.

August: Helped by Krupskaya, Lenin tries to learn to speak again.

September: Lenin receives orthopaedic shoes and can walk a little with the aid of a stick.

19 October: Lenin is driven to Moscow by car; he enters his flat and his office in the Kremlin for the last time. On his way back to Gorki he drives through the Agricultural Exhibition.

2 November: A workers' delegation from the Glukhovo works visits Lenin. 'All the delegates kissed Lenin on leaving. The old worker Kuznetsov was the last to come to him. They embraced each other heartily. Old Kuznetsov, in tears, kept on repeating: "I am a worker, a blacksmith, we are forging everything that you designed."' (Biographie p. 855)

Between 24 November–16 December: Lenin is visited by N I Bukharin,
E A Preobrazhensky, I I Skvortsov-Stepanov, N N Krestinsky, I A
Pyatnitsky and A K Voronsky. 'They talk to him about current work
and reported in Moscow that he had listened with interest but did not
appear to have regained the ability to speak.' (*Lenin und die Kultur-
revolution* p. 460)

29 November: Lenin watches the film 'The Sixth Anniversary of the
October Revolution' together with I I Skvortsov-Stepanov and I A
Pyatnitsky. (Ibid p. 460)

End of December: G E Lozgachev-Elizarov visits Gorky and sees Lenin
again. He made a 'fresh and cheerful impression' but his right arm lay as
before, 'lifeless on his lap'. Lenin has still 'great difficulty in speaking . . .
After breakfast he usually went round the park on the paths which had
been cleared of snow in his wheelchair, pushed by Pyotr Pakkaln. After
dinner a sheet was hung over the door to serve as a screen . . . Very
serious films were not shown so as to avoid causing any nervous strain
whatsoever . . . Since Vladimir Ilich could read a little, the latest newspapers were sent to him in Gorky.' He practised 'writing with his left hand
so as to make up for the distressing loss of speech which hindered his com-
municating with those around him'. (Lozgachev-Elizarov pp. 294–300)

1924

Beginning of January: 'I used to read books to him in the events',
Krupskaya writes later to Maxim Gorky, 'those which he chose from
the parcels which arrived from the city. He chose your book *My Univer-
sities* . . . In Guilbeaux's book [Lenin] found a reference to your
article about Lenin published in *Kommunisticheskii International* in
1918, and he asked me to read this article again to him. As I did so he
listened with rapt attention.' Later she adds: 'I see in front of me Ilich's
face as he listens and looks out of the window into the far distance;
he was summing up his life and thinking about you.' (*Lenin und Gorki*
pp. 266–7)

19 January: Krupskaya reads *Love and Death* by Jack London. 'Ilich
liked this story enormously.' (Krupskaya *Das ist Lenin* p. 117)

20 January: Lenin asks Krupskaya to read again from Jack London.
'The next story we came to was of quite a different type, it was replete
with bourgeois morality . . . Ilich began to laugh and waved it aside.'
(Krupskaya *Das ist Lenin* pp. 117–8)

21 January: Lenin has another attack; his temperature rises quickly, he
loses consciousness and dies at 6.50 pm.

23 January: Lenin's body is moved to Moscow.

27 January: Lenin is placed in the mausoleum in Red Square.

Bibliography

Antonow-Owsejenko W (Antonov-Ovseenko V A), *Im Jahre siebzehn Erinnerungen an die Oktoberrevolution* (Berlin DDR 1958)

Ascher A, *The Mensheviks in the Russian Revolution* (London 1976)

Ascher A, *Pavel Axelrod and the Development of Menshevism* (Cambridge MA 1972)

Badajew A (Badaev A E), *Die Bolschewiki in der Reichsduma* (Berlin DDR 1957)

Balabanoff A, *Impression of Lenin* (Ann Arbor 1964)

Baron S H, *Plekhanov, the Father of Russian Marxism* (London 1963)

Basso L, *Rosa Luxemburg: A Reappraisal* (London 1975)

Braun O, *Über Lenins militärische Tätigkeit 1917–1920* (Berlin DDR 1957)

Carew-Hunt R E, *The Theory and Practice of Communism* (London 1950)

Carr E H, *A History of Soviet Russia* Vols 1–3 (London 1950–3)

Cliff T, *Lenin* Three Volumes (London 1975–9)

Cogniot G, *Présence de Lénine* Two Volumes (Paris 1970)

Communist Party of the Soviet Union *Resolutions and Decisions of the CPSU* ed. R C Elwood Two Volumtes (Toronto 1974)

Conquest R, *V I Lenin* (London 1972)

Deutscher I, *Lenin's Childhood* (London 1970)

Donath F, *Auf Lenins Spuren in Deutschland* (Berlin DDR 1970)

Donath F, *Lenin in Leipzig* (Berlin DDR 1958)

Dornemann L, *Clara Zetkin Leben und Wirken* (Berlin DDR 1973)

Engels F, *The Condition of the Working Class in England* (London 1892)

Feuer L S, 'Between Fantasy and Reality. Lenin as a Philosopher and Social Scientist' in B W Eissenstate (ed.) *Lenin and Leninism* (London 1971)

Fischer L, *The Life of Lenin* (London 1964)

Fotieva L A, *Pages from Lenin's Life* (Moscow 1960)

Fréville J, *Lénine à Paris* (Paris 1968)

Fülöp-Miller R, *Lenin und Ghandi* (Zürich 1927)

Garaudy R, *Lénine* (Paris 1968)

Genosse Lenin Erinnerungen von Zeitgenossen (Berlin DDR 1967)

Getzler I, *Martov: A Political Biography of a Russian Social Democrat* (Cambridge 1967)

Gorky M, *Days with Lenin* (London n.d.)

Gourfinkel N, *Portrait of Lenin* (New York 1972)

Haas L, *Lenin: Unbekannte Briefe 1912-1914* (Zürich 1967)

Hahlweg W, *Lenins Rückkehr nach Russland 1917 Die deutschen Akten* (Leiden 1957)

Haimson L H, *The Russian Marxists and the Origins of Bolshevism* (Cambridge MA 1955)

Harding N, 'Lenin's Early Writings — The Problem of Context', in *Political Studies* (December 1975) pp. 442-58

Harding N, 'Lenin and his Critics: Some Problems of Interpretation', in *European Journal of Sociology* vol VXII (1976) pp. 366-83

Harding N, *Lenin's Political Thought* Two Volumes (London 1977-80)

Hobson J, *Imperialism: A Study* (London 1902)

Keep J L H, *The Debate on Soviet Power* (Oxford 1979)

Keep J L H, *The Rise of Social Democracy in Russia* (Oxford 1963)

Keep J L H, *The Russian Revolution: A Study in Mass Mobilization* (London 1976)

Krupskaja N K, *Erinnerungen an Lenin* Two Volumes (Moscow-Leningrad 1933)

Krupskaja Nadeshda, *Erinnerungen an Lenin* (Berlin DDR 1959)

Krupskaja Nadeshda, *Das ist Lenin Eine Sammlung ausgewählter Reden und Artikeln* (Berlin DDR 1966)

Krupskaya N, *Memories of Lenin* (London 1970)

Lademacher H, *Die Zimmerwalder Bewegung Protokolle und Korrespondenz* Two Volumes (The Hague-Paris 1967)

Lane D, *The Roots of Russian Communism* (Assen 1968)

Lezitch B, *Lénine et IIIe Internationale* (Neuchâtel 1951)

Lezitch B and Drachkowitch M M, *Lenin and the Comintern* Volume One (Stanford CA 1972)

Leites N, *A Study of Bolshevism* (Glencoe I11. 1953)

Lenin V I, *Biograficheskaya Khronika* Volumes (Moscow 1970-)

Lenin V I, *Collected Works* 45 Volumes (Moscow 1963-70)

Lenin *Leben und Werk* (Vienna 1924)

Lenin W I *Biographie* 5th ed. (Berlin DDR 1971)

Lenin Wie wir ihn kannten Erinnerungen alter Kampfgefährten (Berlin DDR 1956)

Lenin und Gorki Eine Freundschaft in Dokumenten (Berlin DDR-Weimar 1964)

Lewin M, *Lenin's Last Struggle* (London 1977)

Liebman M, *Leninism under Lenin* (London 1975)

Losgatschow-Jelisarow G J, (Lozgachev-Elizarov G E), *Gora und sein bester Freund* (Berlin DDR 1970)

Luxemburg R, *The Accumulation of Capital* (London 1963)

Luxemburg R, *The Russian Revolution and Leninism or Marxism?* New Introduction by Bertram D Wolfe (Ann Arbor 1961)

McNeal R H, *Bride of the Revolution: Krupskaya and Lenin* (London 1973)

Mendel A P, *Dilemmas of Progress in Tsarist Russia: Legal Populism or Legal Marxism* (Cambridge MA 1961)

Meyer A G, *Leninism* (Cambridge MA 1967)

Morgan M C, *Lenin* (London 1971)

Münzenberg W, *Die Dritte Front* (Berlin 1930)

Nettl J P, *Rosa Luxemburg* (London 1969)

Page S, *Lenin and World Revolution* (New York 1959)

Pannekoek A, *Lenin als Philosoph* (Frankfurt-am-Main 1959)

Payne R, *The Life and Death of Lenin* (London 1964)

Pianzola M, *Lenin in der Schweiz* (Berlin DDR 1956)

Piatnitsky C, *Memoirs of a Bolshevik* (London n.d.)

Pipes R, *Social Democracy and the St Petersburg Labour Movement* (Cambridge MA 1963)

Pipes R, *Struve: Liberal on the Left 1870-1905* (Cambridge MA 1970)

Plamenatz J, *German Marxism and Russian Communism* (London 1954)

Platten F, *Die Reise Lenins durch Deutschland* (Berlin 1924)

Plekhanov G V, *In Defence of Materialism* (London 1947)

Plekhanov G V, *Selected Philosophical Works* (Moscow 1961)

Raeff M, *Plans for Political Reform in Russia 1730-1905* (Engelwood Cliffs NJ 1966)

Reed J, *Ten Days that Shook the World* (New York 1919)

Rosenberg W G, *Liberals in the Russian Revolution The Constitutional Democratic Party 1917-1921* (Princeton 1974)

Schapiro L, *The Communist Party of the Soviet Union* (London 1963)

Schapiro L, *The Origin of the Communist Autocracy* (London 1966)

Schapiro L and Reddaway P, (eds.) *Lenin the Man, the Theorist, the Leader* (London 1970)

Schwartz S, *The Russian Revolution of 1905* (Chicago and London 1905)

Senn A E, *The Russian Revolution in Switzerland 1914-1917* (Madison 1971)

Shub D, *Lenin* (Harmondsworth 1966)

Sinowiew G, (Zinoviev G E), *N Lenin Sein Leben und seine Tätigkeit* (Berlin 1920)

Sukhanov N, *The Russian Revolution 1917: A Personal Record* Translated and edited by Joel Carmichael (Oxford 1955)

Theen R H W, *V I Lenin: The Genesis and Development of a Revolutionary* (London 1974)

Timberlake C E (ed.), *Essays in Russian Imperialism* (Columbia Missouri 1972)

Treadgold D, *Lenin and his Rivals* (London 1955)

Trotsky L, *The Young Lenin* (Harmondsworth 1974)

Trotzki L, (Trotsky L), *Über Lenin: Materialen für einen Biographen* (Frankfurt-am-Main 1964)

Turin S P, *From Peter the Great to Lenin: A History of the Russian Labour Movement* (London 1968)

Ulam A, *Lenin and the Bolsheviks* (London 1969)

Unser Bruder Wolodja Erinnerungen von Verwandten an Lenin (Berlin DDR 1956)

Utechin S V (ed.), *What is to be Done?* Translated by S V and P Utechin (London 1963)

Valentinov N (Volsky), *Encounters with Lenin* (London 1968)

Venturi F, *Roots of Revolution* (London 1964)

Vom Alltag der Uljanows Eine Briefauswahl (Berlin DDR 1973)

Walicki A, *The Controversy over Capitalism* (Oxford 1969)

Weeks A L, *The First Bolsehviks – A Political Biography of Peter Tkachev* (New York 1968)

Wildman A K, *The Making of a Workers' Revolution* (Chicago 1967)

Wilson E, *To the Finland Station* (London 1960)

Wolfe B D, *Three Who Made a Revolution* (Harmondsworth 1966)

Wolfenstein E V *The Revolutionary Personality: Lenin, Trotsky, Ghandi* (Princeton 1967)

Wolodja unser Bruder und Genosse, Erinnerungen der Geschwister W I Lenins (Berlin DDR 1971)

Wolper I N, *Pseudonyme Lenins* (Berlin DDR 1970)

Wortman R, *The Crisis of Russian Populism* (Cambridge 1967)

Zetkin C, *Erinnerungen an Lenin* (Vienna–Berlin 1929 – new revised edition Berlin DDR 1957)

Index of Names

Place Index

Subject Index

Index of Works